Eleanor,

Happy Mother's Day!

" Friendship is forever + 10 days."

A Love Letter FROM Princess:
LUCKY, MOMMY & ME

AN UNUSUAL MEMOIR OF THE INDELIBLE LOVE, LOYALTY, AND LEADERSHIP OF A ONCE-IN-A-LIFETIME CANINE CANCER COMPANION

by *Princess Sheba Spirit Brooks Pomerantz*
AS TOLD THROUGH HER FATHER,
RICHARD POMERANTZ

Lovingly Edited By
Barbara Brooks Pomerantz

Cover and Title Page Artwork
by Leslie Cauldwell Rogers (Blum) of Jupiter, FL

Family Gallery Paintings of
Smokey Max & Samantha Blackie
And of
Lucky & Princess
By Sandra Severson of Honeybrook, PA

This book was printed in the United States of America.

To order additional copies of this book, contact:
Xlibris Corporation
1-888-795-4274
www.Xlibris.com
Orders@Xlibris.com
86531

A Love Letter FROM Princess:
LUCKY, MOMMY & ME

AN UNUSUAL MEMOIR OF THE INDELIBLE LOVE, LOYALTY, AND LEADERSHIP
OF A ONCE-IN-A-LIFETIME CANINE CANCER COMPANION

by **Princess Sheba Spirit Brooks Pomerantz**
AS TOLD THROUGH HER FATHER,
RICHARD POMERANTZ

Lovingly Edited By
Barbara Brooks Pomerantz

Dogs Are a Man's Best Friend

Dogs are like a dream come true
Playing, pouncing and waiting for something to do
A dog's soul is purely one of a kind
Always waiting for a new friend to find
Running and digging around in the dirt
Keeping their eyes open, always alert
Dogs are a man's best friend

Dogs are always up for a great time
And are always protecting at the scene of a crime
They have hearts as sweet as candy
Are always so happy and dandy
Soft eyes like a fluffy cloud
Walks proudly and swiftly through big crowds
Dogs are a man's best friend. Dogs are such beautiful creatures
Have such warm and friendly features
They are gentle, passionate, sympathetic and caring
Are very proud of the fur coat they are wearing
They are Mother Nature's friendliest breed
Always helping to your every which need
Dogs are a man's best friend

Dogs try to hold out till the end
Although sometimes they can't continue being your friend
When they get older its often very tough
All the surgeries, love, and medication are often not enough
Although their souls will stay with you every day
It comes time for them to pass away
Dogs are a man's best friend

Dedicated to my special dog, Rudy
Lexi Kroll (13 years old)
Toronto, Ontario, Canada

"WE LIVE ON BORROWED TIME"

I never thought that there could be a love like yours and mine
I never dreamed that I would see the day that I would find
A love that feels so right, but here we are tonight
And now the only thing we really need is time.

We live on borrowed time
No one can be sure when the loan will finally come due
But I'm loving all of mine, I know what time is for,
I've borrowed it so I can spend it all right here with you

There was a time when I believed that life held guarantees
There was a time when I was sure my future was secure,
But life had other plans, the future's in God's hands
And knowing that has let me live and love you more

We live on borrowed time
Yesterday is past, tomorrow seems a million miles away
But I promise you that I'm gonna make love last
By living every moment, every hour, every day

Now we may have a year, and we may have a lifetime,
No one can be certain what the future will allow,
But you and I are here, and this time is the right time,
'Cause one thing that I know is that we have each other now, and now,

We live on borrowed time
Let's celebrate and sing as we walk bravely into the unknown
'Cause we're gonna be just fine, whatever life may bring,
We'll face it all together and we'll never be alone
We may not have forever but our time will be our own

Used by Permission
We Live on Borrowed Time
Music & Lyrics by David Friedman
MIDDER Music Publishing, Inc.
Originally sung by Nancy LaMott

DEDICATION

In deciding to whom to dedicate my memoir, I asked Daddy
to research its definition and found it apropos:
"To hold someone in token of affection or esteem."

I therefore dedicate this book to:

Perywinkle, Lionmonkee & Kiss Kiss
Whose comfort to me our family will forever cherish.

and

My Uncle Doctor Greg Hahn
*Who exemplifies that superior veterinary medicine and compassionate care never need be two
solitudes. I thank him for never giving up on me, when others might have.*

and

My Beloved Lucky
We will remain attached at the hip & hearts bonded together . . . forever and a day.

And especially

My Mother—Mommy
*Because of you, I was given the chance to fulfill my potential.
From you, I learned about courage and humaneness and unconditional love.
For you, I have had the privilege to do my job.*

A MOTHER'S FOREWORD

MAGIC GIRL: Princess Sheba Spirit

Princess Sheba Spirit, a majestic Anatolian Shepherd, was my "Magic Dog" from the day we met. My husband and I had to say good-bye to our wedding-gift-to-ourselves, our Coonhound Smokey Max, four months earlier. Though we also had Samantha (a beautiful and truly unique Basset Husky mix) and Lucky (the only real "dog"—make that pooch—we've had, who people always called "Happy" in error, as his tail always wagged), our hearts were broken from our recent loss. My husband and I promised that when the time came, we would go TOGETHER to pick out the next addition to our family pack. We just weren't ready yet.

One day, on the way to work (I was dressed appropriately as a management consultant), my car virtually veered off the highway with a life of its own as it turned onto the street on the way to our local SPCA. We believe in "Karma," so I just went along with the car. On reaching the SPCA, I entered the kennel area where all the strays were held, drawn immediately by a beautiful German Shepherd pup gazing at me. Before I could get there, a true roar from beyond beckoned me—no, ordered me—to *"come here . . . I've been waiting for you . . . Where have you been?"* The command had been barked by the still-most-magnificent-animal I'd ever seen—one who for her entire life, people would stop to meet with the words, *"What a gorgeous dog . . . What is she?"*

Princess joined our pack without ever looking back. We could not imagine why anyone would have let her get away—nor why she could have been adopted out and returned twice. She was amazingly well trained, clearly smart in a way we'd never experienced with any of our many dogs, and at six months, wanted to be part of the family. We learned two days later when we took her for her mandatory spay that she had such severe hip dysplasia, she would either have to be euthanized soon or live a life of pain and near total inactivity. We could not lose two dogs in so short a time, and we had already all fallen in love with our Prinny. So we took a big gulp and had both her hips replaced, something we recognize not all could ever commit to financially nor in terms of what is required for rehabilitation and recovery.

For the next six months, when not at work (she was then crated), I lived together with Prinny in our TV room/den. We ate together, cuddled together, whispered in the dark, and slept together, I on the sofa and she snuggled on a blanket on the floor beside me. The bond we formed was awesome. My husband says I became her mother in her eyes and soul.

Shortly after her full recovery and rejoining the family pack, I was diagnosed with lethal and likely terminal cancer. My husband sat Prinny down and said to her, *"Princess, when you were sick, your mommy took care of you and never left your side. And now, Mommy is very, very sick and needs you to take care of her. I need you, Princess, to stay with Mommy at all times, and to never leave her side. I know you love her . . . I just need you to show her all the time."*

She never, ever left my side. She guided me through years of chemotherapy, radiation, and six major surgeries as she occupied my mind's eye in my meditation. She saved our home by telling us that it was on fire not five weeks after that first day of Daddy's request. She herded Samantha and Lucky as my husband dealt with the fire and instructed her to *"Take care of them—keep them with you until I can come back and get you out to safety."* She became Lucky's "love of his life" and soul mate, even becoming HIS therapy dog as he gradually became deaf and blind, leading him around rib-cage-to-rib-cage. When it was time to say good-bye to Lucky, she knew—she walked over and kissed him (she does NOT kiss, much to our chagrin, but she did that day) then did the same to her Daddy. She filled the huge hole in her Daddy's heart when his "bestest pal Lucky" no longer filled his arms. Today she is our solo dog, starting each day with our post-Lucky ritual of muffins in bed and ending it cuddled by our sides in the still of the night.

She is in our hearts. There is no beginning and no end to our feelings for her of love and awe. She is all encompassing. All who have come to know her speak of her wisdom, her ability to reason, and her intellect. Sounds like just another owner of the world's smartest dog—no, they say, *"There is something once in a lifetime about this particular one."* We've always known that.

Princess Sheba Spirit. Regal in countenance, fierce in her love and caring for us—with that special bond to me, and the spirit of all that is good in nature.

By Barbara Brooks Pomerantz
An excerpt of this essay was published
as a photo essay in the *Palm Beach*
***Post* in May 2006.**

A FATHER'S PROLOGUE

My forever memory of Princess Sheba Spirit was created on October 9, 2007.

Bobbie and I were driving home from Williamsburg, Virginia. We'd been there to carry out something we intuitively knew meant there would be no going back from the next path we had chosen to follow in our life partnership.

It was thirty-four days after one of the most important doors in our life journey had closed, a new one had opened totally unexpectedly, and we'd made the decision to walk through without looking back.

. . .

As we got to the outskirts of Dover, Delaware, right across from the famed NASCAR racetrack, we found ourselves in the middle of a thunderstorm.

Not just any thunderstorm, mind you, but one of those truly scary storms you talk about for years to come: long vivid streaks of lightning that look like jagged scars hitting the ground. Massive explosions of thunder even the music in the car turned up high couldn't hide. The wind howled. The windshield wipers valiantly, if vainly, tried to keep up with the torrent of water smashing against the window.

Some cars had already been pulled to the side of the road, by choice. Others, not so lucky, were strewed every which way, having slid off the side of the highway.

It was one for the ages.

Our mutual decision not to stop, to forge ahead despite the elements, was made wordlessly. For no words were necessary. Neither was stopping. As long as Panda Petunia Ruach wasn't frightened, then there was no reason for Bobbie or me to be.

We didn't need to explain to each what the other was feeling.

If the newest member of our family—a beautiful, eternally cute, tiny, four-month-old Cardigan Welsh Corgi puppy that we had just met for the first time the night before, and then twelve hours later carried in our arms away from the house she had been born in and placed into a brand-new crate for the six-hour ride to her new home where she'd begin her new life—could sleep so tightly, so totally unperturbed, despite the cacophony surrounding her new family's car, then we took it to be part of a sign.

A sign we so desperately needed.

One I had, without any embarrassment, asked for, loud enough for Bobbie to hear, a half hour before, almost in visceral reaction to two songs I adore that had played back to back on a local radio station: Sarah McLachlan's haunting *"Angel"* and Eric Clapton's even more personal *"Tears In Heaven."*

She didn't need me to explain why I asked for what I asked for. Not after the life-altering thirty-four days we had just lived through. At that particular moment in our life journey together, thirty plus years from the moment we had first met, we were reading each other's emotions as well, if not more so, than ever.

· · ·

The storm hadn't completely stopped even as the full scope of the "sign" I'd asked for took full form.

The most magnificent *double* rainbow suddenly appeared on the near horizon, just to the right of Bobbie's side of the car. With multiple vivid colors that transcended the full breadth of the sky.

It was gorgeous!

And it stayed with us for the next few miles as we continued down the road, before finally disappearing from view.

We were overwhelmed.

Even more so when it decided to reappear just a few minutes later, as if it felt, it and we had not adequately acknowledged each other with proper deference.

For Bobbie and me, our reaction was both visceral and very personal.

Awestruck is the only word that can begin to adequately describe what each of us was feeling. Mixed with astonishment and a few tears of sadness and more than grateful elation, we watched the rainbow's coming and going over twenty miles, if not more.

All coincidentally and exquisitely accompanied "without commercial break," almost as if it had been planned but had not, by Louis Armstrong's *"It's a Wonderful World"* and Elton John's *"Can You Feel the Love Tonight"* and Dan Fogelberg's *"Leader of the Band."*

It was eerie.

Bobbie and I didn't need to tell each other what we had just seen, what had just happened. For we already knew.

Our once-in-a-lifetime Anatolian Shepherd, Princess Sheba Spirit, was letting us know in her own way that she was in total sync with what we had decided to do. That she was still with us and would always be, watching over her family which now included her baby sister, Panda—forever and a day, as we had said to each other on countless other occasions.

She was still doing her job.

. . .

Having a big job to do. Looking out for her family was at the core of Princess—of who she was, just as it is at the heart of her quite wondrous breed.

Consistent with her ancestry—to describe her as majestic and beautiful, serious, reserved, strong willed, protective, principled, loyal, thoughtful, strategic, a zealous guardian, courageous, impeccably clean, and a leader with an uncanny ability to reason—only partially speaks to who she was.

For, she always led by example.

And she always personified grace under duress, in pain, and especially in a crisis.

And in so doing, just like the human mother she treasured—having long ago picked out her mother-to-be during a spontaneous visit Bobbie made to our local SPCA—Princess survived, thrived, and fulfilled her life potential as an authentic once-in-a-lifetime miracle story.

. . .

As strange as this may seem to others, for her family and hundreds, even thousands, of others whose lives Princess touched in large and small ways while she was with us, the stories of her life became something we all came to know firsthand. And why so many came to feel about her the way they did. Indeed, for us, Jerry Lewis might have just as well been speaking of Princess when he explained to cynics as to why he does what he does and feels the way he feels about Muscular Dystrophy: *"For those who understand, no explanation is necessary. For those who don't understand, no explanation will suffice."*

. . .

Said simply, for her family and her legion of friends from all around the world, Princess Sheba Spirit will remain forever an indelible once-in-a-lifetime magical presence.

One uniquely beautiful and majestic, yet modest . . .

Innately gifted yet humble . . .

Uncannily intelligent and inspirational, yet quiet and low-key . . .

Unabashedly confident yet a wary leader and guardian . . .

Paradoxically, for one so awesomely decisive, especially in times of dire life-threatening crisis, Princess exuded obvious deliberative and strategic thinking.

And while absolutely fearless, with an ingrained courage that was both undeniable and ever present, she also had a preternatural wisdom: her first choice was always prudence and caution.

Prinny was a contradiction of deep love and intense purpose: as joyfully playful she could be, she was even more reflective, always ready to focus on the job she was born and bred to do.

And despite wondrously individual athleticism, Princess preferred to be a team player. She'd defer to her beloved brother H.G. Lucky so that he would win whenever they played. Intuitively knowing that it made him happy and proud and gave him the confidence he needed to overcome the traumatic abuse he had endured during his earliest years, before he joined our family pack.

Finally, to Lucky especially and all those she allowed to get to really know her, Prinny was a wonderfully eloquent, and yet at times, silent communicator. One who spoke with a look as much as, if not more than, with her voice.

And her way of communicating was fascinating. For depending on with whom she communicated, she did so in her own very different ways.

For instance, as you will learn, with her beloved "bestest" pal Lucky, there was an intimate playfulness. While with those she mentored like Paris, the young Collie who lives nearby, she was very playful yet still reserved. And while with her grandmother she was almost childlike, with her babysitter Brian Hunter, she responded to his natural quietness with a reciprocal gentle submissiveness. And while the way she communicated in emergencies was unfailingly consistent—with clarity and confidence and maturity—for her parents, Bobbie and me, she could just as easily be childlike or directed and focused and *always* affectionate.

In sum, to her proud family, Princess exhibited all of these traits and more.

To us she will always be our indescribably loyal and protective daughter and sibling.

To us she will forever remain our "bestest" girl . . . our Magic Girl.

. . .

A Love Letter From Princess: Lucky, Mommy & Me is Princess's own very real life story. As seen through her eyes. Told in her words, many of which she not only understood but were uniquely hers.

Hers is a life story of extraordinary service, unconditional love, and the remarkable and inspirational impact on *everyone* she met. She was a genuine once-in-a-lifetime presence.

Dick Pomerantz
West Chester, PA, and Jupiter, FL

I believe in miracles.

There are many reasons why I do.
For now, suffice it to point out just two: Between
Mommy and me, we
have respectively survived late-stage and very
aggressive forms of cancer.
Neither of us should still be here. But we are . . .
and we did it together.
That's why I believe in miracles.

A LETTER FROM PRINNY: LIFE PRINCIPLES TO LIVE BY

My Story As Told
Through My Father

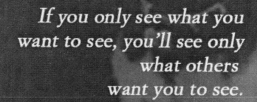

If you only see what you
want to see, you'll see only
what others
want you to see.

One's sense of self worth should be built on
your pride in all that is about
you. Not about looking for what isn't there,
just because it might be in
someone else.

A LETTER FROM PRINNY: LIFE PRINCIPLES TO LIVE BY

Lucky and Princess
As Depicted by Pennsylvania Artist Sandra Severson

MY OWN GLOSSARY
by Princess Sheba Spirit

In reading this book, you may come across some phrases, words, names, and terms that may be somewhat unfamiliar to you but have for years been in everyday usage in our family. In any event, each has come to mean something quite specific to me.

As a courtesy, to ease both your enjoyment and understanding of what you are about to read, I have listed them—in no particular order—with their respective appropriate meaning and where helpful with some further explanation.

Should you wish to take advantage of their expressiveness by using them with those you love as much as my parents have loved my siblings and me, absolutely feel free to do so.

It would be an honor knowing their legacy continues to spread.

- ***The Bestest Girl:*** My parents' term to describe much of what I do, have done, and the way I am.

- ***Magic Girl:*** Same as above.

- ***Snarf:*** There is no more important, no bigger compliment than to be referred to as a snarf. It means all that is wonderful and kind and warm and giving and generous and committed and loyal and loving. It is not limited by any size or type or breeding or skill sets or smarts or particular activity. You know a snarf when you meet one. My parents would say it is very likely that if you have or have had someone like my brothers Smokey and Lucky or my sister Samantha or me in your life, your life has been made better for it.

- *Snarfing:* The sound of a snarf or snarfs anticipating breakfast or dinner; the sound of snarf or snarfs eating breakfast or dinner; the actions and/or sound of a snarf or snarfs just being snarfy.

- *Monkees:* All of my toys.

- *Clump Clump:* The sound of a snarf or snarfs walking up the stairs of your home.

- *Slurp Slurp:* the sound of a snarf or snarfs drinking water.

- *My Parents' Time:* You will see it used in reference to time

- *My Time:* Just like my parents' time, times seven

- *"It's a Wonderful World":* My brother Lucky's favorite song and his philosophy of life . . . whenever I hear it being played I go look for my father, for I know he's thinking about Lucky. Together we sit, listen, and remember.

- *"One Small Star":* An extraordinarily beautiful song of melody and words Lucky and I used to listen to, together with Daddy. When we did, we both knew he was thinking about our brother Smokey. Now when I hear it, I know he's thinking especially about Lucky. And I know he's hurting inside, so I come running from wherever I am to be with him, to let him know I understand fully.

- *Bad Girl:* The one phrase I find most embarrassing.

- *Grandma:* Mommy's mommy. Grandma Beazie as Daddy calls her.

- *Being a Pig:* My sister **Samantha** illicitly eating a five-pound cherry cheesecake.

- *Smokeyism:* Any thought, skill set, instinct, or activity all of my late older brother Smokey's friends would immediately recognize as *"Yes, that was Smokey."* (For example, it ranges from predicting local tornadoes twelve hours prior to their occurrence; telling us earthquakes are about to occur in places as different as the mountains of Turkey and Joshua Tree, California; entering detox for liking beer too much; trapping Daddy's mommy in my parents' kitchen; and other things you will come to learn about.)

- *The Miracle:* You'll read of this in the book. Let me know afterwards if you require further explanation.

- *Housis:* You know these as homes or houses.

- *Serenity* **1**: My "*housis*" near the Pennsylvania/Delaware border which backs onto a forest, not too far from the orphanage where I first spotted and picked out my mother. It also has a second name—a French one—Chateau des Arbres. It means "*home of the trees.*"

- *Serenity* **2**: My "*housis*" in Jupiter, Florida, where I love to watch the golfers playing past the back of our home, behind our pool that borders the ninth hole of the north course, where I have a completely different set of friends from those up north, friends like "Mr. Armadillo" who I met at our favorite "beachis".

- *Goodest Girl:* Another name my parents call me.

- *Pretty Girl:* Like any female will tell you, I just *love* being called this by my parents and by so many others.

- *So My Good:* My parents expressing pride in something my brother Lucky and/or I would do.

- *The Grand High Hazamazzabooboo:* One of my brother Smokey's favorite nicknames; a reflection of my parents' greatest respect and affection. I think it was their way of honoring his having been the wedding gift they gave to each other.

- ***The Little Grand High Hazzamazzabooboo:*** Lucky wore so proudly the "little brother's" version of Smokey's distinguished mantle.

- ***Walk & Crap:*** If you take the opportunity to accompany me on one of my daily sojourns you'd find this expression self-explanatory.

- ***"Batroom":*** A special place accessible through the garages of both of our "housis" which my parents built for convenience purposes, for my siblings and me to use as needed.

- ***Go Tell Mommy What You Did:*** What I proudly do with a tail wag when I have finished going to the "batroom."

- ***Was That A Farto?:*** I sometimes have a problem with gas . . . when I do, the sound literally makes me jump up.

- ***I Think I See a Waggy Tails:*** My parents look for this from me when they think I feel particularly proud of something I may have done. I can do this on command as well, although I only do so when there's a reason to.

- ***Biggest Jumpo:*** Such as, the act of dismounting from a sofa, a bed, and/or from one of our car seats.

- ***Let's Go to Work:*** I am in the office every day with my parents.

- ***You Have a Big Job To Do:*** The words that changed my life forever. Especially the job you'll read a good deal about in this book; that which I am most proud of.

- ***Mr. Sweetness; Mr. Congeniality; Mr. Wack Wack:*** All were other names for my brother Lucky. Names that very aptly described what he was all about and what he meant to all of those who had the privilege to make his acquaintance. The last was the ever present sound of his ever wagging tail hitting a wall or chair or sofa or desk or door.

- **Are You Hungry Now?:** My favorite words twice a day, other than when I am asked if I want to go for a walk.

- **Vitamin Time:** I don't like them. But when I hear these words I know my parents are about to shove something down my throat that's good for me. So I have stopped protesting.

- **Icis Water:** My favorite thing after a long walk and before I go to sleep at night. Especially when I am asked if I want this, I know my thirst is about to be quenched.

- **Porchis:** Behind Serenity 1, it's where I go to watch for deer in the forest. Behind Serenity 2, it's where I go to guard Mommy from the golfers passing by as she swims her laps in our pool.

- **That Was A Good El Crapo:** Just as it sounds. I can do this pretty much on command now too.

- **Muffin time:** There is no better way to begin each day. First thing each morning, it's accompanied by a touch of coffee on Daddy's fingers.

- **Picnic Table:** What Mommy and Daddy set out in front of me every morning before coffee and muffins in bed.

- **Lift Your Left Foot Please:** What I do when asked by my parents if my leash gets caught.

- **Lift Your Right Foot Please:** Same as the above, just with the other foot.

- **Mr. Can:** What my brother Lucky would bring to each meal in his mouth, brought from our parents pantry closet. That was *his* job.

- **Please Turn Over:** What I do when asked by my parents particularly when they are afraid I might fall off the bed, or have not left enough room for Daddy to sleep.

- ***Make Room For Daddy:*** Another term my mother uses to tell me we need to create more space for Daddy. As soon I hear those words, I immediately turn over.

- ***Let's Do A Crawley:*** What I do now when asked to move closer to wherever my parents think I need to be. What I did once, at Daddy's request that stunned everyone who saw me do it at the time. You will read about it in some detail.

- ***You Want Your Basket?:*** At Serenity 1, it's a really comfortable place I go to lie down in the kitchen while my parents eat. At Serenity 2, it's a really comfortable place where I go to lie down in our family room usually after dinner when my parents read their newspapers or watch television. I tend to do so only when my hips are feeling arthritic.

- ***You Have To Hurry Up Now:*** I know my father thinks I am dawdling too slowly when I hear him say those words.

- ***DooToo DooToo DooToo:*** I love these words! When I hear Daddy say them to me I know it's time to run to wherever we're going—outside, or to eat, or to spend some *Daddy Doggy Time* together. Something we do every night for some period of time on the sofa in the television room.

- ***You Know Where You Are, Don't You?:*** Returning once again after some absence to those places that are both familiar and hold very special memories . . . such as the Donald Ross Exit off I-95 outside Jupiter, FL, and Route 926 and our street in West Chester, PA . . . and driving through our development in Jupiter, Florida . . . and past the campus at Westtown School . . . and seeing the always amazing "wild beachis" at the Hobe Sound Nature Preserve near our "housis" in Jupiter.

- ***You Smell Smoke, Don't You:*** What my father asks when he sees my nose in the air when I smell something I will never forget as long as I live . . . Neither will Daddy. It changed our lives forever. You'll read about it.

- *Uncle Greg:* My doctor Greg Hahn who has saved my life on several occasions . . . everybody should have a doctor just like him.

- *Aunt Celia:* My other doctor who helped save my life.

- *Uncle Richard:* The special security guard man for us in Jupiter. He gets out of his car to say hello every time he sees me walking with my parents down the street.

- *Uncle Jim:* There are two: one who drives our car back and forth to Florida with my "monkees" in it and who has been a longtime friend of my parents. The other Uncle Jim takes care of our "housis" when we need repairs. They are both very nice.

- *Aunt Louise:* The nicest lady in the world next to my mother. She's been like a member of our family . . . and has taught me about racial tolerance. And she said I taught her how to love big gentle dogs like me.

- *Uncle Brian:* My baby-sitter up north, someone I feel totally and completely comfortable with. I trust my life with him and know my parents do too.

- *Uncle Ron:* A nice man who does electrician stuff for us up north. I keep an eye on him when he's at the "housis."

- *Aunt Suzanne:* Our very nice next door neighbor up north . . . She was the one who, while hugging my brother Smokey in a final goodbye the weekend before he joined my grandfather in helping to keep our family bench in Heaven warm for the rest of us, told him he had lived his life so fully and intensely.

- *Sneezie Wheezie:* What my parents would say after I would unload my stuffy nose. I learned to do this on command too.

- *Do You See Any Squirrelies?:* I go on immediate alert for birds, squirrels, bikes, ducks, horses, foxes, etc. when my parents say those words. It keeps me young.

- ***Do You See Any Deerzie Squirrelies?***: When my parents ask me this I immediately go on alert specifically for pretty, peaceful, but rather large (bigger than me at least) four-legged acquaintances of mine in the forest behind our "housis" up north or in the fields we drive by en route to take my daily walks.

- ***Do You See Any Squirrely Geeses?***: This phrase means I go on the lookout specifically for my feathered friends that talk loudly and can do something I can't: they can fly. There are lots of them who live near our "housis" up north.

- ***Barbeque:*** When Daddy says this word, I immediately go out to our "porchis" up north and down south and tend to salivate. It means great smells and even the occasional taste from Daddy's finger.

- ***Cowzys:*** Friends who are large and black with four legs. I see them from my favorite spot when walking at the school nearby.

- ***The Box With Pictures and Voices:*** A machine I am sure you and your family enjoy watching almost every evening, although more and more what we see seems quite violent in nature.

- ***Pictures With Moving Parts and Voices:*** You know these as movies.

- ***The Box With Voices & Melodies:*** You know these as radios.

- ***Uncle Connell (CJ):*** My parents' really nice friend who I haven't seen for awhile. But to whom I will always be grateful for flying in from Minnesota to take care of my sister Samantha, my brother Lucky and me for almost two weeks when Mommy and Daddy were in New York City for Mommy's life-saving cancer surgery.

- ***Aunt Allison:*** The doctor who was so wonderful on the most important day of Lucky's long life.

- ***Uncle Dave:*** A doctor I first got to know when he helped my parents understand my natural place as the Alpha dog of our pack.

- ***Fingertails:*** Daddy thought I never knew this meant that my toenails needed clipping . . . something I really do not enjoy.

- ***Perywinkle:*** My very, very favorite monkee! We always travel together in the car on our trips to and from Serenity 1 and 2, where we also share a basket to keep each of us comfortable.

- ***Smell the Smells:*** What all my peers and I love to do when we go on our walks . . . I also do it when I am out on our "porchis" up north which looks out over the forest.

- ***Where's Mr. Armadillo?:*** I have only met him once, the first time Lucky and I ever went to "wild beachis" near Serenity 2. He was pretty weird looking. Rather than saying hello, he escaped down a deep hole right next to the path leading to the "beachis," and he has never come out again. But my parents know to remind me to look for him each time we go there.

- ***It's Time To Weigh You:*** I sit down on the scale at my Uncle Doctor Greg's office when asked by my parents.

- ***Trow-Ball:*** When Daddy uses this term I know we are about to play with one of my favorite round "monkees" which I have learned to both catch and throw with my mouth.

- ***Trows-up:*** Just like it sounds, and not pleasant for your kind or mine. Mommy did a lot of this when she had cancer. And I have too when something I have eaten disagrees with me.

- ***Hold On Tightly:*** Daddy's way of warning me that the car is about to make a turn. If you were sitting beside me, you'd notice I get prepared by pushing even deeper into my seat than I usually do.

- ***Goes My Sleeps:*** When I hear these words I know it's time to put my head down and close my eyes.

- ***You Can Put Your Head Down:*** Same as ***Goes My Sleeps.***

- ***Machine With Wheels:*** You know this as a car.

- ***Give A Nuzzie:*** Unlike many of my peers I do not kiss with my tongue. I have only done so once which you'll read about. However, when asked to give a nuzzie, I love to rub the side of my face against Mommy or against Daddy.

- ***Say Hello:*** An easy one for me . . . when asked to, I do so pretty enthusiastically.

- ***Aunt Merrie:*** Mommy's friend who helped us put our "housis" back together after the fire.

- ***Paris & Snoopy & Sinbad:*** My young Collie protégé, Paris; and my even younger energetic and loud German Shepherd friend Snoopy up the street; and my very old, white Samoyed pal Sinbad who lives next door.

- ***Baby & Chippy:*** My favorite horsey friends who live right across the street from us up north.

- ***Barbaro:*** A kindred spirit who I am often compared to.

- ***"Sweet Survivor":*** Another song I love to listen to with my father, just as he did with Smokey before I was born.

- ***Bring Monkee to Say Hello:*** As long as I like whoever has come to visit, one of the ways I like to welcome them is by introducing them personally to one of my "monkees." Depending on which specific one my parents ask me to select, I'm fortunate to be able to discern from among **Aurora, Blue Bear Monkee, Flying Pig Monkee, Baby Monkee, Ducky Monkee, Pelican Monkee,** and **Holiday Monkee**. (About the latter, all I know is when asked by Mommy on a Memorial Day weekend to get my favorite "monkee" for that particular holiday, I came back to where she and my father were sitting and carried in my mouth the only "monkee" dressed in an American flag.) In any event, my absolute favorite is Lion Monkee, along with, of course, my biggest "monkees" **Perywinkle, KissKiss, Polarsnarf,** and **Fluffy** who are too big for me to carry around in my mouth. But I can also pick them out in a crowd of "monkees" upon request.

- ***Ball:*** Like a "monkee" but something I use for **"trow-ball."**

- ***Doggy Car Wash:*** most of my peers don't like this . . . I love it! As soon as I hear these words, I move over to the hose on the "porchis" because I know Mommy is about to cool me down.

- ***Give Me Five:*** Lucky and I learned to do this on command. He had a way of doing so that really ingratiated him to others.

- ***Huggy Wuggy:*** This expression has always meant something different to me than it did to my brother Lucky . . . When I hear these words I know it's time to have some fun . . . So as long as my hips are feeling up to it, you will always find me flipping onto my back with my legs in the air churning in motion much like a horse does. For Lucky, they meant a special code between him and Daddy . . . Daddy would spread his legs like a tunnel, and Lucky would walk between them where he'd go through and back, again and again. Or he'd stop and Daddy and he would do a dance together.

- ***Buggy Wuggy:*** An expression my parents use to describe small flying creatures, or the tiniest of them crawling on the ground that can get into my fur and make me itchy. ***Buggy Wuggy Medicine*** is the name of what prevents them from doing so.

- ***Aunt Sam:*** Someone I have not seen for a long time. But she drove Mommy to her chemotherapy sessions and also home safely from New York after the cancer surgery, so I will think of her always as someone special.

- ***"Wild Beachis":*** Lucky and I loved all **"beachis,"** but as you will read, **"wild beachis"** was by far our absolute favorite—and for good reason.

- ***Shoezys:*** I wait while Daddy puts these on before our walks.

- ***Growlies:*** I do not do it often. However when I feel we are under some sort of threat or just feel uncomfortable about something or someone, I make this sound to let my parents know. Sometimes I can do it on request. And more important, sometimes I do it *proactively*. The best example is when we once had someone come to the front door where Mommy and Daddy spoke with her for some time. During the whole time I very quietly expressed to my parents my opinion about what I perceived were the intentions of the woman. I guess my concerns got through as she was not hired to do whatever she was being interviewed for. And perhaps it was only coincidental, but sometime later my parents learned she was arrested.

- **Belly Belly***: Sometimes it means I go on all fours and do a "crawley." Sometimes it means I lie on my back to have my belly scratched . . . It all depends on the circumstances.

- **Shake Shake Shake:** Something I do on command after a bath or after being caught in the rain. I also know to do this as hard and as loud as I can, noisily shaking the "necklaces" (you know them as collars) around my neck when I need to catch my parents' attention about something really important.

- **Aunt Anne:** The lovely woman who fell in love with me while editing the essay that Mommy wrote about me, the one that the *Palm Beach Post* published along with our pictures.

- **Keeping Our Family Bench Warm In Heaven:** A special wondrous place of peace and happiness where my mommy's Daddy and all of my siblings and friends are waiting for all of us to be together again.

- **Rainbow Bridge**: You cross it on the way to our family bench.

- **Lucky:** My canine soul mate.

- **Face:** Lucky's name at the orphanage. But **Lucky** is all he ever wanted to be.

- **Aurora:** The very first name I was given as a new born, and happily and suddenly recalled *ninety-one years later* (my time). It was when Mommy asked **Aunt Suzanne** how her cat by the same name was doing during an interview for another book my parents are coauthoring about caregivers. As soon as I heard the name "Aurora," I came running and let Aunt Suzanne and my parents know vocally I knew that name really well. Unfortunately Aurora the cat passed away at the age of seventeen (my parents' time) while I was in the very late stages of writing this book.

- *Velvet:* The name the orphanage (the SPCA) gave me, in large part due to my beautiful coat . . . I still respond to Velvet when I hear it.

- *Mushy-kins:* A term of endearment to which I have always responded to when my mother hugs me. When I was little, Mommy used to say I reminded her of the "Mushy Dogs" who raced in something called Ididarod. Sometimes it's used in concert with, or at the end of, the three names that follow immediately below.

- *Princess Sheba Spirit:* This is the full name I go by . . . the one given to me by my mother.

- *Mommy:* My idol. My hero. My inspiration. My human soul mate.

A GOOD PLACE TO BEGIN

As you already know, this story is about me—my life story. Actually it's about those stories from my life that are of particular interest to me. For whether important or not, they have very much defined who I am.

At my age, I felt it's as propitious a time as any for me to relate them. While I still have all my mental and physical faculties and the energy to do so.

I am no longer a youngster. Although I have been told many, many times that with maturity and even with so many life experiences behind me, I still retain a residual youthfulness. You can see it in my step when I go out on my nightly walks. And in the gait of my now very occasional and very brief runs, which due to my always suspect hips, I have always tried to keep to a minimum.

When I began this project, I obviously had to answer the question, "*So what is it about my life that makes it worth reading about?*"

I'd answer that this way.

No one who knows me doubts the fact that I've lived a rather unique life. One filled with the extremes of life's offerings. From initial depths of despair to real hope; from the mundane day-to-day to hours of extraordinary drama; from an early outlook of only loneliness and aloneness due to no fault of my own to a life replete with warmth and love and loyalty mixed with lots of contentment, uncertainty, and occasional drama.

In short, my life has to date been much like the stories that comprise this book: totally fulfilled and totally fulfilling.

And in that, therein lies the raison d'être for this memoir.

In a day and age of so much negativity, so much cynicism, so much self-indulgence, so much disposability of things that are perceived as "uncool" or inconvenient, and all the other things that complicate this world, my life story, I trust, sends forth a simple positive message.

That message is: *just be yourself and be true to yourself*. And if you do, good things will happen.

As one of Daddy's favorite philosophers, Emerson, put it so well: *"If a single person stands upon her convictions and there abide, the whole world will come round to her."*

That in essence synthesizes what my life has been all about. This is as good a place to begin.

. . .

To reemphasize, there are a couple of points that you should know about me from the outset, for they make up a great deal of who and what I am today.

First and foremost, as I mentioned, I'm adopted, as were Smokey, Samantha, and Lucky, who joined my parents' pack before me. I also don't know just how many other little girls and boys were members of my first (birth) canine family pack or how old they might have been when adopted. But from what I now understand, I was about six months old (my parents' time). I also don't know how being adopted may have affected the lives they've lived and their outlooks on life. But for me, it has had a significant impact on the kind of female I've matured into.

Second, in my case, compounding matters is the fact that I was adopted not once but a couple of times, having been returned, at least twice, back to the orphanage due to no fault of my own.

Why?

Likely because I was born with a physical deformity: my hips weren't attached right. So much so that as soon as I learned to walk and then to run, I also learned, to my chagrin, that when I would stop suddenly, my body wouldn't cooperate.

By that I mean the back of my body would grotesquely collapse under the rest of my body. So while not only terribly uncomfortable for me, it also had to be nothing short of the ugliest and scariest of sights for those who happened to witness it. And so that's why I was returned to the orphanage.

Looking back, I cannot and do not really blame anyone for doing so. Who wants a baby girl if within hours of adopting her, you find out that going forward she's going to face severe medical challenges that are going to cost you a fortune in hospital and doctor's bills!

Besides, while most parents adopting my kind will not readily admit it, deep down they are more than likely looking for the perfect child. Or at least one they think has the potential to be.

At this stage of my life, I guess even I can sort of see their point of view.

Having said that, while maturity and a long fulfilling life have helped to give me such perspective, I can also tell you firsthand how much it hurt—to find myself back in the orphanage before I even had a chance to take in my new environs and before I had a chance to prove myself.

As much as it hurt, however, it's probably a good thing that I was too young then to comprehend what was being said upon my return to the orphanage. Not yet able to understand the full implications of the meaning of *"She's a really good, really smart, really beautiful little girl. It's just we just can't afford to pay for all the bills we know she will bear. So before we become too attached, before we fall in love with her even more, it's best to 'cut our losses' now. And look for one who's healthier, even if possibly not as smart or as good or as beautiful as this one."*

Who knows, but it's possible that had I understood what was being said, I might have given up all hope to find someone who would love me for who I am, and not some idealized version of what they may have wanted me to be.

I hope I do not sound bitter, for I feel no bitterness at all; I'm just making a point.

Being returned to the orphanage for a birth defect is no fun—no fun at all.

So I did the only thing I could do under the circumstances: I went back each time and committed myself again to try again. To do my very, very "bestest" again. To hope in my heart of hearts, once again, that I'd meet a family that would see through the physical deformity.

Third—and this is not insignificant either—I'm very smart. I say so without meaning to sound arrogant or cocky. Honestly I had little to do with it. I was just born that way.

By this I mean that from as early as I can recall, if something was said to me, I'd not only get the gist of it the first time, but also be able to remember it forever. Some say that's been my life gift. It's also why I not only really do believe each of us has our own particular gift, but we have to be lucky enough to find those who will help to nurture, cultivate and celebrate it.

I sincerely appreciate how important my superior memory is. How it, along with my ability to deliberate, evaluate, and assess before dealing with any situation I encounter, has helped me to respond appropriately to the many little and especially not so little of life's issues and challenges, and helped me evolve into the leader I have become. So that when I speak, others tend to listen. And when I decide on a course of action, others tend to follow. And it's allowed my natural instincts to be good, particularly intense and challenging situations. Not just for me, but especially for my loved ones.

· · ·

Chief among those loved ones is my wonderful mother.

She's been the greatest gift to have ever graced my life.

She doesn't know it, but the day I decided to begin this project was the day she celebrated her most recent birthday. This is my birthday gift for her. One that honors her and thanks her for the indispensable role she has played in my life.

It is in fact to my mother these stories from my life are primarily dedicated. For sharing with me her unfettered, unfiltered, and unconditional love—and for showing me what unmitigated, unrepentant, and unqualified love are all about.

She's led by example, and it is her example that I have taken on as my standard in dealing with others. And in so doing, I have tried—successfully, I hope—to live a good life. One in which I have maximized my potential. One in which, I trust I became what she always wanted from me, always expected from me.

To become, as she characterized me as recently as today while stroking my hair as we sat together on my favorite sofa at our "housis" in Jupiter, Florida, her "bestest girl."

. . .

While I may be her "bestest girl," I am not embarrassed to say Mommy is my heroine.

She's the most courageous, strongest willed, kindest, bravest, most compassionate, caring and not uncomplicated of her kind I've ever known. And I've known quite a few during my life. In fact, over the years of my life, I've gotten to meet and know to varying degrees of closeness my parents' colleagues, families, clients, deliverymen, neighbors, friends, acquaintances, doctors, nurses, firemen, policemen, civic officials, teachers, students, employees, clients, clergy, and vendors—from over twenty countries and almost every continent.

And it's fair to say, if asked, most of them—or at least those I would have met a second time—would tell you about one other gift of mine. That is, once someone has met me, I make enough of an impression, so that they never forget me. Just as they can be sure I never forget them. Or anything I may have picked up about them. That's another thing you should know about me from the outset.

. . .

So that I am not remiss, as I have already told you about my mother, let me say something about Daddy.

About my father, suffice it to say I love him very, very much. In just the same way I know he means it when he tells Mommy and Lucky and me he loves us *"more than life itself"* and *"forever and a day"*.

We have a unique father-daughter relationship. He is still today after all these years, my athletic coach, having taught me from our very first day together the joys of playing "trow-ball." But as much as he does special things like that for me and has done so throughout my life, much more importantly, he has also been my comfort zone. The one I would go to tell if I thought there might have been something wrong with my brother. Or that my mother needs his attention right now. Or that a big storm is coming and we need to get ready for it. Like most men, Daddy loves the fact that I'm athletic. Yet he even more loves the fact that I have matured into what I have overheard others say is a *"beautifully elegant,"* *"quite self-sufficient,"* *"self-composed,"* and *"intelligent"* female. In much the same way—but different obviously because I'm his daughter—that he feels about my mother.

I suppose that's the reason it was appropriate that he agreed to help write my story. Otherwise it's more than likely these stories from my life would not have been written.

Simply put, while it's true I can do lots of things some of my peers can do, and some many cannot, penmanship and typing are not, have never been, and will likely never be one of them.

So in my own way, I asked Daddy to help me.

Because I know he loves my mother as much as I do, and she would appreciate it. And because, though he's very much a male, he, like my beloved brother Lucky, happens to be very sensitive.

Something I can attest to firsthand: I listen to the music Daddy listens to. And while I don't always understand everything he hears in the words of a song, I am often touched by many of their lovely melodies, by their sounds which I frequently find romantic, on occasion melancholy, and almost always inspiring and soothing.

It's those moments which have not only brought us very close together, but they have also enabled us to be able to read each other so well.

Which is also why, the fact that we both not only share our deepest love but also an enormous respect for my mother, has never had to be explained by either of us to anyone else, or to each other.

And why I never doubted for a moment he fully understands and appreciates my decision to dedicate this book about my life story, first and foremost to my mother, while recognizing as well others who have been so helpful along the way.

And that's why I have never had to explain to him why I would like a portion of the proceeds of my book to go to fund caregiving for others like Lucky and me, in Mommy's name.

It just seems so natural to honor my mother in this way—for all she has meant to me, to all of my siblings, and of course, Daddy.

She would tell you it's been nothing but a labor of love.

Well, Mommy, so is this book . . .

With all my love,

Princess Sheba Spirit

THE EARLY YEARS
My New Family

Princess: My First Day With My New Family

MY BROTHER SMOKEY

By now you are already aware that I wasn't the first to be adopted in my family. My half-brother Smokey Max Brooks Pomerantz was, fourteen years (my parents' time) before me.

He was followed by my half-sister Samantha Blackie (everyone called her Sam). Who was followed by H.G. (stands for Happy-Go-) Lucky, who became my absolute "bestest" friend in life, and canine soul-mate forever.

I trust you won't mind my getting away from technicalities, but hereinafter, I will be referring to all of them as my brothers and sister without the reference to "half."

For in my mind, and I assume all adopted siblings feel this way, there is no "half" in any of us.

In my view, we are no different than any brothers and sisters. We just have different biological parents, and a mother and a father who love us now no differently than if we had been part of their lives from the outset.

I feel the same way about adoption. Sure I've known for as long as I can remember I was adopted. It didn't take much to figure that out.

I look nothing like either of my parents. None of us did.

But that didn't make any difference to us. Nor has it ever made my parents feel any different about any of us.

Indeed, if they have taught me anything at all it is that being adopted doesn't mean you're any less appreciated, or loved, or important. It doesn't mean you're less valued, or somehow "tainted" or "disposable." In fact, it means *we were chosen* to be loved. I really think that's something every adoptee should take to heart. Something every adopting family should remember before they decide to adopt.

. . .

In preparing for this book, I had to think long and hard about what exactly I could tell you about my parents' first adoptee: my oldest brother Smokey. For the simple fact is I never met him.

I only wish I had.

In some ways though, I feel as if I have known him all of my life. That in some ways we are intrinsically connected.

This may be due, in part, to the fact that his presence in our family is ubiquitous. In old photographs and family movies. In all the stories I have heard told about him by all of those who knew him, from his earliest days in Charlotte, North Carolina, and then Minneapolis, and finally where we live today.

If there is one common theme that runs through every single description of my brother, it is the word, "spirited." That in a nutshell was Smokey.

It is also why my mother incorporated it into my full name.

As far as she is concerned, Smokey sent me to find her after he left to join up with our grandfather in Heaven, keeping our family bench there warm for us. As far as both of my parents are concerned, it is Smokey's undeniable spirit which flows through my veins that has helped make me the survivor I am, against all odds.

Whatever!

What is undeniable for certain, however, is that Smokey's life story was nothing short of remarkable. The type of which books are written and movies are made.

It had a little bit of everything . . . and more.

Just like mine.

I guess that's why I found myself stymied by the challenge of what would be the "bestest" way to tell you what you should know about him, without making it too much about me, and not enough about him. Said differently, how does one accurately sum up the life of one whose spirit runs through my veins, yet one I never met?

The solution came to me in the middle of the night: You needed to hear it from someone who knew my brother far more, and far more realistically, than the almost mythical figure he has come to be known to me. From someone who knew him "bestest."

The father we shared.

It dawned on me that I had actually heard the remarkable saga of my brother's life best summed up in an emotional musical farewell Daddy had assembled based on a short story he had written. A few months after Smokey was reunited with our grandfather in Heaven.

The first time I heard it was when my parents had some friends over for a dinner party a long time ago, and everyone was recounting their favorite stories about their own respective family adoptees.

There had been lots of laughter . . . then some silence . . . then more laughter. From our vantage point in the television room just down the hallway, Lucky, Samantha, and I got the strong impression everyone was having a really wonderful time.

Then we began to hear something different. Four really nice melodies —three of which I would later learn were composed by a man named Yanni, and a fourth was called Pachelbel's Cannon.

And then I overheard the unmistakable sound of some sniffling. Whatever it was playing on the box with voices and melodies was making people cry. So I decided to check it out for myself, quietly moved into the big hallway that runs from the front to back of our "housis."

There I lay down to listen to:

OUR WEDDING GIFT: A LIFETIME OF MEMORIES

"It was to be our final weekend together, after thirteen years.

Three presidents (Carter, Reagan, and Bush) had come and gone. A new one had just been elected.

He had lived through the 'It's a new morning in America;'; Mandela; the Berlin Wall; Gorbachev; Yeltsin; the demise of the USSR; two hostage crises at least; Beirut; the shooting of the Pope and John Lennon; Tiananmen Square; "Iran-gate"; the LA riots; the San Francisco quake; the superstardom of Ted Koppel and Larry King (with whom we had become acquainted professionally) and Oprah; the rise and almost fall of Prime Minister Brian Mulroney (whom I had once known well in Canada). He had lived through the devolution of GM and IBM; NAFTA; Thatcher's leaving; LES MIZ; PHANTOM; MISS SAIGON; Charles and Diana—had married and separated; the saving of the Minnesota Twins; the explosion of Microsoft and the MAC; the notebook computer; Rap as a lifestyle; the Thomas-Hill hearings, and the EXXON VALDEZ. And even the dream home we moved into. Oh, and yes, Joe Montana was still around.

Personally, he had experienced two tornadoes, had been hit by a car, and survived parvo, a life-threatening disease which killed too many of his peers. He had saved us from a fire, and once jumped into the pool to save his mother. And he had the uncanny ability to predict earthquakes and tornadoes.

His mother is American; father, a Canadian. He had witnessed their evolution together, their partnership in marriage and business—from the corporate hallways to radio and television (where he had listened to their talk shows and watched avidly the news commentaries), and then to worldwide strategy consulting.

They traveled a lot . . . and missed him greatly. But he was always with his two adopted siblings—a brother (almost 4) and a sister (8) whom he cherished, and they him.

. . .

It was to be our final weekend together . . . As a family, as a complete unit . . . Thirteen years to the day of his arrival within our midst . . . Handsome and strong, although now weakened by the process of time . . . Alert but hurting . . . Ever the enthusiastic trailblazer . . . Slowed now, dramatically so, having lived life so intensely and fully . . . A survivor . . . A companion . . . A genuine friend . . . He was my soul mate . . . Gone now, but never, ever to be forgotten.

. . .

I knew it was the right time, Thursday evening, the 18th of December 1992.

. . .

I called Bobbie from the car.

As elated as I may have been returning from my last trip of a very difficult, draining year of travel, her message was short, full of grief, and poignant: 'I don't think I can take care of him anymore.'

For almost eight months, every night— well at least 6 out of every 7—there had been numerous "gifts" to clean up. Several rooms in the house had been destroyed in the process.

Sick? Not according to his doctor, a shy and gruff practitioner with whom our son had developed a rapport of mutual respect—a trust.

Diseased—no, not according to the diagnostic tests.

Rebelling? Well, the personification of same when younger, he had matured into a quiet, confident, secure, natural leader who gave out his affections selectively. But if he was your friend, there was no one more devoted—ever.

Except by now he was no longer quiet and confident, nor secure. He wanted you by his side constantly. The incessant din told you so.

Friday the 19th at 10:30 a.m., I called his doctor from our office. 'It's time,' I said. 'We'll see you Monday.' And then laying my head down on my desk, I cried . . . cried like I hadn't in 15 years.

. . .

Bobbie and I left the office for home early that day.

A day we had spent huddled together behind closed doors . . . crying . . . rationalizing . . . seeking alternative solutions that did not come. Solutions which, we knew in our hearts, did not exist. But before we left, we pledged to make this a very special weekend. To forge even greater bonds of love and affection and gratitude. For the gift he had, in his own stubborn and curmudgeon-like way, bestowed on us from the outset of our first meeting thirteen years before.

Adopted as a baby with an ingrained courage so strong, buttressed perhaps by an immediate love for him we could not contain, his will to live simply would not be denied. In fact, every day of those thirteen years he lived had been a legitimate miracle.

You see, five days after we met, we were told to prepare ourselves for his death: 'There is nothing we can do. We don't know or understand what's killing him.'

It was a verdict we could not, would not accept.

We stayed up with him for 48 hours in what became his favorite chair, shooting through a syringe, a mix of honey and water down his throat to keep him going.

Until he underwent a massive blood transfusion, the one that saved his life.

And so we had each given the other the opportunity to grow into a family unit together . . .

. . .

Our final weekend together—that Friday, Saturday, and Sunday—was a maze of family activities. He got to eat the foods he loved: steak and kasha. He played with the toys of childhood. He walked down to and around the lake he felt he owned and ran and walked in the woods he loved, amidst the smells and sights he knew so well.

We held him frequently that weekend and listened to the music we had listened to together over the years . . . and posed for a photographer's camera.

He played with his brother and sister, who, it seemed to us, could sense, too, that Smokey would soon not be with us. They kissed him frequently and, on several occasions, even slept by his side—which was unusual for them.

He loved his grandmother. A surrogate love initially perhaps, after his grandfather passed away—it had grown into an unbridled love for each other.

She stroked him. He comforted her.

. . .

And then too there were his friends of nature who came that weekend to bid him farewell.

Another miracle of nature we suppose now . . . in awe perhaps.

He loved white-tailed deer. A born hunter turned pacifist, over the years he would sit and stare for hours at the deer, almost statuelike, whenever they showed up, wherever we lived. Except they hadn't been back for months, almost a year we reckoned.

They came back in a herd that weekend two times, for extended visits. As he sat in his customary place on the deck he truly loved.

So did the woodchuck come out near the lake that weekend on two occasions too, even though he had not been around for months, and indeed we have not seen him since.

. . .

Time passed by too quickly.

Every second seemed loud.

Every moment stood still and then passed on, almost as if it meant—and it did—that we were one moment closer to Monday.

Friday, our neighbor said her goodbye.

Saturday, we decided upon his burial place . . . seeing it made it harshly comforting. His grave digger shed tears for someone he had never met, yet seemed to know only too well. Together, we planted a bush-like tree in his honor. A dogwood bush—it was so appropriate.

Sunday evening, we sat together for hours. It was a piece of time we had long ago carved out whenever we were home together. It was a time of peace we had both come to treasure. He knew it as Daddy-and-Doggy time. Alone at times, I sat stroking his flanks, his ears, and his muzzle (so white now, but resolute and firm).

Through tears I endeavored so hard to hide, I let him know how proud I was of him. He had been everything and more than I could have ever expected. He had fulfilled his potential, having 'lived a full and good life,' as our neighbor said while hugging him closely in her farewell. God, I loved him so. It was so hard to accept the fact that twelve hours later, he would never again be there to meet and greet us at the door . . .

. . .

By the time we went upstairs, his grandmother had returned to her home nearby, after she too said her final goodbye.

He fell asleep in his usual spot. In his basket, wrapped tightly against the cold winds that never came, secure in the knowledge that his family was all around. Interestingly, his brother and sister were more clingy than usual. Both decided to sleep close by our sides.

For Bobbie and me, sleep could not come right away. The early hours were spent sharing our grief, each privately replaying in our respective minds the inevitability of the events that were to come the next morning. Finally, perhaps out of exhaustion, if not despair, our mutual silence evolved into the darkness of sleep . . .

. . .

Was it 7:00 a.m. already?

That was the first thought when I awoke with a start, awake and alert. No, it was not yet 7:00 a.m. Indeed it was only 2:15, when again for the last time during what had become a lifetime of a weekend and a weekend of a lifetime, again one more miracle of nature was to play itself out. Almost as if it was a television script, but one whose plot no one would dare accept to be realistic.

Through the moon's light streaming through the window beside our bed, I saw him standing at the top of the stairs waiting, staring back at me with a sense of quiet urgency. How did I know? I don't know, to put it simply. There had been no alarm . . . no noise . . . no bark . . . just an awakening.

He needed to be half carried down the stairs, and then, he followed his traditional route out the door.

When he came in, I told him how proud again I was, and he stood up as tall as he might, and gave me a loving and affectionate kiss. It was as if he were now saying, 'it's all right.' That we were in sync, and that our feelings of guilt should be assuaged.

He went upstairs while I lay a while on the sofa in the television room. To collect my thoughts . . . to regain my emotions . . . to strengthen the resolve required for the next eight hours or so . . . and to record the moment. With that hug, for me, it all came together and apart simultaneously. But, now I knew that with God's help, I would be there for Bobbie and the family.

. . .

At 6:40 a.m., all five of us were in the bed together. But the poignancy of that bittersweet moment was countered by the harsh knowledge that this would never ever occur again.

By 9:00 a.m., we were on our way. I sat with him in the back of the car. 'Majestic' was how everyone had always described him. And now, majestic and curious as usual, his eyes sought out the familiar sights. A rolled-down window gave entry to his favorite smells as we passed by the lake.

Bobbie was driving, and I knew she was suffering inside. Truthfully, we both were. But she had become his (and my) Rock of Gibraltar over the past few years of interminable travel.

However, all he heard on that final ride was how handsome he was. How much we loved him. And how proud we were that he had come into our lives. At our destination, he and I waited outside while his mother paved the way . . .

. . .

His final minutes of life with us are an indelible marker in a lifetime of memories.

He was quiet, not agitated, as I lifted him up. Holding him gently and firmly, I quietly let him know, 'We are so proud of you . . . so proud of you. You are so brave. You will always be part of us. We love you so much.'

I could feel Bobbie so close to me, holding onto me, knowing that the journey in our life partnership was entering into another era.

Every second became a lifetime of emotions.

The silence in the room was broken only by the quiet cadence of the words spoken in prayer.

And finally, as I held him, his incredible current of life gently dissipated in my arms. Within seconds, there was only the peacefulness reflected on his beautiful countenance, almost as if he were so very young again.

The bond between Bobbie and me at that moment was never stronger, never more fragile. A bond cemented over years of common and individual dreams and ambitions. A partnership of love—tested and tried—and all chronicled through his eyes. Eyes that would no longer ever see, but whose wisdom, his friends and we had long ago come to accept. He had been witness to it all . . .

. . .

Gently and lovingly, we dressed him in his favorite sweater with a red bow, just as the first day he came into our lives.

We were so gentle . . . Aware that he could not feel our touch, but knowing that he had touched our lives, our hearts, and our souls forever.

With the fierceness within only the proudest of mothers, Bobbie turned down all overtures to help her carry him out for his final ride home. She had carried him home underneath her coat, against her breast, the first day thirteen years before. She would carry him home on this—his final—journey home.

Then, having been given the choice, she asked me to stay with him in the back of the car.

. . .

That final ride home, I held his head firmly and yet so gently.

I stroked his head, his ears, and his face. Through my tears, I saw others pointing and looking sadly at me through our back window. I whispered to Smokey and told him where we were. How close we were to the one place he truly loved. Outside, in the back of our home, on the edge of the woods, where he would always be close to us and smell the smells of his wild nature.

. . .

At home, Bobbie carried him to his final resting place.

Together, we laid him down gently, wrapped in his favorite sweater and blanket. Surrounded by that and those he loved: a bone . . . a baseball cap . . . a picture of his family.

*And we said our final goodbye: a prayer of gratitude and hope, a
thank you for a life so well lived, and so well deserved.*

. . .

From my study window, he is never beyond my view.

And in our hearts, he is never beyond our thoughts or feelings.

*For he was—nay, he remains the best, most sustainable wedding gift
ever bestowed on Bobbie and me.*

*Our Coonhound, Smokey Max Brooks Pomerantz, was the wedding
gift we gave each other thirteen years ago."*

. . .

That it was in Smokey's sense of spirit I am named, I have always
taken to be nothing less than a huge compliment and a huge legacy to
uphold.

With two big caveats.

Unlike my big brother, I never did anything violent. And I've never had a
drinking problem. Certainly not the kind he did.

The fact is, at one point in his younger years, Smokey had an unfortunate
encounter with someone he thought posed a threat to him and quite
possibly to my parents. So he did what came quite naturally to him: He
used his teeth on her! And as a consequence, almost immediately, he was
forced to go on the lam from the law!

You see, while he didn't know it, my parents certainly did at the time: If
Smokey was caught by the Charlotte, North Carolina, police, the likelihood
is he would have not been subject to a fine or imprisonment—but rather
capital punishment! A point radically different from how Mommy and
Daddy viewed the matter: Yes Smokey had made a bad mistake, but not
one necessarily so bad that he deserved to die for it.

So they found him a farm to hide out at, thirty miles away from their
"housis" in Charlotte, North Carolina. Where he lived with one of the
many listeners to Daddy's popular radio talk show. And where one day,
about a month later, when they felt things had calmed down a bit and it was

safe to do so, my parents went to visit my brother and the radio listener, Clete, and his wife who were responsible for Smokey's safekeeping.

What they saw when they arrived shocked them beyond belief: My brother was drunk as a skunk!

It seems that at 4 o'clock in the afternoon, every afternoon, Clete would finish off his daily six-pack of beer, and Smokey, not wanting to be a bad guest, would down a full can of his own. So that by the time my parents found out about it, my brother had become a full-fledged, staggering, falling-down, dead-drunk, beer-dependent canine.

So much so, that while eternally grateful to the couple for taking Smokey in when they did, my parents decided this was not the best environment for my brother. Certainly not one they had ever intended or could have imagined for him. So they took him home that very afternoon. And the very next day, enrolled him in doggy detox.

It must have worked.

For although he never lost his hankering for the taste of beer, I am glad to say it never got the better of him again.

MY SISTER SAMANTHA

In January 1981, my brother Smokey and my parents moved from Charlotte, North Carolina, to the Twin Cities of Minneapolis-St. Paul.

They had to, in part, for their own safety.

No it wasn't due to something Smokey did.

Rather, unbeknownst to more than a handful of my parents' friends, there had been a very serious death threat against my father from the Klu Klux Klan, after one of his television shows in Charlotte. That forced my parents to live in not inconsiderable fear, under police protection, for almost three weeks prior to their acting on their decision to leave.

Yes, it's almost sure my parents would have left there anyways at some time of their choosing in the future. Daddy's radio and television talk show career was exploding. He was in demand, including by the people who ran the station where he worked. They wanted him to stay for at least another three years.

But the death threat and my parents' sense of insecurity there certainly made their decision a lot easier.

I can relate.

As I have always believed, there is a reason for everything. This was no different. The fact is that had the death threat not happened, quite possibly my parents would have been more inclined to stay where they were.

And had they done that, Samantha Blackie would never have become the second family adoptee in 1984, when after five years (my parents' time) of being an only canine child, Smokey gained a sister.

As was the case with Smokey, it was Mommy who found Sam. This time Mommy was at the orphanage known as the SPCA of Golden Valley in Minnesota. That's where she went one afternoon to purchase a large traveling cage for Smokey. Instead Mommy walked out with an utterly exotic-looking female canine with a velvet-like muzzle not unlike mine. She also had over-sized, basset hound-like ears that felt like velvet too, and two exquisite, different-colored, almond-shaped, sad-looking eyes, much like a Husky.

Sam's physical beauty lay in her unorthodox looks. When he first laid eyes on her, Daddy summarized the best description: *"Samantha,"* he would say, *"looks like two different ends of a car that don't match."*

He was right.

I also understand there was also never a question her name would be Samantha; I just never learned why.

What my parents were much less sure of, however, was how Smokey would react to this baby newcomer to the family.

They needn't have worried.

As soon as my mother took Sam from her arms and put her on the floor, Smokey walked over and gave her a couple of sniffs. To which she responded with a smile that said, *"I like you too . . . a lot."*

And from that very first moment, they remained frequently affectionate, always mutually respectful, and on occasion even playful "buds." For the most part, theirs was a close sibling relationship comprised, on the one hand, of an intense brooding loner type, Smokey, and on the other, the always smiling Samantha, who reveled in soaking up all the attention and affection she was given. Theirs was a friendship whose dynamics would stay consistent and predictable and only began to change some five years later (my parents' time). That was when a new brother joined the family, turning what had been a comfortable canine twosome into a pack of three.

. . .

My relationship with Sam was a little bit more complicated . . . actually a lot more.

Let me put it this way.

I guess we have all heard of families in which sisters are inseparable, the closest of confidantes and best friends.

Well, that wasn't the way it was at all between my older sister Samantha and me.

Yes, she was my sister.

And yes, as a consequence in my heart of hearts, I did love her—sort of. And yes, she did love me too—sort of. And yes, we respected each other—sort of. And yes, I suppose one could even say there were times we actually liked each other—sort of.

But, by no means were we best friends or confidantes. And we were certainly not inseparable.

Other than on two occasions when we did have to be separated— because we didn't see eye to eye about something. Those were the two times she had to be taken to the hospital for stitches.

You see, the truth is, she never wanted a sister like me. I'm big. I'm confident. I'm used to being in charge. I'm a natural leader—all characteristics Sam would very much have preferred a younger sister to not have. And that's only if she had to be encumbered at all by the sudden presence of a new and very large "baby" sister.

. . .

From the outset, it's fair to say Sam and I were destined for an acrimonious relationship . . . not a rivalry, mind you, just conflict.

It first came to the surface when I was still very young, had overcome my hip replacement crisis, and finally felt good enough to take my natural place in the family pecking order.

Sam would continually try to test my otherwise inherent tolerance, patience, and resiliency by doing rather irritating things. She'd try to sleep on my side of the bed. She'd steal my toys. She'd try to eat from my dish. Or simply attempt to disrupt whatever it was that I was doing, particularly if it involved crossing the unwritten boundaries in the relationship between Lucky and me, or between our parents and me.

I suppose, in retrospect, I finally ran out of patience.

I know that's not a good thing. Never losing control has always been something I have prided myself in. But it just got to the point with Sam's antics I simply couldn't take it anymore.

So I snapped.

Which is why, ever since, I've always regretted that my sister ended up at the hospital. I wish it didn't have to come to such ugliness. I realize even more today, many years later, that violence of any kind is not a suitable response, even if when provoked. I feel terrible for the inconvenience and pain the conflict caused our parents.

· · ·

As I said earlier, however, I think it was inevitable. A view shared by our family psychologist Doctor Uncle Dave.

He surmised that Mommy and Daddy probably didn't know what they were doing with Samantha and me once I no longer had to remain "cooped up" after recovering from my hip surgery.

After observing Sam, Lucky, and me interact with each other for just a few minutes, he told my parents, "*They (we three) are not the problem. You are. Just because Lucky's a guy doesn't mean he wants to be the pack leader. In fact, he doesn't want to be that at all. He likes it when someone else in whom he can have confidence does the leading."*

This, though, is where it got a bit more complicated. Samantha, he told my parents, thought *she* should be the leader (he called it being the Alpha) because of her older age. However, he also advised them that would not fly well with me, as I am a natural Alpha, no matter what, even if I happened to be the youngest.

It's fair to say at first Sam didn't take well to Uncle Dave's assessment of the situation.

But she was forced to live with it, and eventually learned to deal with its most obvious consequence: from that day forward, I was the one who my parents would turn to first when it came to deciding what to do about anything involving the three of us.

This made Lucky very happy. Sufficiently so, he gave me his *permanent* proxy.

As for Samantha? Well Uncle Dave came up with a really good solution. She was "rewarded" with her own very private time with our parents. Time they made sure to carve out for her each and every day for the rest of her life.

Putting this new approach into place, however, was not as easy as it may sound.

For you see, Mommy and Daddy felt a little sad for Samantha at the start. However, in due course, they were pleasantly surprised how things among the three of us began to fall into place, with even Sam eventually becoming comfortable with her new place in the family.

Lucky, as I mentioned, was quite happy to leave decision-making among the three of us up to me. Still he too, at the beginning, had a difficult time adjusting. Clearly empathizing with his older sister's change of rank, for some time he thought he could put things back to the way they were, if he could only get Samantha to accept his suggestion of her putting a stop to challenging me all the time. And when that didn't work, he tried using shuttle diplomacy, racing frantically, running back and forth between wherever I was and wherever Samantha might be, trying to keep both of us happy.

It was a good try on the part of one who in his heart simply wanted everyone to get along, and didn't understand when and why they couldn't. As a consequence for a period of time, he found himself physically and emotionally betwixt and between Sam and me, as a sort of peacekeeping, shuttle-diplomat, acting on behalf of the two sisters he dearly loved.

Looking back on it all, I sincerely believe had he pursued a different career, Lucky would have been a very able arbitrator. It's pretty obvious why. In my brother's constant pursuit of making everybody happy, he was forever looking for common ground to bring rival forces together. He was really good at it. And it said so much about him.

You know, volunteering to take on such duty takes extraordinary courage. For it means being prepared at any time to face the potential wrath of those he was trying to help.

It's just one of the many reasons I came to admire him so much and why I came to love him *"more than life itself."*

· · ·

I like to think, but will never know for sure, that given more time Samantha and I would possibly have become sisters more like those I have heard about: each other's closest friend and confidante.

However, with the rocky start we had early on, and then later, a prolonged illness that seemed to draw Samantha away from Lucky and me, it was not meant to be. It was not in the cards.

· · ·

Today I am comforted by the knowledge she continued to enjoy her brother's affections and her parents' unconditional love until the very last day of her life, just three and a half years later (my parents' time). An unconditional parental love, which resonated especially when Sam was finally ready to join the others keeping our family bench warm, in Heaven.

Mommy and Daddy did a wonderful job on that day. By equating their unconditional compassionate love for Sam with clear concern for how her passing would affect Lucky and me, they made sure they did all the right things the right way by all three of us.

For instance, on her very last day, Samantha's final moments with her family were spent in our parents' embrace next to our Doctor Uncle Greg on a very pretty blanket Mommy had spread out wide on the lawn right near Smokey's bush, next to the forest behind our "housis" Serenity 1.

After Samantha bid her final breath in farewell, with Uncle Greg's kind and gentle assistance, Mommy and Daddy brought Lucky and me over to say good-bye in our own way to our sister. By doing so, they allowed us to see up close what our senses could not ascertain from a distance: that she seemed so much at peace. Her face no longer marked by the strain of the chronic illness she had been fighting off and on.

While the scene was quite emotional for both of us, it was especially so for Lucky. For him, Samantha represented an earlier time in his life: happy, carefree, playful times when they were both quite a bit younger. And then having mutually shared the loss of their revered older brother Smokey, they had come through it stronger and closer.

And so it was with this as a backdrop, my brother had his own very personal way of saying good-bye to his older sister. He gave Samantha two kisses on her nose and one on each of her ears. This was his personal way of recognizing her for the really good and eventful life she had lived, for the joys they had shared. And for her unique contribution to our parents' family legacy.

Shortly thereafter, Uncle Greg carried Sam away, gently and lovingly, in his arms.

· · ·

Samantha Blackie Brooks Pomerantz, the little girl who never grew up and liked to eat everything in sight, will always occupy an important place in my parents' journey together.

That's why they and I carry "her box" with us, whenever we drive to and from our homes Serenity 1 and Serenity 2.

. . .

One example of the irrefutable impact Samantha made on our family legacy is reflected in the role Doctor Uncle Dave, the psychologist, played in our relationship.

It would be many years and a lifetime of experiences later before I next bumped into him, occurring very recently in fact, when we enjoyed a reunion of sorts.

Upon spotting me, it was pretty clear he was proud of what he saw: how much I had matured since our last collaboration more than eighty-four years ago (my time).

Mommy and Daddy had brought me to see him to get his thoughts on a very delicate and personal question: Was it possible for me to develop friendships with anyone who wasn't my brother Lucky who had left us a few months earlier for our family bench in Heaven?

To make a long story short, to everyone's surprise and pleasure, I could and did, and demonstrated I could do so with two of Uncle Dave's closest friends. One was a male. The other was, like me, a female. The two times we got together at Uncle Dave's "housis," we had lots of fun. Although it probably didn't hurt that we did so under close supervision of both my parents and Uncle Dave.

On both visits, particularly the first, I let everyone know I was incredibly happy to have been given the opportunity to make new friends. And while they weren't family—obviously neither could replace my Lucky—they were okay. And ever since, I must say I have felt better about my life in general and really myself in particular. And even happier knowing my parents feel better for me as a result.

• • •

Seven years (my parents' time) after my sister's passing, my favorite memory of Lucky, Samantha, and me together is etched crystal clear in my mind.

It was one time only, not necessarily a very good one for Daddy in particular, but very funny and eventful for sure.

While I don't remember *all* the details surrounding the event in question, I sure remember what happened.

Mommy was out somewhere. Maybe she was in Florida for a few days or maybe at the hospital in Boston. Whatever and wherever she was that day, she wasn't at home.

In any event, at some point during the afternoon, Daddy was leading us out to the garage so that we could use the dog run. When without thinking, he opened the door that separated the rest of the "housis" from the garage. And did so without looking!

Someone had left the garage door open! Who it was, or how it was opened no one knows to this day.

It certainly didn't matter at the time!

In a flash, Lucky and I decided it would be lots of fun to run as fast as we could out the garage, so as to take a good look around our environs without the usual encumbrance of our leashes.

Realizing that Sam had reacted somewhat more slowly to the opportunity, Daddy was able to get her to stay where she stood and to place her in our dog run where he knew at least she'd be safe.

Then he started chasing after my brother and me.

However, by then, Lucky and I were relishing the fresh air and opportunity to stretch our legs while racing as fast as we could against one another. Having never had so much fun, we got caught up in the moment. Truthfully it never struck us Daddy might have been concerned about what we were doing.

(Years later, we know better, and Lucky and I did offer an apology immediately afterwards).

In any event, the more we ran, the more he chased us. The more he chased us, the more he called us, and of course the more he called us, the more we raced ahead. That's the way it went, all the way up the street. I've never measured it exactly, but I have heard people estimate it's over half a mile.

Frankly it had to be a really funny sight: two four-legged sprinters being chased by a middle-aged man dressed in a suit, long sleeve shirt and tie, and black shoes, desperately shouting out their names at the top of his lungs!

• • •

All of a sudden, Lucky and I spotted something ahead of us that made us run even faster. It was something on wheels, and it seemed to be driven by someone, but we could see it bore no resemblance to the type of machine with wheels we drive to and from Florida. In fact, it was very different, quite distinct-looking: a one-person vehicle with one seat that offered no overhead protection from the rain.

It seemed to us that it was both odd and interesting, if not a little intimidating.

The further it/he went, the more we tried to catch up. Although truth be told, what exactly we intended to do with it had we actually apprehended it was something to which Lucky and I hadn't given a second of thought.

In hindsight, it was not one of our "bestest" moves.

Moreover, we began to notice it seemed to be slowing up the closer it got to the intersection. So as it slowed down, we slowed too, as the reality set in that we might have to decide on its disposition, should we capture it.

What we didn't know, of course, was that Daddy was *not* slowing up his pace. We also didn't know how frightened he had become that we might get lost and he would have to explain to Mommy what had happened.

· · ·

All of a sudden, Lucky came to a screeching stop! Toenails on asphalt! As soon I saw him do so, I too immediately put on my brakes.

We both had to!

For in the blink of an eyelash the tables had been turned on us. The weird-looking mobile had suddenly pivoted completely around and was now heading back in the direction Lucky and I were coming from!

My brother and I had only a split second to think, just enough to catch each other's eye and let the other know *"We gotta get out of here!"*

And so that's exactly what we did!

· · ·

It couldn't have been more than thirty seconds later after we had done a complete about-turn when we literally bumped into Daddy.

Right there and then I let him know we wanted to go home *now*. We had enough freedom on the run. For his part, Lucky said it in a different way. He simply lay down flat on his stomach and started crawling back to Daddy, right there on the street!

All three of us still breathing very hard after our respective long runs, we returned to our "housis" where Samantha was waiting patiently for us, wondering what she had missed.

But not until after Daddy had profusely thanked our neighbor in the wheelchair for being so concerned about our welfare.

· · ·

At home, Daddy didn't know whether to be grateful we didn't get lost or to be mad we had run without thinking. So he simply went with his gut. He told us how much we meant to Mommy and him, and said that all of us needed to be more careful in the future.

He did the right thing. It was the right approach. Lucky and I already felt bad enough for the fuss we had caused.

He also made sure to praise Samantha *"for guarding the house. You did exactly what you should have, Girl, and I am so proud of you for doing so."*

It made her so happy she slathered him in sloppy kisses.

Later that evening when all three of us and Daddy were together in the den, watching the box with pictures and voices, I mentioned for all to hear we had learned two good lessons that we would forever take to heart.

In the future, we'd think before ever again deciding to run off anywhere . . . *and* we assume our parents will also always make sure that no door would ever be left open, from which we might accidentally escape.

And with that epiphany stated, all of us including our very tired and relieved father fell asleep on the sofa.

Daddy Leading His Pack:

Me & Samantha & Lucky

MY BROTHER (HAPPY-GO-) LUCKY

L ucky was always the sweet one.

He was also my canine soul mate and the "bestest" friend I ever had in the world.

How he gained a family and filled ours with love is a story as inspirational as it is moving.

To help put it into perspective, it might be best to start from the end and work backwards.

. . .

It's been a year and five months (my parents' time) since he left the three of us: a mother and father whose love and respect for him knew no boundaries and me, his sister with whom he shared a love of a lifetime. Our love was one of a kind, as my parents tell everyone, that they were privileged to observe, witness, appreciate, and even to be a part of.

As I write this, it's true all three of us still hurt. For his father and mother, it's a sadness that runs as deep as any hurt can, at times so emotionally painful as to be overwhelming and debilitating.

Of course, I too miss him so much; however, nature has given me the tools to move on.

But he's always in my heart and is very much part of my soul.

He's with me every minute of every day. With every smell in the 'housis,'' with every toy we'd share together, at all the places where we'd run and walk and play, it is simply impossible for me to forget him, and even if I could, I would never want to.

However, as deep as is our loss, there is something else just as profound: the comfort we share knowing he is now in my late grandfather's caring embrace. No pun intended, but it is a match made in Heaven. For no two of God's creations could be better suited for one another. Both are good and tender and unassuming and gentle souls who sought from their lives nothing more than the happiness of others.

My parents and I are equally comforted by the knowledge that their son, my brother, is in a better place, where he is rejoined once again with the older brother Smokey he once hero-worshipped from the second they first met, and his older sister Samantha with whom he shared a warm and loving friendship of the heart.

So while our hurt is still deep, at times even overpowering, we take great comfort in knowing that he is in that better place.

A place where love is the only currency and where no one hurts.

A place where he can once again romp and jump and run like a bunny rabbit (as Mommy always described it).

A place where he can also once again fully take in every one of the sights he used to peer at with such intensity and with such obvious curiosity.

A place where he can again smell the smells he used to guide him and us around the places he loved to visit every day, no matter where we were.

A place where all of us can again visualize him cocking that expressive head of his at all those sounds he missed listening to for so many months when he was unable to hear much if anything at all.

A place where, once again, he can just simply be Lucky. For to be Lucky was all he ever wanted.

. . .

He was not only my brother. Lucky was my canine soul mate, my absolutely "bestest" friend in the world.

. . .

It was his eyes that first drew him to our father.

They were as wide and round and bright as they were scared and sad and innocent. So full of hurt and despair, they were at once both incredibly compelling and yet too full of sadness to hold in your gaze for too long. He sat there first looking at Daddy—no, it was more like he was looking right through him, staring out through the bars of a cage too small by half for one his size.

It's generally not an easy thing to convey from one's distant memory, the first sight of someone you would eventually end up loving so much it hurts, now that he's gone.

But in Lucky's case, it's as stark and real and true and clear in my father's mind's eye as it was back then. Simply put, if there is such a thing in the dictionary as the visual definition of a "haunting forlorn goodness," my brother's eyes would fill that page.

Eyes which immediately told all who matched theirs with his that he had quite a story to share, maybe even some deeply kept secrets. And that given the opportunity, very possibly a real-life contribution to make.

Eyes that told of suffering and disappointment and despair, but also of a hope and prayer for something better and more, from what up to then had been a very tough existence.

Eyes that frankly cried out, as much as did the rest of his sad browbeaten visage, the sad reality that he hadn't yet been given, nor did he think he might ever get, a fair shake in life. Eyes that would share his story. And reveal those secrets.

And under the circumstances of his life to that very day, who would or could blame him for holding such sad thoughts?

The fact was he had already been abandoned at least once, possibly twice. Left behind, waiting to be rescued from being tied to a chain-link fence, beaten and starving, for who knows how long.

From where, he was finally brought to the canine orphanage, the same one I would find myself in a few years later.

Where thirty-two days later (my parents' time) he was still waiting . . . waiting for someone to come for him. Someone prepared to take a chance on what on the outside looked like one of life's losers.

. . .

If his history had not been pretty, his appearance also had to play a not insignificant role in putting off potential adopters.

For he was not a pretty picture.

He was terribly, terribly bony. A body frame that would eventually accommodate sixty-two pounds carried just half that. It was covered by an ugly, tangled, mangy coarseness, much closer in texture to steel wool than the tender feel of a healthy puppy's soft fur.

And his demeanor didn't help much either.

Sure, it's possible it may have elicited some initial sympathy, even pity, from a few. But it certainly did nothing to help him come across as the kind of happy, healthy, vibrant, attractive young new arrival a family pictures joyfully and playfully scampering around one's "housis."

In short, the little boy who would become my bravest, "bestest" friend in the world was terrified—terribly, painfully, frighteningly scared.

He was scared of strange sounds even if they were but the enthusiastic calls from the scores of his peers at the orphanage, doing whatever they could in nearby runs and cages competing for attention to be noticed by passers-by.

He was also terribly scared of men's voices no matter how soft their intended intonation.

And he really never ever did get over the terror he felt from what he perceived to be any sudden movements. Notwithstanding how innocent those motions were, and unintentionally provocative they might have been.

In short, when he and my father first met, Lucky was scared of anything and anyone who was not the one kind female attendant who Daddy soon learned was the sole human being to take the time to try to get to know him. The only person to get to know him, to feel for him, to show him a patient gentle sense of human compassion, mixed, I'm sure, with not a little bit of pity.

I later learned from Lucky that she was the only person to really try to help him—to refuse to give up on him. But who at that moment was also making it no secret she was keen on dampening Daddy's growing curiosity about this sad-looking representative of God's many creatures, shaking like a leaf, in his presence.

In fact, she was quite intent on discouraging any further interest whatsoever in him.

. . .

In so doing, her tone was not unfriendly, just matter-of-fact.

"His name is FACE," she said. *"As you can see from the sign, he's been here for thirty-two days. He's a truly wonderful animal who surely deserved something better in his short life. But our space, as you can also see, is very cramped. We need to create more room for those who haven't even found us yet."*

As she spoke, my father said nothing. But neither could he take his eyes off the tragic, frightened, quivering, living entity peering out of his cage.

Her tone was flat, friendly, and factual.

"Mr. Pomerantz, he is a real sweetie you know. But with all the baggage he carries, I hate to say it, but I think even I have come to the conclusion he seems to be one of the 'un-adoptable' ones. And so as sad as it is—and I hate this part of my job—but he's about to be put down very soon.

So can I interest you in any of the others? You know there are some really terrific animals here waiting for a good home like yours."

"Why is his name FACE?" Daddy asked.

"I don't know really, but if my experience with him is any indication, it seems most appropriate," she replied.

"He sure is quiet. Does he bark?"

"No, in fact you never hear anything at all from him."

"So how does he communicate with you?" Daddy wondered.

"The same way he seems to have already done with you . . . with those eyes of his. At least that's been my experience with him. But I'd bet few, if anyone else around here, would see what I see about FACE. While two or three of my colleagues have mentioned his gentle sweetness (it's impossible to miss), I think it's fair to say even they view him as nothing more than a sad, abandoned, abused stray who we happened to come by a month ago, and whose time I am sad to say is now up."

"Truthfully I can see their point of view. We gave him a chance. Now we have to give that chance to others. FACE's time has come and gone. I don't have to tell you that it's the cruelest reality of what we do here."

· · ·

The fact is my father hadn't gone to the canine orphanage near our "housis" to look for another dog.

My parents already had two.

One was Smokey Max. Then about nine years old, he had been their wedding gift to each other—a very proud and regal and unquestionably rebellious Coonhound who had already lived an incredible life including, among other things, the miraculous survival from the insidious disease parvovirus that had killed nine out of 10 of his peers the year of his birth (1979).

Their other canine was Samantha Blackie, a magnificent, if strange combination of Husky and Basset Hound. She was the result of a 1984 visit Mommy made to another orphanage in search of a cage for Smokey.

Actually, on the day my parents first met FACE more than fifteen years ago (my parents' time), the real reason they had gone to the orphanage was for what they called a *"mental health break."*

It was something they did quite regularly to escape the tensions of their growing consulting business.

In my parents' view, there was no better place to get away from the realities of business. With its demands for a kind of laserlike focus that can turn into a kind of narrow-minded self absorption. That too often is accepted as the norm in a business world my parents have long viewed as too often unnecessarily ruthless, hypocritical, and destructively Machiavellian.

I look at it this way.

For my parents, their visits to a place that housed those who only have the simplest desire—to live—so as to love and to be loved without any pretense or hubris, was their way of staying in touch with who they were and have remained at the core.

That day in particular would exponentially reinforce that conviction of theirs, especially so for the next one hundred and seventy-four months (my parents' time) that followed.

For they were about to learn that if there ever was one of God's creatures who only wanted to love and be loved without any pretense or hubris, at that moment, Lucky's name was at the very top of the list.

. . .

"I understand your concerns about him, and God only knows if we could, Bobbie and I'd take all of the dogs here home with us, but what I'd really like you to do is bring him out of that cage, if only to give him a little bit of space before you have to do what you have to do with him," my father suggested to the attendant.

She nodded her head and pointed to a place for them to meet. It was just beyond the large rather imposing noisy room which housed all the dog cages. Where a rather small but accessible spot had been filled with sand, where the dogs could be introduced on more neutral ground.

"But before I bring him out, let me say again FACE is going to disappoint you. The few times anyone has asked to see him, he's been too frightened to go anywhere near them. Are you absolutely sure I can't introduce you to any others?" she asked, this time with a little edge in her voice.

Daddy's reply was polite but resolute.

"No, I'd prefer not. Let me be clear about it: I meant what I said. We did not come here to adopt another dog. I just came to see them, probably a dumb mistake on my part, but so be it. But I guess everyone has their idiosyncrasies . . . going to the SPCA is mine . . . my wife's too. So while I appreciate your caution about FACE, why not let me see for myself what you mean. What the heck does either he or I have to lose?"

. . .

The attendant could not have been more correct!

FACE turned out to be a terrified bundle of shaking, tangled, mangy, ugly, and coarse fur. No more. No less.

No matter how much Daddy tried to engage him, to merely reach out to pet him, no matter how gently he tried to encourage FACE to come a little closer to him, my future brother retreated to safety behind his friend, the attendant's, legs.

Not that he wouldn't look at Daddy—he did. Throughout those first few minutes when for the first time the two of them met up close and personal.

However, as often as my father would try to get my brother to come closer to him, FACE would retreat.

So, Daddy would wait.

And FACE would stand his ground, trembling, with those sad eyes staring up at Daddy from behind the attendant's legs.

So Daddy would try again . . . In fact he tried six times.

Until it became very clear neither of them was making any progress. That it was futile.

So much so that now comfortable in the knowledge she had once again tried and failed, the attendant took FACE by the rope by which she had held him and, without comment, started back through the long rows of dog runs, back to the cage which had become FACE's zone of personal safety for the past thirty-two days (my parents' time).

Where he would inevitably, in short order, meet his final fate.

. . .

As she had said from the outset, *his* time *had* come and gone at the orphanage. She could assuage her guilt: They had tried and failed.

. . .

As Daddy watched, they began to disappear from his view, the attendant and FACE in tow. He recalls even today what he felt and what he saw then as if it were yesterday. It wasn't a matter of being angry or frustrated or even sad. If anything, maybe just a little disappointed.

The reality was FACE and my father had not been able to connect.

Daddy knew only too well from experience that the reality is those things happen more often than not when it comes to strays like us looking to be adopted. It was something one learned to accept with some sense of inevitable, if reluctant, equanimity after frequent visits to the orphanage.

So frankly, at that point in time, Daddy believed there was nothing he could do to change things.

. . .

Although truth be told, I heard him tell others years later, there remained a niggling little thought. Part hope, part wish, part prayer perhaps that while FACE's short sad existence on this earth would very shortly come to an end, maybe at least he'd leave it with the innate knowledge that this one human being with the deep male voice had already fallen head over heels in love with one of God's creature's with the gentlest of souls.

. . .

The memory of the next few moments is pictorially burned into my father's brain.

Just as FACE and the attendant turned the final corner, FACE stopped and looked back to where he and Daddy had tried but hadn't succeeded to bond.

My father could see the attendant urging FACE on his way with a less than gentle tug at his rope. She was in a hurry now. There were others who could better use her attention.

Still, my brother stood his ground with a long silent stare—one our family would come to know well.

It wasn't defiance on my brother's part that my father and the attendant were witnessing. Rather it seemed more like confusion and desperation.

Or perhaps it was simply the relief he was still feeling in being free of the cage that had been his refuge for thirty-two days (my parents' time). Even if it were just to be a period of those few minutes.

Those are, of course, just a couple of possibilities.

However, to be honest with you, *I* tend to think there was something else at play.

Maybe, just maybe, it was fate beginning to take its natural course. In retrospect, it certainly seems so.

• • •

For just at the very moment, FACE seemed once and for all ready to acquiesce, to give in to the attendant's insistent prodding to move forward, and even started to move in the direction he was being pulled, just as abruptly he stopped. FACE sat firmly down on the floor and gave her a look of quiet resolve with which my family and I would also become quite familiar with over the years that would follow.

He was going nowhere!

Evidently caught totally off guard by his sudden action, the attendant pulled again, this time far less gently.

Just as resolutely FACE refused to budge.

And while for him to do something like this would turn out to be so out of character, at that moment in his life, he seemed quite comfortable with what he was doing.

Perhaps he felt he had no other choice.

Perhaps from his perspective, he was making his final stand.

I happen to think he was right.

• • •

He stared directly back at my father with those eyes of his—as Daddy stood watching this small incidental life drama between human and canine play out no more than fifteen yards from where Daddy stood, his mind in overdrive.

FACE simply felt compelled to respond. He needed to take some action that might break the obvious stalemate.

What FACE didn't know of course at the time was that Daddy had taken my brother's stare as a quest for advice.

FACE seemed to be asking, *"What did Daddy think was the right thing for me to do under the circumstances?"*

. . .

Whatever it was he was *thinking*, Daddy knew what the right thing was for him *to do*—and did it immediately!

Calling out to the attendant, he politely insisted she bring FACE back to try *"just one more time."*

He had made up his mind. Whether that *"one more time"* meant a minute, an hour, a day, a month, or a year, he was going to do everything in his power to convince FACE he had a good family waiting for him. That they would give him the love he had never known and the freedom to fulfill all the potential his new life could grant him.

. . .

This time, when FACE came out, it's not that he wasn't still leery of Daddy—for he was that and more. His innate shyness still dominated his every move.

However, there was something not quite the same as before. This time, if you looked hard enough, you would have seen what Daddy saw. That there was a discernible, if just a little, bounce to his step.

This time FACE and his caregiver stopped much closer to my father, no more than ten feet away from where he was standing.

With a slight nod to Daddy but saying nothing audible whatsoever, she dropped the rope that tethered FACE to her. And together, she and my father waited to see what would happen next.

FACE looked up at Daddy with those eyes of his, then back at her, and then at Daddy, and then gave what would come to be his (our family's) very most private signal for the next fourteen plus years (my parents' time): the slightest, very, very, very slightest wag at the very, very tip end of his tail.

Daddy took it as a sign. Of exactly what, he was not really certain at that moment.

Without saying anything, Daddy gently fell to his knees and from there got totally prostrate in the sandpit. Where FACE, not my father, was supposed to be and Daddy looked up in search of my future brother's eyes.

In doing so, my father's thinking was that he'd likely find FACE backing away warily, or at best perhaps standing right next to the attendant while all three considered their next moves.

That's what Daddy counted on.

Happily my brother proved him fallible.

For instead, as Daddy looked up, he came face to face with those wonderfully sweet eyes of my brother, and that wonderfully soft muzzle of his. And as their eyes met in tandem, Daddy thought he could see my brother seemingly trying to process this new development going on in his life.

"Can I really believe that my world is changing? Or am I imagining it? Can I trust that this human I've never met has really just walked into my life and actually cares about me?"

. . .

"Hello again," Daddy said softly. *"You know we're friends now don't you?"*

FACE's response said it all.

As in almost everything he did over the remainder of his life, his actions immediately spoke so much louder than words: He gave Daddy a kiss!

A fleeting one, but a kiss on the nose nonetheless. His tongue almost furtively darting in and out of his mouth, much like the little lizards we would meet near the "beachis housis" when we were older. And exactly the same way as he used to do it to me, kissing my ears and face in the years that followed, every single night after we'd finished our dinners.

My father was touched. However, he thought it best to move cautiously. To respond to my brother in a manner he might best appreciate: with silence and a kiss on my brother's forehead.

And that's the way they sat until the attendant's voice broke the comfortable silence between them.

"Mr. Pomerantz, you now know why we call him FACE. He does that only with the very few with whom he is comfortable. He very obviously bonded with you."

Daddy asked her what else she knew that he didn't know about FACE.

"Well, for sure he scares easily."

"Why, do you think?"

"All we know is he was found chained to a fence. He was all skin and bones (still is as you can see). He had clearly been beaten. He's terrified of anything that seems to him to be a loud sound. But having said all that, as soon as we took him in a little over a month ago, he's just been a trooper. He never ever goes to the bathroom in his cage. He is never aggressive to anyone here. He just seems to be the type of animal who is a good soul, who needs a break in his life. But when people come in here, he is so afraid of anything that is strange to him, he simply shies away."

"But you said he gives kisses reasonably readily."

"Yes, but not once has he given a kiss to anyone other than the people who work here like myself. He has never done what he just did with you. That's the first time I have ever seen him kiss a stranger, so to speak."

As they spoke, FACE's eyes moved in concert with their voices: from the attendant to my father . . . from my father to the attendant . . . back and forth . . . back and forth . . . back and forth.

As they conversed and my brother followed along, it was almost as if the three of them were oblivious to the fact they were not alone. In fact, there were by now several other people taking their measure of other dogs within a twenty foot radius of where they were. FACE sitting, the attendant standing, Daddy still on his stomach.

But FACE could not have cared less about any of the others. He just sat there, never giving the slightest hint that he wanted to run away. He was focused on the discussion underway between the person who had been his caregiver for the past thirty-two days (my parents' time) and this other human being who he had just made friends with. He just kept listening and looking up at her . . . and then back at Daddy.

It was a posture of his our father would never ever forget from that moment on. Never failed to appreciate, and never ever took for granted, the rest of their days together.

· · ·

The conversation must have gone on for maybe a good ten minutes more when, while still lying flat in the sand, Daddy turned one more time from the attendant back to FACE, with the question that would change both of their lives forever.

"Why don't you tell me what you want to do . . . would you like to come home with me?" he asked almost in a whisper.

FACE's unspoken response once again told Daddy all he needed to hear.

Another kiss and another little wag at the very tip of his tail.

· · ·

No more than five minutes after that, FACE became Lucky for the rest of his life.

Just how that happened was so typical of him, a moment in time both special and simple.

It occurred as he and Daddy were about to leave the orphanage.

Just as they were finalizing arrangements for payment, his license, and a new collar, the cashier suddenly broached a subject Daddy had not had any time to consider.

"Mr. Pomerantz, I am so happy for FACE I could almost cry. He's had such a tough life, you know. What a wonderful thing for him. I really have a special feeling about him. I think he is going to turn out to be something very, very special. You know he really is such a sweet one, don't you? Maybe this will be the start of a brand-new, happy-ever-after life for him."

She smiled. So did Daddy.

My brother looked up at both. He seemed to understand he was the one being talked about.

He wagged his tail. This time not just at the very tip, but all of it and very enthusiastically—the very first time Daddy saw him do something he would repeat many thousands of times for years to come.

"What do you think we should call you?" Daddy said, looking directly at my brother.

I guess the cashier thought the question was meant for her.

"Well, whatever you decide to call him. I know one thing for sure: This is his lucky day."

And that's how FACE became my "bestest" friend, Lucky.

MR. CONGENIALITY

There was a connection between Lucky and me from the minute we met. It was both instant and kinetic.

And it remained that way for more than seventy years (my time).

Our incredible bond was formed the moment Lucky spotted that my parents had brought home a "stranger" . . . except he never treated me as one.

In fact, he never treated *anyone* as a "stranger."

From his perspective, any friend of his parents was a friend of his.

It is a perspective we always shared.

. . .

When Lucky came over to say hello, I liked what I saw in him immediately. He was darkly attractive, with almost handsome, if somewhat unusual features. He had a terrific smile and an even nicer demeanor. There was an inner confidence about him, almost a presence. He walked with a bounce in his gait, yet he also conveyed an immediate gentleness, a kindness, even a vulnerability of sorts.

They remained among his best traits . . . until the day we said good-bye.

What he saw in me that moment he never really said.

As long as I knew him, he tended to speak in actions not words. His first, like his last, were his norm: a kiss on my nose, a kiss on both ears.

In this way, he really knew how to get his point across. He was a practitioner of the precept that "Less is more."

There was one other attribute he had that was very special, a true gift.

Simply put, he was incredibly nice.

By this I mean he never felt superior to anyone nor did he ever feel that someone else was not up to some preconceived standards of his. He disavowed phoniness, arrogance, or false airs. He was always upfront, open, and honest. He never wanted anyone to feel left out. He abhorred even the possibility of someone feeling envy or jealousy or anger or disappointment or disenfranchisement or despair or disillusionment or defeat. He would do everything he could to ensure no one got hurt, no one felt excluded, and personally see to it that everyone was happy.

All of this was just part of his makeup. It was built into his DNA. It also epitomized his life philosophy of *"It's a Wonderful World,"* the title of a song he and my Daddy would never tire listening to together.

My parents had a term for it. And so, they called my brother **Mr. Congeniality**.

I have often thought it would be a far nicer world if everyone were like my brother.

· · ·

I saw Mr. Congeniality at work, up close and personal, on more occasions than I can ever fully recall today. However, I do very much remember the first time. It was within minutes after I first came into the "housis." Immediately after he and I had made each other's acquaintance and instantly bonded.

At the time, I didn't think much about it. In retrospect, however, having come to recognize more and more just how tough my arrival on the scene must have been for our sister Samantha, I have also come to appreciate the significance of what Lucky did that day.

It had to be very tough on Samantha indeed . . .

And shocking, dismaying, disorienting, discombobulating, discomfiting, even disillusioning.

You see, by the time I walked through the doors for the very first time, Samantha had finally found *her* niche in the family.

As the second to join the family after Smokey Max, I can't imagine how much of a challenge it must have been for her to establish herself, to make a real mark on her adoptive parents who loved her intensely but who's first adoptee (Smokey) was the wedding gift they'd given to each other. And who with all the trials and tribulations that made him so unique, tended to soak up so much of their attention.

It's easy to see why it had to be extraordinarily challenging for Samantha to live in that shadow.

Still, from what I understand, she was quite content to do so. For she genuinely admired her older brother; she would do anything for him.

Such as the time she would not stop bugging the living daylights out of our parents until they understood that Smokey was not lying listless on the sofa in our den because he was tired, but instead because she realized that there was something else going on.

In fact, there was something very wrong with him! He needed medical attention! And he needed it quickly!

She was so right!

Within an hour, Smokey was diagnosed with a low grade, but increasingly serious virus. He had had it for awhile, but it had gone undetected.

The truth is if it hadn't been for Samantha, it could have turned into something very serious. This was Sam being Sam. Happily leaving the limelight to her older brother, she found contentment basking in his presence.

· · ·

And that's the way it was.

Until Lucky, Mr. Congeniality, came on the scene a few years later . . . without prior notice or fanfare.

His arrival to Samantha meant *she* now had found a younger playmate (albeit at first, a painfully skinny, scruffy, mangy, emaciated-looking one) with whom to romp and lord over whenever she felt like it.

And in many ways, that is just what happened.

For Lucky and Sam did greatly enjoy each other's company, happily spending many hours sharing their toys, having fun on the "porchis", playing tug and soccer and "trow-ball" (a game Daddy made up just for them), as well as joining their older brother and our parents for walks down at the lake at the school near our "housis."

As good as it was between them, there was one caveat.

As much as she may have wanted him, she could not have Lucky totally to herself. She could not. Not as long as Smokey was still around.

You see, Lucky absolutely hero-worshipped his older brother. There was nothing Smokey could do that was wrong in Lucky's eyes. Even if it meant on occasion disappointing Lucky, which did happen. For as Smokey got older, like some elderly we have all known, he became crankier, more cantankerous, more idiosyncratic, more of a loner.

So the more Lucky requested time with his brother, the more Smokey wanted to be left alone. As far as the latter was concerned, whatever time he had available, he wanted it to be only with his father, who unfortunately was then traveling constantly.

For his Daddy, Smokey was prepared to wait. He'd lie at the far end of the sofa, saying little or nothing for days on end, looking out the window of the den until Daddy would get home from another trip.

At that stage of Smokey's life, there was just about only one thing he looked forward to doing, even if it were only for a short two-day weekend before our father would have to pack again for another trip. The two would make time to go on one of their own private walks, after which they'd just sit on the sofa together. Where my father would stroke him, and quietly remind Smokey of his youthful days of mischief and wonder. And together they would listen to hours of the music they never ever tired of.

It would be accurate to say Daddy and Smokey were as close as close can be. They were as strongly bonded at the heart as my mother and I would eventually become, and as close as Lucky and I eventually became.

Not only that, but like my mother and I are today, Smokey and Daddy were so much alike in many ways.

Both were shy; others confused it with arrogance.

They were both iconoclastic; others confused it with standoffishness.

And without a doubt, both were always a little wary. They had both gone through so much, been hurt in the past, so they tended keep most things close to the vest.

And so when my brother Smokey passed away, not surprisingly Daddy's heart was broken. Smokey and he had been through so much together.

It took my father a very long time to get over losing someone he had genuinely come to think of as his "bestest" friend—other than Mommy of course.

Indeed after Smokey left to join our grandfather in Heaven where he was keeping our family's bench there warm for the rest of us, it took a long time for Daddy to fully allow either Lucky and for that matter, even me, (a few months later) into his heart.

Lucky and I understood fully: Daddy was afraid of being hurt again.

However, with Mommy's wise and gentle encouragement, he eventually did open up. In a very, very, very big way for both of us.

• • •

So you can understand that while Smokey was still alive, Lucky would keep trying, more often than not in vain, to get his big brother's attention. He invested a lot of energy, time, and effort that Samantha would surely have been very happy to have had lavished on her.

Yet, no matter how much more distant Smokey became from his younger siblings, Lucky never forgot what he felt was his primary task in life. That was to be Mr. Congeniality.

Which meant that rather than Lucky sulking around his brother, even in the face of Smokey ignoring him, his smile never left his face.

It meant Lucky never blaming or criticizing his older brother, even as Smokey became more remote from his younger brother and sister.

And it meant that Lucky constantly made certain to remind Smokey—with a kiss on the nose and ears—that his younger brother understood his moods. And promised he would continually look out for him. And communicated that he would always be there for him, if and when Smokey needed him.

• • •

And as Smokey aged, Samantha finally got what she had really craved for years: someone's almost full attention.

That someone, of course, turned out to be her obliging younger brother Lucky, Mr. Congeniality!

In a word, for a few months they became best buds and constant companions. They never argued, never fought, never criticized or even competed against one another. And they both still loved their older brother.

However, with the passage of time, they intuitively understood Smokey increasingly had other priorities and pressing needs. So it was quite natural for Lucky and Samantha to turn towards each other.

And that's the way it was until Smokey said good-bye in December 1992. And the way it remained right up through April 15th, 1993. The day I walked into their lives.

The day I would see, for myself, for the first time, Mr. Congeniality at work.

. . .

As soon as Samantha saw her Lucky amble over to welcome me to my new "housis" and family, she was shocked, even hurt.

I could see it in her eyes. She couldn't understand what had driven my parents to once again raise to three the number in our canine pack. In Samantha's view, it wasn't necessary. Everything in her life by then was copasetic, calm, in order. Our parents had each other, just as Sam and Lucky now had each other. In Sam's view it was a tight knit group that simply didn't need the disruptive force of a newcomer.

I watched my parents watching my homecoming unfold right in front of them in the main hallway of our "housis" that runs the depth of it, and leads to my favorite "porchis" overlooking the swimming pool to the right, and the lush green heavily treed forest straight ahead.

I figured that they figured it would all work out in time, that we'd all find our respective place to fit. Today, they would be the first to admit they were only half right, but I'll get to that later.

There was obvious tension in the air. And silence too, interrupted only by Sam's heavy sighing.

The fact is we might all still be standing there today if the situation had not been saved, as it was, by the actions of my new brother Lucky. The one I would soon learn had several names, one being of course Lucky and the other, Mr. Congeniality.

Upon seeing the horrified look on his older sister's face, Lucky's reaction was natural and intuitive and instinctive. He ran back over to his "bud" Samantha, cocked his head slightly upwards to the left, gave her two kisses on her nose, and then more on each of her ears. And while he did so, he kept looking back at me, whereupon he reiterated his *"welcome to the family"* message with an enthusiastic wag of his tail.

So with that out of the way, the three of us met in the middle of the hallway, where we proceeded to take full measure of one another by sight and scent.

This was classic "Mr. Congeniality" at his best. Something I would come to even more fully appreciate with time. He had done *his* job—an act of genuine diplomatic kindness—the first of many I would see him carry out during the course of our life journey together.

Said simply, my brother Lucky was one of those gifts of nature who not only always saw the "bestest" in others, but would do whatever he could do to get others to see the positive in everything, in everybody, and in every situation. His was the eternal quiet voice of conciliation and reason and *"let's work together"* spirit of doing the right things the right way.

It is an unusual skill. An important leadership quality so few have in this day and age.

To my brother, it was always about sharing in his good fortune.

Being Lucky was all Mr. Congeniality ever wanted to be.

THE FIRE:
THE DAY EVERYTHING CHANGED

There's a time, or a day, or an event in your life journey when everything changes. When it's time for you to step up and begin to fulfill your life mission, no matter how young (or not so young) you are. And when you do, that's the time, or day, or event that changes everything in the relationship with someone close to you. The way they look at you. The way they feel about you. The way they think about you. Even the way they talk to you.

For my father and me, and really between Daddy and all three of us—my brother Lucky, my sister Samantha, and myself—that would turn out to be the day our house caught fire. The 29th of January 1995 would turn out to be the unequivocal turning point not only in our respective relationships with our father, but in fact how all three of us siblings would relate to each other in the future.

At the time, I was a little over two years old (my parents' time), comfortable that I had adopted the right family for me, even if I was still considered to be the "new kid on the block" in our family pack.

. . .

It was not a good time in our lives.

Mommy had been hospitalized for the very first time with her cancer. She had collapsed after one of her chemotherapy and radiation treatments had put her system into something called septic shock. From something bad and very painful called peritonitis.

As I understand it today but did not fully comprehend at the time, Mommy had a tumor inside her that was the size of a grapefruit. If doctors had tried to cut it out without first making it smaller, they would not have succeeded in getting all of it. And so, aggressive chemo and radiation had to be given. As a result it was not only not a fun time for her (and therefore not for us), but far worse, the more she was treated, the weaker and weaker she got, week after week.

My siblings and I could see the difference every day, especially when she would come home from the hospital.

She didn't look like the person we knew.

She was never hungry.

She walked very slowly, and only if she was up to it.

She didn't talk to us in the same way we were used to.

And as much as Daddy tried to hide it from us by doing things to distract us, like playing "trow-ball" and other forms of play or by playing music unusually loudly, we couldn't help hearing Mommy doing "trows-up" in the "batroom." Or crying. Crying a lot. Or both.

Like I said, it was a bad time for our family.

So knowing that and recognizing there was little we could do to help Mommy medically, instinctively I decided to do what I had to do.

To take the lead with my brother and sister, to ensure the three of us did whatever we could in other ways to help our mother.

For example, if we needed to go to the "batroom" out in the dog run, I not only knew not to ask Mommy to walk me out, but also convinced Samantha and Lucky they too needed to be patient. No matter how badly we had to go, we all had to wait till Daddy was available to take us.

I also quietly suggested we not ask Mommy to feed us, trying to not bother her in any way, even if it was our regular eating time. Again it was a matter of us being patient. Till Daddy was able to get to us, after he'd made sure Mommy was comfortable upstairs in bed.

Moreover, I persuaded my siblings to trust that on the few occasions Daddy couldn't get back from the hospital on time to feed us, he would make sure someone else would step into the breach to help out.

· · ·

The "bestest" way to explain it is that despite being quite a bit younger than my siblings, I instinctively sensed that I had a job to do.

To take charge so as to ensure Lucky, Samantha, and I did whatever we could to be as good as possible so as to not overly tax Mommy's strength, which she badly needed for her treatments.

And I determined that the "bestest" way to do my job would be to lead by example.

I figured that if I was calm, my brother and sister would be calm. And if I exuded confidence and optimism in the wake of such bad times, the more confident and optimistic Samantha and Lucky would be that all would work out well.

In short, leading by example meant if I behaved "bestest," they would follow suit. And to their ever-lasting credit, they did so beautifully, without a word of complaint or the slightest waver.

And so, from the time Mommy started her treatments, this was the family pattern we followed day in and day out. Along with our daily hope and prayer that Daddy would say to us privately that things would get better soon, when our family could once again return to some sense of normalcy.

· · ·

That was our intention—and our hope.

What none of could have foreseen, however, is that things would get much, much, much worse over the next few weeks. Before they ever began to even begin to get better. During which time, we not only almost lost both the Mommy we so very much loved and cherished, but also the "housis" my siblings and I had come to think of as our family den.

. . .

It all began at eight o'clock the night of January 28th when Daddy gave Mommy a kiss on her forehead along with his nightly silent prayer of love from all of us.

She was not awake at the time. She was in fact in a deep sleep in her hospital bed.

You see, we wouldn't know until many weeks later and even then only upon overhearing Daddy recount the story to others that Mommy was, at the time, actually falling in and out of consciousness. In a sort of semicoma state from which her doctors didn't know for sure if, and, or when she would ever recover.

Yet as bad as it was, and as strange as it might seem, in some ways, it was a blessing for Mommy. For when she was awake, she was in terrible pain which made it very difficult for her get around on her own. Especially when she had to go to the "batroom" (which was often), as she was tethered to a contraption made up of wires and pipes and stuff that forced fluids into her system.

That evening, as always when leaving her room, Daddy whispered to Mommy that he loved her and that she should be brave. But that if she decided that it was too hard, that would be okay too. That if she felt it was time to join her daddy on our family bench in Heaven, she should *"feel free to let go."* That she need not worry. He would take good care of Grandma and my siblings and me, as he had privately committed to Mommy's daddy long before he went to our family bench in Heaven.

He also told her that, unlike almost every other day when he would try to get to the hospital as early as possible after making sure we were comfortably settled in for the day, he would not see her till late the next afternoon. Daddy, we would learn later, had been asked to go to New York City by the only client our parents' consulting firm had continued working for after Mommy got sick, in order to lead a very important meeting. It was to be between one of the client's senior executives from England and their corporate chief operating officer who was flying in from Boston the morning of the 29th.

Point of fact: All of my parents' clients had been informed, as soon as Mommy and Daddy found out she had cancer, that their office would be closed until further notice. Nevertheless, this client had suggested, *"Let's keep the relationship we have for the time being even if we never call you . . . It's one way to thank you for all you have done for us in the past."*

In retrospect, I guess that in asking if Daddy could help them this one time, they must have really needed his help.

In any event, before agreeing to the one-day trip to New York, Daddy had asked Mommy's doctors—her radiation oncologist, the oncologist, and the surgeon—what they thought of the idea of his traveling that day. All three insisted it might be a good thing for Daddy to do.

"You need to get away for a day if only to clear your brain. Nothing is going to happen in the few hours you'll be away. That we are absolutely sure of. And you know if we do happen to need you for anything unexpected, we'll know how to contact you."

In whispering to Mommy his plans for the next day, Daddy also made sure to mention he would say hello for her to friends in New York City, and that he'd stop over at their favorite church there, St. Patrick's Cathedral, to say a special prayer for her.

Then, with his usual mixed feelings, he left her . . . very much alone in her room. Which he always felt some guilt in doing. A feeling I understand only too very well. It's exactly what I experience whenever I am unable to do my job looking out for Mommy, whenever she is away from home.

. . .

That night Daddy ate dinner at 9:40 p.m., after which he played with us out in the back yard far longer than usual. My siblings and I could sense that he seemed distracted, preoccupied, bothered by something. But whatever it was, he thought it "bestest" not to share it with us. More than likely because he's always preferred to have us think only positive thoughts.

Moreover, he knew that after our having been cooped up most of the time that day, save for when someone came over to let us out to go to the "batroom" and to feed us dinner, playing outside in our back yard on the edge of the forest would be great therapy for us. It was. And I think for Daddy too that night.

Especially since there had been a snow storm just a few days before and it had remained cold. So the mounds of snow provided a really fun place for Lucky, Daddy, and me to play "trow ball" together. A most welcome opportunity for my brother and me to romp, and run, and retrieve, and laugh, and chase each other all over the place, while Samantha found plenty of fertile spots to do something she loved to do: eat snow. It was a night of fun made even more memorable when Lucky decided to share his speaking voice, one of the very few times he ever did.

By 11:45 p.m. or so, Daddy and we were all settled comfortably in bed together.

He was pooped . . . and so were we.

Which is why, within minutes, the room was filled not just by the pictures and sound from the box with pictures and sounds, but also by the rhythmic snoring of my brother and sister, and a good deal of snow-related gas from the latter.

• • •

While Lucky and Samantha slept, Daddy didn't sleep a wink that night . . . not one.

I know, for I didn't either.

Whatever it was that was bothering him had now permeated my consciousness too. For the truth was that something had been disturbing me all day. Something I had trouble expressing in words. But something nonetheless I could sense —and whatever it was, it was really, really important. So I hoped that in some way whatever it was I was sensing, would somehow be conveyed to Daddy, so that he too would be aware of whatever it was.

I guess that's what occurred.

For he and I tossed and turned from "lights-out" all the way through to 4:00 a.m. The harder we tried to fall asleep, the worse it got.

So Daddy tried a variety of tricks: a late-night movie, reading, even stroking me. Nothing worked.

. . .

All the while, I could sense some sort of ambivalence in my father about something, something dark and strange and inexplicable, but very much not good. I thought for a while it might have had something to do with Mommy. But my intuition told me otherwise. I guess Daddy's did too.

Were I to be asked to describe it today, I would call it a sort of gloomy sadness or a feeling of doom taking over your whole body and brain. The same thing I had been feeling all day.

So I decided to stay right beside him that night. I would not let him get even an inch beyond where I lay. If he moved, I moved. If he turned, I turned.

. . .

By 4:15 a.m., Daddy was up, showered, dressed, and drinking coffee.

By 4:20 a.m., he had called and cancelled his train ride to New York City.

By 6:00 a.m., Daddy had called the man from Boston, who was flying to New York City to meet my father and the other man from London, who was by then in New York, to say he would not be there for the meeting.

In all honesty, Daddy did not tell him the whole truth as to why he felt he should not go. And while all of us had been raised by our parents to tell the truth at all times, I really think this might have been a proper exception to that rule.

Let me explain what I mean by that. How could anyone—even my father—tell another person he knew professionally, but not personally, that his personal intuition was telling him something terrible was going to happen that morning—and he felt he needed to stay close to home?

I can understand the quandary Daddy was facing. He wanted to tell the truth but found it difficult to put the exact right words together. It's the same sort of challenge I have when I need to communicate something is going to happen in the near future, like an earthquake or a tornado or a thunderstorm.

How does one do that without seeming to be an alarmist?

So I can't blame Daddy for not saying so directly.

. . .

Either way, he needn't have worried. In hindsight, in fact, with all that was happening in our family, that should not have been a concern of Daddy's. But, he like us had learned never to take anyone or anything for granted and to always assume nothing. And especially under the circumstances of such an important meeting, Daddy did not know how the client would respond.

So he decided to blame his absence on a cold he thought might be coming on, and did not wish to exacerbate, particularly given Mommy's situation in the hospital.

It didn't matter. The Boston man was very nice about it. He simply suggested Daddy facilitate the New York City meeting being held later that morning, and do it instead from the study in our "housis." By telephone. My sense is he trusted Daddy enough to know if Daddy thought he shouldn't be some place he had committed to be, then there had to be a very good reason.

Here's why.

You see, sometime before, Daddy had been one of the first contacted by the man from Boston for advice regarding a terrible emergency of his own. While I am sure it was not intentional, a hospital that the man headed had just accidentally killed one of their highest profile patients.

He asked Daddy how he would deal with it were he in the same position as Chairman of the Board of Directors. Instead of giving what he would have characterized as a knee-jerk reaction, Daddy said he wanted to give it the consideration it was due.

Upon reflection, he came to the conclusion that since the damage had already been done, perhaps a broader more strategic response might be better for everyone concerned over the long haul. Rather than just a typical public relations approach. Daddy's thinking was consistent with something he and Mommy, in their work together, had grown concerned about: the *"Managing by PR"* philosophy of business—which included explaining away mistakes being justified by something called *"CYA."*

Daddy felt even more strongly about this since it involved a hospital.

He could identify with the dead patient's family members.

His view was that while nothing would bring back that person, they deserved something more substantive than patronizing gobbledygook written by those who didn't even know what had really happened.

Within a couple of hours, Daddy had written a series of strategy recommendations that not only dealt with the immediate need for what to say to the media, but based it on a longer-term plan. One that would ensure that every single process that the hospital undertook in the past that might have led up to that accident would be reviewed and revamped if necessary, so as to prevent future tragedies.

The hospital did just that.

So that today, while certainly not perfect, it has the reputation for being one of, if not the very, very "bestest," of its kind in the country. And it's patient-friendly too, just like my Doctor Uncle Greg's office.

. . .

By 11:00 a.m., the conference call meeting Daddy was moderating had been underway for an hour and a half.

From the desk in his study, Daddy could easily see Lucky, Samantha, and me playing on the "porchis" in the back of the house where he had put us because it had turned unusually warm. Almost 70 degrees in the direct sun, even with snow covering much of the area we were playing on.

It was then when Lucky, Sam, and I all began to sense something happening.

We smelled smoke.

For a short while none of us were terribly concerned. The strong scent of smoke had been something we had become quite accustomed to. Several neighbors, including Aunt Suzanne who lived next door to us, had wood stoves. And these always gave off that really nice smoky aroma into the air. So initially we weren't particularly worried.

To her credit, Samantha was the first to realize this was not the standard wood stove smell. Clearly agitated, she began to call out to Lucky and me. In a way we had not heard before, but which *she* had heard often when growing up with our late brother Smokey.

I can only describe it as a howl, like that of a wolf! It was a sound which both puzzled and alarmed us. For we sensed she was trying to tell us something and it was clearly very urgent. But we couldn't determine what exactly it was, as we had never heard it from her before.

Part of the problem was logistics.

For at that very moment, Lucky and I were at the other end of the "porchis," a distance from where Daddy's study is. And so as things would have it, we were also quite far away from where Samantha now was looking straight up into the sky.

Seeing her posing that way, I decided to check things out for myself. So with a slight nod over to my brother to follow me, I quickly ran over to where she stood —where I could look straight up into the sky in the general direction of where Samantha's howling seemed to be directed.

I couldn't believe it! There *was* something very, very wrong!

It was something big and scary looking. Something I knew I had never seen before. Something sort of a bright yellow, with blue and reddish things, was leaping from the top of the gutter on the edge of the garage roof!

And it was moving very fast!

Before we knew it, within seconds, there were little yellow bits of debris flying through the air, followed by a louder and louder hissing sound that seemed to grow even louder as the big yellow thing up high grew in size and began to move towards Daddy's study.

· · ·

As soon as Lucky caught up behind me, he didn't wait a split second: He started to yell with that deep voice of his. This time though his voice had a tone of desperation to it.

Daddy would later characterize it as being *"not unlike how the late Nicole Simpson's Akita was described when neighbors heard, 'the plaintive wail of a dog.'"*

Hearing Lucky, I joined in as loud as I could. I knew we needed to catch our father's attention! And we needed to do so as quickly as possible!

· · ·

I guess he eventually heard us.

He came out through the kitchen door not long afterwards, although much too long for our liking, to be totally honest with you.

Even before he got close to us, we could hear him asking what was wrong.

But none of us could answer right away, as we were all caught up doing what we were doing, and besides, we intuitively thought it might be best for him to see for himself what it was we were talking about. We thought, that way he would know what to do. And that he would give us some guidance as to what we might best be doing, besides yelling and howling.

Assuming, of course, our instincts had been right in the first place. That what we were seeing for the very first time in our lives was indeed something terribly out of the ordinary—and likely terrible. And that it needed Daddy's immediate attention and would require us to help him any way we could.

I guess our instincts proved prescient.

As soon as Daddy saw what all three of us were pointing up to, he literally jumped into immediate action. It was a scene I have replayed over and over and over in my mind since then. For while I would have described it at the time as almost frantic, there was also a real clarity to what he started to do. There was a preciseness, almost a surreal calmness, in every move he made and in everything he would say to us, over the next few minutes. It was almost as if on the outside our father's body was moving a thousand miles an hour, while inside all was under control and moving at a much more measured pace.

· · ·

He cautioned us to be careful, to not touch anything, but to follow him all the way back to the kitchen door on the other side of the "porchis".

I fell in right behind him.

Upon seeing me do that, Lucky and Samantha followed right behind, directly in my footsteps.

As soon as we got into the kitchen, Daddy became a sort of whirling dervish.

He picked up the phone and told the men in New York City that our house was on fire, and then wished them luck with the rest of their meeting. I can only imagine what they must have thought at the time!

He called Emergency 911, told them what was happening and gave them instructions.

He dialed my parents' office to ask Aunt Karen to organize some of the people there to come out to our "housis".

He called Uncle Bob, our babysitter at the police station, and left a message for him.

He called Aunt Merrie, our contractor, and left a message for her.

• • •

Just before he did all that, however, he had given me a quick, direct, and succinct order: *"Princess, go to the top of the stairs to the bedroom. Take your brother and sister with you. When you get there, sit and wait for me. I want to find you all of you sitting still and straight like soldiers. I will come and get you. Just wait there. Okay, girl???"*

He didn't have to tell me twice.

This was an emergency unlike anything we had ever experienced before as a family. And I knew that he knew he could count on me.

I bounded up the wooden staircase to the master bedroom. Where, as soon as I got to the very top step, I turned around and sat up in the middle of that step like a soldier, straighter and taller than I had ever done before, figuring that that if I did that, Lucky and Samantha would follow my lead.

They were wonderful!

They ran up the stairs as quickly as each could and took their seats beside me—one to my left, the other to my right—where we waited patiently for Daddy to tell us what our next move would be.

• • •

In the meantime, he knew what else he needed to do before coming back for us.

He ran into the room where he and Mommy kept some important stuff, including their favorite pictures of us, and took them outside for safekeeping.

He ran through the fire, racing to take one of the cars out of the garage, as the roof burned and embers flew, and parked it out on the street beyond the house.

Then he ran into the "housis," picked up our three leashes hanging in the closet on the way in, and then came back to get us.

· · ·

"Good girl, Princess! Good girl! That's my 'bestest' girl," Daddy said at the sight of the three of us sitting proudly and quietly, waiting for him at the top of the stairs.

"You too, Sam . . . you're the 'goodest' girl too," he replied in response to my sister's request for equal time.

As was his bent, Lucky neither asked for any special attention nor did he seem to want any individual praise from Daddy. Instead, he just sat straight and tall and calmly acknowledged that all was well (and would be fine) with a small but discernible wagging at the very top of his tail.

And when Daddy quickly but calmly strode up the stairway to put my brother's leash on first, Lucky made sure our father knew what each of us had wanted to say at that very moment—that we all loved him and trusted him implicitly.

Lucky did it his way, of course, by holding out his paw to be shaken by the man who had saved his life once before, and was about to do once again.

What we would not find out till later that night was that Daddy viewed it all totally differently, and still does till today, as I recount what happened that day. As far as he's concerned, *we* saved him, the "housis", and everything Mommy and he treasured—most of all, us.

· · ·

Once we had all been leashed, Daddy held onto all of us as we carefully but quickly navigated our way down the stairs, through the main foyer, and from there out to another hallway that leads to the smaller foyer that leads out to the garage.

It took maybe thirty seconds all told.

Obviously, we could smell the heavy smoke. And once in the garage, we could see small pieces of wood with that yellow, blue, and red tinged stuff flying all around us.

But Daddy kept us *real calm* by keeping us *real focused*, while he opened the door to the remaining car that was waiting for us in the garage. We were so calm and focused, we didn't stop to think about the hot embers on the floor as we ran into the car. We were on a mission.

As soon as Lucky jumped onto the backseat where Samantha and I were already sitting, without another word Daddy closed our door, ran to the driver's seat, started the engine and then we drove right out through the already open garage door, minutes before big pieces of the roof started crashing down where we had just stood.

For a second, Samantha started getting excited, thinking, I figure, that we were going for a drive. But she quieted down as soon as Daddy pulled the car to the side of our front lawn near the street.

There, we could already see people come running out of their "housis" to see what all the noise was about, a noise I have remained sensitive to throughout the years since that day. Sirens are still scary to me.

. . .

They infer somebody has a big problem just like we did that day. And I cannot help it, but when I hear sirens now, I find myself anticipating the smell of smoke.

And I'm not the only one: I see Daddy doing the exact same thing when *he* hears sirens.

It's something Mommy has commented about many times to others.

• • •

The rest of the afternoon went by in sort of a blur.

People would come over to us in our car. Some would peer in. Some were more subtle about it. Some would smile. Some would sort of shake their heads sadly.

Honestly, we hardly noticed.

All we were focused on was our father, who stood not too far from us out on the edge of our driveway talking to the men in helmets. The ones who kept coming to and from our property, and kept going in and out of our "housis," and whom we saw climb to the very top of it onto the part of the roof not yet burning.

We were so very happy to see Aunt Karen arrive from the office. She came by to comfort us and brought each of us a biscuit.

Sometime later, someone else was nice enough to take each of us for a brief walk so that we could stretch our legs and go to the "batroom."

Throughout the afternoon, at least four times an hour, Daddy would walk over to see how we were doing in the car. As soon as we'd see him wave to us, we waved back with our tails. And when he opened the door to say hello, Lucky and Samantha gave him kisses while I made sure to give him a "nuzzie" with my head.

• • •

By 5 p.m., everyone had left, except Aunt Karen and Aunt Merrie, Mommy's contractor friend, and a few others who worked for her.

I can't remember who it was, but someone held onto the three of us really closely, as we all walked through the rubble that had destroyed part of the "housis."

It was bad. But it could just as easily have been much worse.

The smell of smoke was a bit overwhelming at first, but the more we walked around, the more we sort of got used to it.

During the walk-through, Daddy made the decision to stay in the "housis" overnight, having been convinced by the police and fire people that it would be "bestest" if we did so to protect what was left. Especially since the "housis," on one end where the fire had been, was wide open with no roof and only what was left of burned out walls.

Upon hearing Daddy announce our intention, my siblings and I knew we would be called upon to help one more time. Something we were more than happy to do. For this was our den too! And we were prepared to protect it any way we could.

And that's exactly what we did that night.

. . .

Fortunately the part of the "housis" where the master bedroom is located had not been damaged, other than by smoke. Consequently, to make sure none of us could be poisoned by the deep smokey smell, Daddy kept all the windows in the bedroom wide open that first night. Even though the temperature outside dropped to less than ten degrees above zero, and we had neither heat nor power. Since it was so very cold, Daddy invited each of us to lie under the covers with him.

What he didn't know though was that my siblings and I had already decided among ourselves we had two core responsibilities that night.

The first was to keep the "housis" safe from potential intruders. Every once and a while I would get up off the bed, go over to the open window and give a loud warning to no one in particular outside—but just in case. No one asked me to. I just figured it was the right thing to do.

The second responsibility was obvious. It was our job to do what we could to keep Daddy warm all night.

So Lucky slept the whole night across Daddy's chest, while Samantha slept right next to him on one side and I slept on the other. All of our heads were snuggled right next to his.

Every once in a while one of the four of us would cough from the overwhelming smell of the smoke. Nonetheless we got through the night just fine. So much so that by the next morning, we were ready to tackle anything we might be called upon to do that day.

. . .

It's been many years since the day of the fire, a day I have thought a lot about—as you can well imagine.

We all have.

It was harrowing yet exhilarating.

It was obviously scary. Yet it could have been much worse.

The point is we got through it together as a family. A family unit that survived as more united and more trusting of one another than ever, as a result of what we had experienced.

We're also grateful, very grateful that Mommy wasn't there to have to go through it. Had she been with us, in her much weakened state of health, who knows what the consequences might have been.

. . .

It's fair to say the events of that day changed each of us forever.

Thereafter, no matter where we were, Lucky and I would look to see where the other was whenever we'd hear sirens or smell smoke, no matter where we were.

And after the fire, Samantha, Lucky, and I found we responded to Daddy even more promptly than we had ever done before when he'd call our names, even though we'd actually been pretty good before the fire.

And one more thing. From that day on, Lucky and I became *incredibly* close.

He had trusted me to lead the way for the three of us when Daddy had given me the instructions to wait for him up at the top of the stairs. As a result, our sister followed suit, and we were where we needed to be when Daddy came back to take us to safety outside.

. . .

As a leader, I learned a great deal from all we experienced that day.

I came to realize how helpful it is not to panic when there is an emergency, no matter how bad the situation might seem.

I also learned from my father the importance of communicating quickly when needed, and to do so clearly, concisely, and succinctly so that those in your care are not frightened even more than they might be under difficult, or even dire circumstances.

I learned that leadership is not always about being the first to do something, but rather to do things right when someone else is in the leader's role.

And I also learned that love may—or may not—be about never having to say you're sorry. But it is surely about being prepared to do everything and anything to ensure your loved ones will be safe, no matter what!

Finally I have learned since that day just how much our father was grateful to all of us, especially me, for helping him keep all of us together and united throughout what was one of his biggest life challenges.

Which I have overheard him express this way: *"There's an awe I have felt towards Princess since the fire. She is an amazing animal, amazingly smart, the best that nature allows herself to share with us. If it weren't for her leadership, her ability to think, to ensure the others would be where I needed them to be when I needed them to be there, all with just one instruction from me for there was no time for more than that, I don't know what might have happened. As far as I'm concerned all three—Lucky, Samantha, and Princess—saved our house with their barking. And Princess saved all of us with her magic leadership."*

I feel exactly the same way about my father. And Mommy knows I have lived every day since the fire to show Daddy just how strongly I feel that way.

"YOU HAVE A JOB TO DO."

T hose are the most important words I have ever heard in my whole life. I first heard them from my father.

It was in the midst of the single most important discussion he and I have ever had.

It happened in mid-March 1995, not long after the fire.

It would change my life forever.

For in that moment, I formally transitioned from the carefree youthfulness of childhood, to assume serious responsibility for those under my caring watch. To fulfill what my Anatolian Shepherd heritage has all along fated me to do.

That is: we take our jobs very seriously.

With that simple instruction, *"You have a job to do,"* everything about the life I had led up to that point in my life changed—absolutely everything.

Thankfully at the time, due to his inner contentment and self-confidence, my brother Lucky was able and willing to adapt very readily to the change. Even to embrace it, even if it meant—and it very much did—the nature of our relationship would be affected. An act of magnanimity I will not only always love him for, but truly admire him.

That's the way I will always feel about Lucky.

• • •

By now you know my mother fell ill—very, very, very ill not long after she and Daddy adopted me.

It was a very bad time in the life of our family.

In fact, Mommy almost died on a couple of occasions. It was touch and go whether she would leave prematurely for our family bench in Heaven that her father, Smokey, and others have been keeping warm for all of us.

However, you also already know by now that very fortunately for Daddy, Lucky, Sam, and me, it turned out not to be Mommy's time to go.

Like me she's a survivor. Like me, she carries the label of being a miracle.

In my case, with all the health issues I have had over the years—my double hip replacement, two bouts of cancer, my stomach crises, other surgeries, etc.—everyone logically knows I shouldn't still be around. And I wouldn't be, without the help of those like my Doctor Uncle Greg and the loving diligence of my family.

The same is true, even more so, about my mother.

Her survival from cancer is miraculous. The kind of story about which books are written and movies are made.

The kind of inspirational love story the Hallmark Hall of Fame people like to adapt for television. The kind of story my family and I have always enjoyed watching.

In my situation, the doctor had been accurate in his assessment of my problem, when as a child I was diagnosed with a very severe congenital hip disorder. It's just a miracle that my parents refused to take his advice to *"put her down."* Instead they found one of the very few doctors at the time willing and able to try experimental hip replacement surgery for those in my situation. His name is Doctor Uncle Dietrich Franczuszki and he saved me.

Mommy's circumstances could not have been more different.

Over a period of about ten months (my parents' time), she was misdiagnosed at least twice by two different doctors.

The first missed it, pure and simple. That was in October 1993.

The second didn't recognize it for what it was. That was in the summer of 1994.

And so it was just a few months later, in early December 1994, that my father was informed *"there's an 80 percent probability of (my mother) dying within eight months, and a 100% probability she will be dead within 18 months . . . If I were you I'd begin to get her affairs in order."*

Needless to say that last prognosis proved to be not just inaccurate, but plain wrong.

For that doctor had underestimated my mother's incredible courage and will to live, the love of her family, and our commitment to do whatever needed to be done—from finding the right doctors, to creating the right environment for her miracle to happen.

It wasn't easy by any means.

It had its ups and downs many times.

It was life altering to say the least.

Indeed, the whole experience changed almost everything about the lives my parents (and we) lived before her cancer was diagnosed, and that which has followed since.

But looking back more than ten years later (my parents' time), I am proud and grateful to be able to say she—and we—prevailed.

· · ·

The fateful conversation between Daddy and me that changed everything forever took place in mid-March 1995.

Mommy had just been carried gently upstairs after arriving home a few minutes before.

It was the end of a tiring journey after being "ambulanced" back by chauffeured stretch limousine (the back of which had been converted into a comfortable mobile recovery room by Daddy) from New York City. It was there in New York that Mommy had been hospitalized for a long time. Where she underwent massive, life-saving, and traumatic life-altering surgery for colon cancer. The doctors called it "monster surgery."

Lucky, Samantha and I knew something very big had happened but didn't know exactly what. It was almost like Mommy had disappeared from our lives without notice.

Over the prior three weeks (my parents' time), we knew she and Daddy had held many conversations about a doctor in New York who worked at Mt. Sinai Medical Center, where Mommy's old college friend, our Aunt Wendy Goldstein, was the president.

This coincided with my parents' firing the first surgeon at the Hospital of the University of Pennsylvania (I heard it is also called HUP) who was supposed to do the job originally. They had good reason to do so: He seemed very content to leave Mommy with more questions than answers whenever she'd asked him anything, which quite understandably left Mommy feeling rather uncomfortable.

My siblings and I could fully understand why. We could easily put ourselves in our mother's shoes.

Simply put, my sister and brother and I always hated when someone would tell us something they thought we wanted or needed to know—but said it in a way we couldn't fully understand, often talking down to us. In our view that's just a sign of a poor communicator. Or someone who doesn't have much respect for your intelligence or, worse, is just too insensitive to care how what they say is received.

In my view, there's nothing worse than ambivalence when it comes to important issues that can affect your future. At a minimum, one would think you are owed the courtesy of a *"we're not certain . . . but . . . "*

So when that first surgeon answered one of Mommy's questions with his comment that *"I will not dignify that question with a response,"* he was "toast." My parents fired him.

And likely he probably still can't figure out why!

In any event, at the time, our parents were probably were a bit too busy to see how relieved the three of us were on Mommy's behalf. In our hearts, we knew our parents were doing the right thing. And that even if it meant having to go to another city to get better, even it meant Mommy would have to be away from us for a long time, we were very comfortable with that course of action if it would help her to get well for us.

· · ·

I'll leave it to Mommy to tell her own story sometime, about how she and Daddy found the new surgeon, and about her surgery, and the lengthy recovery she went through.

But let me tell you what I saw when she got back, and what I did as a result.

Mommy had endured a lot from what was traumatic surgery.

So much so, that by the time she got home thirteen days (my parents' time) after what we heard was called her "monster surgery," she was very weak, quite thin from not eating and clearly still in lots of pain.

While she was away, all we knew was what we overheard when Daddy would call home to Uncle Connell. He was a good friend of my parents from the days when they lived in Minneapolis where my sister Samantha had been born. He babysat us when Mommy and Daddy were away, when Mommy had her big surgery.

Evidently Mommy's cancer was very large.

The surgery had been lengthy and massive. But thankfully, the doctor was confident he got all of it.

He was good enough to forewarn Mommy and Daddy that her recovery would be painful and difficult while in the hospital—and then lengthy and very challenging once back at home. However, given time, good follow-up chemotherapy and radiation, and with God looking out for her, she would be okay . . . and we would all be okay.

. . .

During the thirteen days (my parents' time) they were in New York City, Daddy came home for one night when Uncle Connell had to fly home for a family event. Otherwise Daddy slept in Mommy's hospital room or in a hotel.

Truthfully, Lucky, Samantha, and I were happy he was with her. We never had to tell him we were being good while he was there, even when he would ask to speak with each of us by phone every night. Uncle Connell would hold the phone to each of our ears so that we could hear our Daddy. Of course, by the time he'd call us, we could tell how tired he was. So my sister, brother, and I got into the habit just being good listeners, as he filled us in about how things were going and kept reassuring us, *"Mommy will coming home soon. She loves you very, very much."*

I can't tell you how comforting it was to hear those words each time he called. If he could have seen us through the telephone, he would have seen our tails wagging in unison. But we suspected he couldn't, so we let him know by our heavy panting in response.

. . .

I can't explain how we knew it, but the morning before Mommy actually arrived home in the late afternoon, all three of us intuitively sensed she would soon be with us.

It's an instinct we would be able to count on for all of our lives. It actually helps one prepare mentally for what's about to occur, especially if it's something significant and might call for some adjustments to be made.

This was obviously one of those situations.

Part of it involved making certain Mommy would be comfortable upstairs in our bedroom, where up to the day of her return Lucky, Samantha, and I had all been sleeping with Uncle Connell.

Part of it also involved making certain Mommy would not be adversely affected by the remnants of the big fire that had occurred just a few weeks before, causing considerable damage to one-third of our "housis." Fortunately, it had not been the side of the "housis" where Mommy would eventually spend the first phase of her recovery.

Finally, part of it involved making certain that Mommy would feel welcome and not alone upstairs, while she was getting better.

This was important because the "housis" kind of sprawls out and if you are on one side and someone else is somewhere on the other, it is not impossible for your calls for help to go unheard.

So these were the kinds of things Daddy wanted to talk to me about, after Mommy had been carried upstairs and had settled in as comfortably as possible.

. . .

Oh yes, there's one other thing I forgot to mention. And it's *very* important.

Maybe it was due to the surgery or her great pain. Or maybe it was the enormous number of painkillers she was forced to take. Or maybe it was simply due to the fact that this was the longest stretch of time she and I had ever been apart since I had spotted her in the orphanage. Whatever was the reason, Mommy told Daddy she was very afraid that *"Prinny will forget who I am."*

So strong was her fear, she had repeated it numerous times during her hospital stay.

And each time she'd do so, Daddy would quietly reassure her, *"Boulie,* (one of Daddy's nicknames for Mommy) *that will never happen. The two of you are joined in your hearts and souls . . . a child never forgets who saved her life . . . you'll see."*

Deep down, Daddy believed what he was telling Mommy. He's never for a second had any doubts about me, and certainly not since the fire.

What he did wonder about though was how I would react to the sight of my mother totally weakened, scared, and scarred, and filled with pain-killing drugs. The same mother who, when leaving for New York two weeks before, looked on the surface at least like she was well on the way to recovery from what had been another previously harrowing and terrible life-threatening cancer-related experience. One I hope she will decide to tell you about in her own words someday.

You could understand my father's concern.

He already knew what my brother, sister, and I were about to see for the first time.

That the mother we loved so much now looked really sick, with all kinds of needles and tubes sticking out of her, all over her chest and arms.

That our mother once so strong and confident and so full of life less than two years before (our parents' time) when I first spotted her at the orphanage, now seemed terribly beaten down by a disease I did not then fully understand (but with which I myself would become very familiar just a few years later).

Those were Daddy's real concerns.

Still, Daddy never shared them. Not with Mommy. Not with us.

That was in keeping, I now know in hindsight, with his overall philosophy as a caregiver for Mommy. Through all the years she had the worst of the cancer. Simply put, *"there's no sense wasting emotional energy focusing on negatives."*

He believed then and still does today that *"you look at bad situations from all points of view. You think through all the possible alternatives. You follow a plan that takes these into consideration but does not allow them to paralyze you into inaction, and you do your best to make it all work."*

That's exactly what he did with Mommy when she had cancer.

That's also been our parents' approach in dealing with life challenges posed by my siblings and me.

As it has been the philosophy and approach that I have adopted—and used—ever since.

$$\cdots$$

Daddy brought me into the room with the box with pictures and voices for one of our private chats.

At the beginning, I will admit I was pretty excited. Although they were not with me in the room, so too were Lucky and Samantha.

Who wouldn't have been?

Mommy was home!

Daddy was home!

Aunt Sam, our friend the limo driver, was here!

Uncle Connell was still with us!

There was also a nurse or two.

What I remember most was feeling like, *"Okay, everything will begin to get back to normal now."* So I was pretty bouncy to say the least. Moreover, I couldn't wait to visit Mommy upstairs, barring her being too tired or asleep, of course.

"Prinny, I need to tell you something very, very important—it's about Mommy."

I have always loved it when Daddy would speak quietly to me in that really mellow deep voice he has. For when he speaks to me that way, he conveys a confidence in me that makes me so proud to be his daughter. He neither speeds up nor slows down his speech pattern. He doesn't change it in a phony way, for example, by talking in a higher pitch, or by talking down to me like I might not understand what he is trying to say.

In fact, the way he spoke with me that day is exactly the way both my parents have communicated with me all of my life. Almost as if they knew from the outset that, even as a young adoptee, I fully comprehended what they told me the first time they said something, and never felt they had to repeat it.

All I can say is they were right.

And so you can imagine how surprised and pleased they were when years later—quite recently in fact—they found out that it is one of the most telling characteristics of my Anatolian Shepherd heritage.

In any event, that's the way Daddy talked to me late that afternoon in March of 1995.

And as I said earlier—it would turn out to be the most important thing he would ever say to me, and in doing so changed my life forever.

What's interesting, also in hindsight, is that almost intuitively, even before he started to talk, I had a really strong sense he was about to tell me something truly life altering that I needed to hear. Which is why I settled myself down, sat as I usually do in these types of circumstances, immediately in front of him with my head and body fully erect, and my tail wagging ever so slightly in anticipation.

As soon as he saw I was ready, Daddy continued.

"Prinny, you remember when you were young and Mommy found you and took you home, and promised to take care of you the rest of your life."

Since it sounded more like a rhetorical question than something requiring a response, I thought it best not to respond and just listen. It's a lesson I actually learned from Lucky. More often than not, the most valued response—the one most appreciated—is to say nothing, and to just listen.

"I'm sure you remember as well, Prinny—I'm sure you do—when you went to the doctor to fix your hips and then came home, you had to stay really, really, really quiet. You remember you weren't allowed to go upstairs, and when you had to go out to the 'batroom,' Mommy or I would put a towel under your 'belly belly' and help move you like a wheelbarrow so you wouldn't have to strain your hips to walk."

"Do you remember—I am sure you do Big Girl—how Mommy used to sleep beside you down here almost every night for all the months you recovered from your surgery . . . and how she would talk to you before you both would go to sleep? She'd tell you how much we adored you, and how wonderful your life would be after you had recovered from your surgery."

"Do you remember, Prinny, how she slept on the sofa but would not open it up into a bed so that you wouldn't be tempted to jump on it, because that would hurt your hips?"

"And because Lucky and your sister could only see you for a few minutes at a time so that you wouldn't get too excited, we would bring them both there to say hello. And then before you'd go to sleep, I would bring Lucky alone to say good night to you . . . and he'd kiss your ears and your nose . . . and you did 'waggy-tails' for each other."

Observing my posture and eyes and my tail wagging ever so slightly, Daddy could see I was taking it all in. So he continued without any hesitation.

"Well, Prinny, that's the way Mommy is now. She needs all of our help—but particularly from you."

"And, Big Girl, I know there is no one else who can do what I am asking you to do—and I know you will do it beautifully."

I didn't move an inch . . . I just kept looking up directly at Daddy's face. I could see his eyes were tired, even a little sad, and beginning to glisten.

"Prinny, Mommy loves you more than life itself, and she would do and will do anything for you as long as you live."

"So here is what I want from you in return: I want you to know something . . . to take it into your heart and never ever let it go."

"You have a job to do!"

"Your job is to take care of Mommy all the time, no matter wherever we are. When I am home, you can relax a bit, but otherwise **you always have a job to do.***"*

"Wherever Mommy goes, you go. **I never want her to be out of your sight**, *no matter when. No matter what the circumstances, I want you to stay so close to Mommy she'll think you're her shadow. Do you understand?"*

I leaned my head into his hand like I always do when he talks to me like this. It's my way of saying, *"Sure, I understood"* . . . more than he could have ever understood at the time. More than Mommy could have known either.

But they both certainly do now.

I not only had **a big job to do**. Somehow instinctively I felt I had been born for this very moment. And while just to be asked in the manner in which my father did felt wonderful—almost fulfilling—it was not like a burden at all. It also felt almost as if I had been waiting for this opportunity all of my life!

"So now let's go to tell Mommy what we just decided."

And with that last bit of encouragement, my father and I headed out of the den, down the hallway, into the foyer, up the staircase which leads to the room where I knew our human soul mate was waiting for me on my parents' bed.

. . .

At the very top of the stairs, we were forced to stop!

A gate stood all the way across the opening to the room.

I couldn't be sure, but I figured it had been placed there to discourage me from doing my usual flying leap onto the bed. Like I had done every day—sometimes several times a day—ever since I had fully recuperated from my hip surgery.

Through the railings of the fence that separated us, I could see Mommy. She looked like she was asleep. Just to see her there was thrilling.

I looked up at Daddy and then turned back to fully digest the scene in front of me.

I can't be certain when it was exactly, but at some point while standing there, I realized that something in my line of sight was really different. Something about Mommy I had never in my life seen before. Something strange, even gruesome and scary-looking.

She had all these weird tubes and things sticking out of her body!

I felt Daddy bend over me really low, and heard him whisper something into my ear, something else which I would never, ever forget.

"Prinny, now you know what I meant when I said downstairs that Mommy needs our help . . . needs **your** *help . . . As you can see, Mommy is very sick . . . She needs us to be* **very** *gentle with her and* **very** *quiet . . .* **very** *gentle and* **very** *quiet . . . "*

"You have your job to do now, and that means being **very** *gentle and* **very** *quiet . . . So let's see you do that now."*

"Just remember though, Mommy is **very, very** *sick . . . And you* **need** *to be* **gentle** *and* **quiet** *. . . I know* **you** *can. I know* **you** *will, and you'll do it beautifully because you're a big girl now . . . you're our* **'bestest' girl.***"

I guess Daddy may have been speaking just a bit louder than he thought, for right then, I saw Mommy open her eyes and start to smile from her place on the bed.

"Hello my **Big Girl** *. . . I am* **sooooo** *happy to see* **you** *. . . Do you remember me?"*

Even though her voice sounded scratchy and very weak—of course I remembered her!

How could I not?

She's the one who I picked out at the orphanage to take me home.

She's the one who stayed by my side and soothed my pain every night after I had my hip surgery.

She's the one I have known was my human soul mate from the moment we met.

I figured she already knew all these things. So rather than say something, I decided to let my actions speak for themselves.

First, I shook my head as I always do when I am about to undertake something big. And then, as soon as Daddy removed the gate, I started to move towards the bed.

However, not yet having taken more than a couple of small steps, I could plainly see the look of fear on Mommy's face, clearly rattled by the sight of her Big Girl coming towards her.

"Oh, Rufie (she was calling for my father), *I'm afraid she'll hurt me . . . "*

"No Babes . . . don't worry," Daddy said quietly. *"She knows she has a job to do—don't you, Princess—and she will do it just the way you would expect her to."*

. . .

Before Mommy could say anything else, I moved right to the foot of the bed. Where I stopped, in the exact spot where I'd usually begin my leap.

I could hear Daddy's words in my mind: *"Prinny, Mommy needs your help . . . You have a job to do . . . but she is very weak . . . very sick . . . so you need to be very gentle."*

I could literally sense Mommy was scared that I would jump up and possibly accidentally hurt her in some way.

Yet I also knew I had a job to do.

So I quickly made a decision—actually I had begun to think about it when Daddy was talking to me downstairs—on a course of action which would both alleviate her fear and yet allow me do what I needed to do.

"Prinny . . . be careful my baby . . . "

Mommy's voice was faint; her fear wasn't.

Then I heard my father's voice again: *"Gentle, Prinny . . . gently now, girl . . . now let's see you do a* **'belly belly,' 'crawley crawley'** *for Mommy."*

This was fantastic! Daddy and I were obviously on the same wavelength!

I would do *"belly belly"* and *"crawley crawley"* to get on the bed without having to leap, and do it without causing any part of the bed whatsoever to move at all.

. . .

Within seconds, I was laying right next to my mother, resting my head gently on her shoulder, the one spot on her body that had no needles, no tubes, no wires hanging from it.

I had successfully pulled off the *"belly belly," "crawley crawley!"*

It meant moving my front legs as far as I could in front of me while my hind legs stayed on the floor at the very end of the bed. And then as slowly and gently as I could, without jostling any of the blankets covering my mother, I lifted myself up as hard as I could using whatever leverage I had from both the front and back pair of legs. After which, having climbed up on the bed, the rest was a no-brainer: I got on my stomach and crawled like I had always pictured, in my mind, what my late brother Smokey Max the Coonhound might do, when stalking someone in a field.

"Belly belly," "crawley crawley" was something Daddy and I had been practicing privately on the carpet in the hallway for months, well before the fire, well before Mommy went to New York City.

While at the time, I thought it was a fun thing to do, today I have a very different take on things.

There is, as my parents say, a reason for everything, even when we don't know it at the time.

. . .

When I got to my destination, I looked back to where I had been standing a short time before, beside my father and several others who had joined us.

He and they were all smiling through their tears.

I could sense my father's pride in his "bestest" girl.

I slanted my head a little towards Mommy to see how she was doing. She was smiling and crying as well. Obviously very happy to see me and apparently very relieved, she told me later, that I had remembered who she was.

I suddenly felt very tired. It had been a long day and an even longer two weeks (my parents' time). I hadn't realized how much the focus I'd needed and the tension I had internalized, leading up to the very moment I hopped onto the bed, had worn me out. It helped a lot that I could feel the familiar comforting sensation of Mommy's hand stroking my ears and neck. I loved the feeling of safety that came with her smell and feel.

Our mother was home. And I was where I was supposed to be: lying right next to her, watching over her, caring for her, comforting her.

I was just doing my job.

As I have ever since.

So I laid my head on her shoulder, and fell fast asleep snuggled beside her face.

. . .

A closing thought about my job.

Except for meals and walks and brief time-outs for play with my brother and sister, lying beside Mommy was where I spent the vast majority of my time over the next few weeks while my mother regained her strength. Right up until she was able to start joining the rest of us downstairs on a regular basis.

I had a new life responsibility. What mattered then, now, and forever was doing my job "the bestest" I knew how—just as Daddy had asked me to do.

I am grateful to both of my siblings that they seemed to understand, particularly my brother Lucky, with whom I had become especially close. On those occasions when we'd get together, he would let me take the lead in doing whatever we did. He never argued, debated, or sulked. He understood I had become our mother's support, and he had become mine, which allowed me to do my job as well as I could.

Thereafter, I never forgot to let him know how much I appreciated what he was doing. Neither did our parents.

And we never ever failed to revel in their uncompromising, unconditional love for each of us.

• • •

A follow-up postscript to this story occurred several years later. When I overheard my mother tell my father as they spoke by phone, *"I think there may be something wrong with Princess."*

At the time, Daddy happened to be in New Zealand where he was then doing *his* job, the very first day of his very first trip after years of being home making sure Mommy was okay. By then she was doing much better. So much so that when they got a call from a former client of theirs asking for assistance, she suggested that if he wanted to take on some work, he should feel comfortable doing so.

"Why do you think something's wrong?" he asked.

"Well I think something might be very wrong. She's acting strange! Like something is either wrong with her or maybe she thinks there's something wrong with me that I don't know of."

"I'm sure everything's fine," my father assured Mommy, *"but why don't you tell me what happened that has you so concerned."*

"Well, from the moment you left she's been acting weird. She's been hanging all over me. She won't let me out of her sight! For instance, when I took my shower this morning, she would not stop scratching at the door until I let her into the bathroom. I mean she simply refuses to leave me alone for a second! She's following me around like my shadow!"

For a minute or so, the silence in the room where I was lying next to Mommy was broken only by the sound of my own breathing, and then by my mother's loud exclamations that bordered on astonishment.

"She's amazing . . . she's really amazing, isn't she?!"

That's when I knew for sure what she had just been told by Daddy.

The night before he left, he had sat me down like he had that day when Mommy returned from her surgery in New York City. He said I needed to know that he was counting on me to take care of our family in his absence. That I needed to know that while Mommy would likely put on a brave face, she might be a little scared too, for this would be Daddy's first long trip away since Mommy had gotten sick.

Daddy said I still had my job to do. And that he knew I would continue to do it beautifully.

And that he would know I was doing it as "bestest" as I needed to, when he'd hear these words from Mommy: *"Princess is following me around like a shadow."*

. . .

I turned my face back up to gaze at my mother. She had a look of joy and amazement. She was also crying.

"Princess, you know how much I love you, don't you? You are, you will always be, my Magic Girl! You are the prettiest, 'bestest' girl in the whole wide world."

I wagged my tail at the sound of some of those favorite words of mine. I was happy she was happy.

It's so satisfying to know you're doing your job well.

A job I have been doing ever since Daddy changed my life with the words: *"You have a big job to do."*

A job I have been carrying out anywhere and everywhere my mother happens to be.

If she's at the kitchen counter, I am right next to her. Or if she's there and I am out on the "porchis," she's sees me looking back at her through our kitchen window from my vantage point atop a three-foot-high serving cart just outside. When she swims in our pool, I watch over her from our "porchis." If she is in the car driving with Daddy and me, I get up and move forward from the back of the car every half hour to see how she's doing. When she takes me shopping or to make a deposit at the bank or to buy newspapers from the convenience store, she knows to leave the car parked so that she's in my line of sight all the time.

And if she's away for a night, she knows I need to hear her voice at the other end of the phone just before she goes to sleep . . . so I know all is well and can sleep easy.

It's all just part of doing my job. And it will remain that way.

Right up to the very moment when it will be my turn to join my grandfather and my siblings to help keep our family bench warm in Heaven.

Doing My Job:

Caring for Mommy with Lucky

THE MIDDLE YEARS

ARE WE *THERE* YET?

O ur first trip to our new "housis" in Jupiter, Florida, almost wasn't.

Mommy, Daddy, Lucky and I were going for the very first time to stay in SERENITY 2. The new "housis" Mommy had built for Daddy. She always only half-joked afterwards that she had done so *"for his next wife"*—in the event her battle with cancer would have had her join Grandpa and the others keeping our family bench warm for us in Heaven.

But Lucky and I always knew better. We knew she'd recover, and the "housis" was for our parents and us.

In any event Lucky and I should have been very excited.

Instead we got stressed out.

This was a brand-new experience with a lot of commotion going on before we were to leave. Candidly, we didn't know what to make of all the planning, packing, and last-minute frantic *"Did you remember to . . . ?"* this or that. So it was all very upsetting at the time, with all the bags and suitcase and boxes and everything else lying around.

We kept wondering what was happening? Where it was that someone was going. And who was going? And more importantly were *we* going too?

Today my parents have it down to a science.

. . .

That first trip was billed as something that was supposed to be a fun thing to do. A time for us to help Mommy to relax. To help her recover from one of the big cancer surgeries she had undergone.

In the build-up to it, Daddy had already told Lucky and me to expect a *"long drive,"* but one we would really enjoy. However, in those days, we had no idea what a *"long drive"* consisted of exactly. Since our average drive was no more than ten minutes to Uncle Greg's or to Mommy's mommy's "housis." And the longest drive we had ever taken up to then was on one of our infrequent magical mystery tours that maybe lasted at most *an hour* (my parents' time).

It also hadn't escaped our attention that something dramatically different was up when Daddy started to take us on other drives in the vicinity of where we lived, but to places that were not familiar to us.

I realize now that this was a pretty good idea—conceptually speaking. He was simply trying to get us comfortable with the unknown. Places we had not been to before. Smells and sounds that would be unfamiliar to us.

As I said, it was a good idea . . . in principle. Things, however, didn't turn out exactly as planned.

You want to know what it was like?

If you have ever seen the Chevy Chase movies about the Clark Griswald family vacations, well, it was just like that!

• • •

The process started off less than propitiously.

By the time we got everything that had not already previously been packed—including Lucky and me—into the car the morning of our departure, my memory of it now is one of overwhelmingly massive tension permeating the car.

Lucky, in particular, normally so placid and calm, kept whimpering. He and I were in the back seat of our car, and he couldn't decide whether to sit or where to lie down.

I was pretty irritated myself: If only my parents had asked me, I would have told them that *this* car simply wouldn't do. We needed something more comfortable and spacious like the car we drive in now, where the passenger seats are rolled down, opening up the back half of the car for us. Where there is a soft, sort of mattress-type bedding for us to lie down on. Where, as well, there's enough room for someone my size to stretch or to ask Mommy for a carrot or water or a biscuit. And where there are always some of our own toys with us. Such as my "bestest" monkee Perywinkle, who's dark, very big, incredibly soft, and very affectionate.

Today, we know better. Along with LionMonkee, Fluffy, and Polarsnarf, Perywinkle goes with me on every trip. Perywinkle enjoys it when I lay my head on him, allowing Lucky to lay his head on my rump.

However, as I said, this is the way we travel *today*.

Unfortunately, it could not have been more different on that first trip!

We should have left by 9:00 a.m.

We didn't get started till a little before noon.

In part, because Lucky couldn't decide if he had to go to the "batroom" before we got started. So we waited around to see what he wanted to do. By the time he did, I was ready to do so too.

Then, after we finally got underway, when we had gotten to an intersection to stop for a red light, Lucky and I looked at each other with anticipation.

We got real excited!

We started wagging our tails!

We started breathing really hard!

I even thought about but did not say to Mommy, *"I told you we would be good. This was no big deal. You see Daddy and you might have had your doubts about us, but like we told you all along, we were ready for something like this."*

Let's just say, it's a good thing I didn't.

You see, Lucky and I figured we had arrived at our destination.

Problem was, we had gone exactly 2.2 miles!!!

Daddy asked us—well, not *asked* exactly—to calm down.

He said we only had another eleven hundred and five miles to go.

That did it!

Lucky started whimpering again. I thought my rather long loud sigh was more subtle.

"Just in case"—Mommy's suggestion that we should stop right then turned out to be a very good thing. Lucky almost didn't make it out of the car.

Fortunately for all of us, he did.

. . .

When we got to Highway I-95, just outside of Wilmington, Delaware, I really began to worry.

"Where the heck are we going? We've never been this way before! Maybe Daddy doesn't know the way and needs some help!"

So in the spirit of trying to be helpful, I decided to tell Daddy. He told me he didn't need my advice. I suggested otherwise, even more loudly.

Mommy suggested *"enough is enough"* and told me to lie down.

I still wasn't satisfied.

Worse, all the commotion had woken up Lucky who had actually fallen into a peaceful slumber.

So now it was *his* turn to be concerned.

He was afraid our parents might decide to leave one of us behind right there and then, if I didn't quiet down. So he started to whimper again.

That got me so upset I told Daddy rather loudly he *"needed to stop"* the car immediately! Now *I* needed to go to the "batroom"!

By this time, we had driven a total of nineteen miles!

$\cdots$

But that's what we did. We stopped again . . . and then again, after another twenty miles . . . and then one more time . . . just outside of Baltimore . . . maybe fifty miles further on. After which Mommy conceded it might be a good thing for Lucky and I to take a small sedative *"to help calm down."*

It must have worked. I don't recall much about the next several hours after that.

$\cdots$

By 8:45 that evening, Lucky and I had begun to feel the pangs of hunger in our bellies.

This was way past our usual dinner time! However, we didn't say anything for fear it might upset Daddy's concentration. But we weren't terribly displeased when we overheard him telling Mommy he was beginning to feel *"less than comfortable"* trying to navigate our way past all of the humongous 18-wheelers that all of a sudden decided to join us side-by-side out of nowhere. So shortly thereafter, we decided to stop for the night.

In a place called Fayetteville, North Carolina, where the people talked with an accent that Lucky and I had some difficulty understanding when we first heard it.

It was okay though. Just being there made us happy on two counts.

The first was we knew we would soon be eating.

The second was my parents had picked out a motel for all of us to stay in. We had heard good things about the hotel chain before leaving for the trip.

. . .

What a dump!

The room was dirty, dank and dark. And it smelled of tobacco and the remnants of others like Lucky and me who apparently, along with their parents had previously rented the room.

It was not just a disappointment; it was atrocious!

In fairness, of course we didn't know at the time it was the only hotel or motel within sixty or seventy miles that would allow Lucky and me to stay with our parents.

Whatever! It didn't matter. We were so tired we were ready to sleep anywhere. So we got through the night. As we also did the next night where we stopped in the town of Daytona Beach, Florida, at a motel right outside a really huge stadium that's used for something called NASCAR stock car racing. This was after we'd been rejected from an ocean side hotel not far from there. Which was probably a good thing, as the street was very busy with cars and those of our kind were also not allowed on the "beachis," so there wouldn't have been many places for us to go to the "batroom."

That motel was okay though.

Put it this way: It certainly was a whole lot better than the motel in Fayetteville, North Carolina.

. . .

The next day we got to Jupiter. All of us were relieved to have made it.

It had been a very long ride. But not so long as to stop us from getting a good laugh at something Lucky did upon our arrival, the memory of which still brings us all a good chuckle today.

You see, as soon as Daddy pulled the car into the garage of our brand new "housis," Lucky and I couldn't wait to run in to see what it looked like. It's fair to say we explored every bit of it while Mommy and Daddy unpacked the car. And then when they finished doing that, they started fixing dinner for Lucky and me. All of which gave me some time to relax and unwind. So I lay down on the carpet in the living room and promptly fell asleep.

. . .

I woke with a start! I thought I heard the terrifying words: *"Lucky's missing!"*

"That simply can't be," I said to myself. *"He was just here!"*

The problem was that *"just here"* was by now actually ten minutes later (my parents' time), during which time I had been in a deep slumber.

Mommy, Daddy and I ran to the "porchis" first. But Lucky was not there. So the three of us then hurried into the master bedroom where we proceeded to even check the clothes closets. But Lucky wasn't there either.

Next, we scoured the den. He wasn't there, nor in *its* "batroom," nor in the guest bedroom and not in *its* "batroom" either.

No luck—there was *no* Lucky!

By now it was clear that what I had only *thought* I had heard in my sleep was in fact no dream at all! If anything, it was becoming a real-life nightmare. My brother, my "bestest" friend in the world, my canine soul mate was missing!

Mommy and Daddy were dumbfounded—how could my brother go missing in a "housis" where none of the doors that lead to the outside were open? So they decided to retrace their steps once more throughout the "housis" . . . but to no avail.

That's when I decided on my own to take a step back. To do what I do "bestest" in times of crisis: calm down and think things through strategically. I decided to take a look for myself. To quietly explore a place my parents had not already searched, but where—knowing Lucky as well as I did (and vice versa)—I thought I might find him.

· · ·

Within seconds I found myself frantically gesturing. Trying my hardest to gain Daddy's attention, as he stood nearby—clearly exhausted from the drive, exasperated, obviously now very concerned—in a state of absolute disbelief about Lucky's disappearance.

First I gave him a shout from where I was standing, maybe thirty feet away. When that didn't work, I ran up to him, gave him a "nuzzie" on his hand, all with the intended purpose to let him know he and Mommy needed to follow me.

It worked! They both followed as I led the way. To the door in the hallway that separates the garage from the rest of the "housis."

There was Lucky!

He was waiting for us!

He had hopped back in the car!

And I immediately knew exactly why.

Having fully explored this place—our lovely new "housis," Serenity 2, that had been the cause of such a fuss to get to in the first place—*Lucky* was ready to leave again. After three days of driving, he later confirmed to me that he thought maybe our trip hadn't ended, and he was just trying to be good, to make Daddy proud by getting a head start.

· · ·

As our parents smiled for the first time in what seemed ages, Lucky stared back at them. He didn't know whether he had done something right, wrong, or just plain embarrassing. He wagged his tail slightly, and in that charming way of his he half cocked his head as he looked up, as Daddy, obviously relieved and happy, walked over and bent down to give him a kiss on his forehead.

"Mr. and Mrs. Snarf, would you like to eat?" he asked while smiling at both of us. To which, in turn, my brother and I both gave our standard response: a big smile and a windmill turn of our tails. Neither of us had to be asked a second time. After three days on the road, we were ravenous. We almost flew into the kitchen.

Perhaps it was all the excitement or now just pent up hunger; whatever it was, dinner tasted better than usual that night. After which, we tried out the new dog run for the first time ever, and then went to bed lying side by side as we always used to.

The fact is our first trip to Florida had ended on a high note: We had arrived safe and sound, if exhausted, and no one got lost.

· · ·

We didn't wake up until eleven o'clock the next morning . . .

FROM THE TOES

Lucky was never the talkative type.

But that didn't mean he didn't communicate.

Indeed there have been few others in my lifetime who have been more expressive than my brother. It truly was one of his most redeeming features.

He just never felt the need to be the vexatious, bravado-spewing, loud-mouth braggart you see so often today talking business or politics or whatever on the box with pictures and voices, and those who clog up the airwaves with seemingly little more than rhetoric, not enough reason, and a whole lot of self-important ranting.

Lucky was the total opposite.

He never felt the need to yell or scream to gain someone's attention.

As far as he was concerned, there is too much noise and too much screaming in our lives. And that destructive partisanship of every kind is being passed off in the name of passionate concern. All the while, there's far too little genuine *listening* to what others would like to say.

· · ·

From the very first day we met, he and I shared the same life philosophy. That you don't build yourself up on someone else's weaknesses, deficiencies, poor timing, or just plain bad luck. As such, he was also not the kind to castigate or denigrate or criticize or put others down if he needed to make a point of his own.

And he never did what so many people in business, politics, and other for and not-for-profit organizations seem to do today in their attempt to look *"leader-like."*

He never ever took someone else's meritorious idea or suggestion or recommendation and then peddled it as his own. To the contrary, he gave credit where credit was due, and communicated such, in his own way, for all to know. To do otherwise, he believed, would have been disingenuous, and being perceived as anything less than absolutely truthful was a reputation he would have abhorred had it been ever even remotely attached to his name. Which, of course, it never was.

I recognize that in a day and age that excess and the "celebrated" are worshipped, where lying and cheating and fraud are explained away as idiosyncrasies or as momentary lapses in judgment or "misspeaking" or even worse, saying it is someone else's doing, being sincere and genuine and honest and ethical and aboveboard may seem like old-fashioned, even antiquated, qualities. But they were at the core of my brother's soul. Just as I trust others would say the same about me.

The fact is he and I never tolerated phoniness well. Frankly for him and me and most, if not all of our kind, insincerity is something rather easy to detect no matter how deeply someone tries to cover it up.

So why do it?

Unlike like my brother Smokey, who if *he* thought you were a phony, instinctively and simply didn't like you and was not at all averse to let you know with a hint of a threat, Lucky always tended, as I still do, to make the point far more simply and subtly . . . but no less effectively.

For example, if we ever found someone making a "fuss" over us that we felt was disingenuous, unlike Smokey who would confront you on the spot, Lucky and I would simply turn away. By doing so, we let our actions speak a whole lot louder than any words (or bite) might.

. . .

Said simply, for Lucky communicating was, and for me remains today, as much about what you *don't* say as it is about what you say. Consequently, unlike so many in this era of so much blabber and blather, Lucky spared the rhetoric when he communicated. Instead of bluster, he allowed silence to be his ally. So much so that when he did speak out loud, you found yourself listening intently, and for good reason.

You see, my brother was turned off by those who confuse poorly thought through doctrine with having a mere difference of opinion to share. Just as he could not empathize with those who misconstrue destructive and angry, rabid name-calling, for constructive questioning. And those who attempt to justify blatant self-indulgent, self-centered Machiavellianism, with the excuse of *"sharing one's pain."* And those who manifest heated, vituperative rancor by intentionally mislabeling it as civil discourse.

Instead, Lucky viewed the use of communication very differently. To him, communication almost always had to have a single objective: *to find common ground.*

As such he became renowned among the many around the world who knew him for uniting, not alienating.

Which is why without exception, everyone loved my brother. He was what he was. He never strayed from who he was. We all got from him exactly what we all we saw in him: sincerity, gentility, modesty, decency.

Plain and simple, Lucky was a "good egg."

That's why I respected him so much.

That's why I loved him so much.

. . .

Over the duration of our long relationship of more than seventy years (our time) of unconditional love, I heard Lucky actually speak . . . maybe four . . . maybe five times at most.

I know it may sound a bit strange, but those are the facts. I never questioned it. I just took it for what it was.

It was who he was and what he was about.

As I indicated before, as far as everyone who knew him would attest, it was in his quietness that my mostly silent brother was a terrific communicator.

That having been said, however, I am very grateful that my parents got to hear him speak on at least two or three of those occasions. Because if they hadn't, I wonder if at some point they might have concluded something was wrong.

There wasn't.

It was just Lucky sticking by one of his life principles. As a genuine advocate of the precept *"less is more,"* Lucky just didn't feel the need to go on and on about anything.

And so you can really appreciate our shock the first time we heard him actually speak. Shock, yes, but also a very pleasant surprise.

. . .

It had to be at least twenty-eight years or so (my time) after I had first joined the family.

And while today I don't recall *what* it was that first drew him to the exact location where we would get to hear him speak for the very first time, I do remember very vividly *where* it was: in the kitchen. Not far from where we both ate.

At a spot that looks out the corner of the window overlooking our pool and forest, where whatever it was that got his attention there, soon got mine too.

So I walked over to where he was standing and staring outwards.

While at no point deviating from the target of his focused stare, he, as always, acknowledged my presence in his usual polite manner. With a slight nod of the head, a quiet smile on his face, a little wag at the very tip of his tail, and his customary kiss on my nose and ears.

In turn for which, with a subtle turn of my face, so that my eyes caught the corner of his, I let him know I was equally happy to be in his company. And then we stood there not moving . . . motionless . . . silent . . . anticipatory . . . for at least five or six minutes (my parents' time).

As we did so, in the background I overheard Mommy and Daddy comment on our posture, about our overall demeanor. They weren't being critical, just inquisitive. Sufficiently so, that soon they too joined us at the window.

Although, to be fair, I don't know what *they* saw or even what they thought they were supposed to be looking at. The truth was neither did I!

Only Lucky knew whatever *it* was that had attracted his intense curiosity. A curiosity, which had by now, morphed into almost vigilant attention.

All we knew is that he seemed totally captivated by what was going on in a way we had never observed before.

And that's what all three of us found so engaging.

· · ·

It began the way an earthquake does . . . with a soft rumble. And then *it* became like the sound made by a tornado when it passes over or very nearby . . . a deep rumbling in the distance that progressively hardens and intensifies the closer it gets. With a clarity that is both striking and indisputable and filled with potential impact, even if at the initial onset it's a bit confusing as to both its source and ultimate direction.

It was Lucky! *It* was his voice we were hearing!

Stunned by its suddenness and its depth, all three of us actually jumped back from the window.

We weren't the only ones! Lucky did too, only further and higher! We couldn't help ourselves. Neither could he.

None of the four of us had ever heard him talk before!!!

It continued on . . . Rising up, it seemed, right from the bottom of his toes, passing right through his body, until it came involuntarily out through his voice box.

He looked at me.

I looked at my parents.

They and I looked back at him. We didn't know what to say. Apparently neither did Lucky.

If anything he seemed more embarrassed than upset, and shocked, yet not terribly surprised. Almost as if *he* knew what *it* was —even though we did not. Especially since he hadn't done *it* before.

Then he looked at us with that quite appealing shy shrug, the half-cocked head with that wonderful half smile of his as he looked back up at Mommy and Daddy as if to say: *"Yeah, I know. I did it! I BARKED!! For the very first time! But it's no big deal."*

How true to form it was that by the time we'd sufficiently overcome *our* collective shock, ready to congratulate him on his new life experience, Lucky had already shrugged it all off and was ready to move on.

I understood why: To him this was no big deal. He was just happy my parents and I were there to listen to what he had to say.

To him it didn't matter this was the first time.

The only thing that did matter was now that there had been something he felt worthwhile expressing out loud, he had clearly asserted what had to be said, what he wanted all of us to know.

. . .

As I indicated before, over the years I have forgotten what brought it all about.

Although, if I were to hazard a guess, it might have been that he had seen a squirrelly navigate the narrow fence that separates the south side of the front lawn from the pool. The one that leads to the exterior wall that could potentially be scaled, for example, if a rodent were aiming for the master bedroom upstairs where we all slept at night. Indeed it's quite possible he was giving us a heads-up. A warning as to what he was seeing. Knowing my brother as I do, I am sure he didn't want the squirrelly to get away with impunity.

Maybe that's what he saw that day. Who can remember that far back? So much has happened since then, really I can't say for sure. Moreover, if you don't mind me saying, it really doesn't matter.

What does matter was the sound of his voice!

It was unbelievably deep and resonant and smooth and confident.
The fact is he would have done well on radio, just like our father.

To me it sounded sexy and endearing.

To my parents it conveyed maturity and confidence. It filled them with pleasure and pride. Something they would wait for years to hear in the future. And they did a couple of more times in the same tone as the first.

But other than that, he was almost always silent.

The rare exception being when Lucky would let us know with a sort of whispered whimper he was scared or in pain. *That* sound used to cut through all of us like a knife. To be certain when any of us heard *that*, we'd come running from all corners to see how we might comfort him.

. . .

Still, it goes without saying that the very first time we all heard Lucky's actual speaking voice was a very special moment for all of us. And it remains one of my very most treasured memories of a cherished relationship.

THE TIME THE WORLD STOOD STILL

From the moment our parents walked into the "housis," Lucky and I instinctively could tell something very bad had happened. Or was still happening . . . or might still happen.

Exactly what, we didn't know. Nor could we tell. We just knew something was really wrong. Sort of like that time, but not exactly, when Mommy came home and we found out about the cancer.

All we knew is that when they walked in after returning from what they said was to be a two day business trip near our "housis" in Jupiter—where they usually were so happy and relaxed—our parents seemed seriously distracted, disconcerted, and disturbed . . . even a bit depressed.

All Lucky and I knew is that not long after they'd left us with Uncle Brian, they and he were constantly on the box they speak into that rings. In addition to which, just as conspicuously, all the boxes with pictures and voices in all the rooms were always turned on. And whenever we overheard Uncle Brian speaking, it was always in a kind of tense whisper.

We didn't know why, but we sure could sense the tension . . . inside and outside our "housis." Especially as those big machines that fly high in the air flew over us day and night, much nosier and more numerous than ever before, and very different looking. Almost as if they had pointed noses to shoot something from.

As I said, all we knew is Mommy and Daddy had planned for what they said would be a trip of a day or two: "*. . . Fly in, go to a meeting, and fly out* *right after"* was how they had described it to Lucky and me as we watched them pack lightly for the trip.

Honestly we didn't mind.

We always felt safe with Uncle Brian (I still do).

He kind of made it feel like camp for us. And unbeknownst to Mommy and Daddy, Lucky and I always hoped he'd secretly invite girl friends to visit. Because we knew they'd make a bit of a fuss over us, which is always nice.

Surprisingly, the promise of a day and a half turned into three, almost four (our parents' time). And even more surprising was when they did finally return, Mommy and Daddy showed up in our extra car. The old one we keep in Jupiter to go to the "beachis."

It turns out they had no choice; they had to. For all the flights had been cancelled.

And it's fortunate they had our "beachis" car waiting for them there, since apparently everyone down there was trying to do the same thing—leave town quickly. In fact, so many were trying to get back to their families all at the same time, there were no more cars to rent. Daddy and Mommy had even met a man who finally found a rental car and set off from Florida to drive all the way to Seattle by himself, as it was the only way he could get home!

. . .

It would be weeks before Lucky and I could put all the pieces of the puzzle together. However, from the many tense conversations we overheard Mommy and Daddy have with others, here is what learned.

The morning after their flight to Florida, they were in our "beachis housis." Daddy was on the phone with a business client from Toronto, and Mommy was getting dressed after a shower, listening to the morning news shows on TV in the background as we always do when we are together.

Mommy ran to where Daddy was sitting to tell him something terrible had occurred and he turned around to look at what she was talking about and seeing on the TV what he saw, he suggested the client do the same at his office.

What they saw was not only horrifying, it was also being reported—incorrectly—as a small machine that flies hitting a large tower. The story was being told far too quickly and inaccurately by media people apparently trying to be too smart by half, expressing opinions without knowledge. That made it even worse. Especially when everyone saw what happened soon thereafter: another crash by another plane into the adjoining building, resulting in terrible fires and the eventual collapse of both towers. Even Lucky and I knew that this was not caused by some small machine that flies—we see plenty of those all the time in the sky outside our "housis."

This was a once-in-a-lifetime experience (at least we hope so). Something so large that, as Daddy described later, *"it was like watching life imitating art in one of those disaster movies."* Unfortunately and excruciatingly sadly, it was real life.

. . .

Over the next few hours, we learned later that Mommy and Daddy in Jupiter kept watching the news reports, and calling us, and taking calls from all over the world. I guess everyone everywhere was seeing the same thing. And so when someone called to ask my father whether he still planned to go to the meeting he was expected at, the one he'd come for in the first place, he told whomever it was *"this is **not** the right time to hold a meeting. It's a time for prayer."*

Although some apparently disagreed, and were even taken aback by Daddy's comment, I guess most were convinced. The meeting ended up being cancelled.

It was the right decision.

By then Mommy and Daddy had decided they desperately wanted—they needed—to get home to us as quickly as they could. Simply put, like so many parents they did not want to be separated from us.

So by about 2:30 that same afternoon, they left as quickly as they could repack their clothes, load up the car, and close up the "housis" . . . wondering if they would ever see it again.

. . .

It didn't take long for them to find the main highway we always use between our two "housis" swamped with others trying to do the same thing. And police were everywhere.

Even had they wanted to listen to music as we usually do when traveling by car, my parents would not have been able to. There was none playing at all. Only scary-sounding police news reports and dire warnings telling people in cars what to do, and conveying instructions they had no choice but to follow.

Like the one about two cars to look for: one a silver Toyota, the other a red something or other. Both suspected of holding *"dangerous chemical or biological material or weaponry. If you spot these either of these cars, do not try to stop them. Please call the police immediately."*

Like the one about a car the police were looking for, possibly leaving, or having just left, a private airport in Vero Beach where people are trained to fly small machines that fly.

Like the one they heard driving into Richmond, Virginia, the next evening en route to the Jeffersonian Hotel, usually one of Daddy's favorites. This was a warning for the people who lived there. Because the Federal Reserve's vaults are stored deep underground in that city, Richmond was a likely target for attack by the same people as crashed the machines that fly.

That wasn't all.

Just as they were about to cross the Florida/Georgia border, they drove into a huge storm, characterized by the weather people later as "hurricane-like" that had started out on the west coast of Florida and crossed the state. As a result, our parents decided to do the right thing—stop till it passed over and then drive on a bit.

It's fortuitous they did so. For as Daddy was paying for gas and some snacks, a really rough-looking but very nice man advised Daddy to *"forget about heading north. There's a huge backup . . . miles and miles because of an accident. It's a standstill."* He had heard about it from another truck driver friend of his on something called a CB radio.

That's why Mommy and Daddy turned around and headed to the nearest hotel they knew from memory, the Ritz Carlton on Amelia Island. Where, some years earlier, Daddy had made a presentation to a client's Board of Directors and senior management, and later that same day, Mommy had caught a shark from a boat chartered by their client's Chairman of the Board.

The surrealism of everything that had already happened up to then did not end. On arrival, as soon as the hotel people heard our parents had come from Jupiter and were en route to Pennsylvania, they were upgraded to a massive suite, given free champagne and food at half price. They stayed indoors all night, watching the news. Likely the seven other guests in the hotel that night did much the same as the hotel staff did everything to be kind to all of their truly unexpected and apprehensive guests. That night and the next morning, Mommy and Daddy saw no one at all at the pool or the "beachis" which their suite overlooked.

From that hotel all the way till Richmond, Virginia, the highway was almost deserted, which made for easier driving for Daddy. Deserted except for the big noisy machines in the sky with funny turning motors on their roofs that would come out of nowhere from time to time and hover over the highway. Still, it was easier than what we usually experienced when all of us traveled to and from Jupiter.

I can only speculate that the people at the Ritz Carlton Hotel in Amelia Island must have told the people at the Jeffersonian Hotel in Richmond to be really nice to our parents. For the unusual even unprecedented kindness my parents experienced the first night was repeated the second—this time with an upgrade to The Presidential Suite at half the rate of a deluxe room. Free meals. Free wine. Free breakfast the next morning. And again as in Florida, only a few anxious guests were in the hotel for the night. Mommy and Daddy said it was outright eerie.

And then the next day, when they got to Washington, DC, where frankly the traffic is always worse than terrible, there were very few cars. However, there were military vehicles everywhere and machine gun posts were visible to the naked eye. And a very strange-looking machine that made noise and had a funny looking thing on its roof flew in the sky. One that had only been seen in news pictures until then. As Daddy and Mommy silently drove on a street they call "The Beltway" around Washington, this strange flying machine circled the city over and over. Later we heard Mommy say it was *"an AWAC."*

Mommy called her "bestest" cousin Lisa whose daughter was a student at a university near where they were driving. Cousin Lisa said her daughter was spooked by the sight of tanks perched ready to protect the campus outside her apartment, across from the State Department. The same tanks, perhaps, Mommy and Daddy spoke of seeing as they drove around the Beltway. Mommy and Daddy hoped to pick up Lisa's daughter and take her with them—but no one could leave. And it was impossible to get into the city.

It was not too much longer, about mid-afternoon, when Lucky and I saw our parents pull up into our own driveway. Honestly, we were not surprised. In fact we had given Uncle Brian a heads-up sometime before, Lucky with a kiss and me with a "nuzzie" and a push to the garage door. I guess it was our natural instinct at work again. Our ability to discern the impending arrival of either of our parents—well before they ever turn the corner of the street that leads to the next street that leads to our street that eventually leads to our "housis."

As soon as the door opened, we literally jumped up as high as we could to welcome them. The kissing and stroking and "nuzzying" went on unabated and unabashed. Until Daddy asked us quietly to follow him into the den where our parents and Uncle Brian compared notes, in very hushed, serious even ominous tones, about everything they had seen and heard reported over the past few days.

· · ·

By Friday evening of that same week, neither the overwhelming shock nor the sense of fear, nor the mind-numbing sadness that enveloped our neighborhood (others too I am sure) had worn off. Nevertheless, or maybe in spite of the fear and sadness and shock, Mommy and Daddy made one other critical decision that played itself out in remarkable ways that evening. They decided to go to the Mann Center, in a big park just outside of Philadelphia, to listen to a musical concert for which they long had tickets, starring two of their favorite performers, the singer Linda Eder and pianist Marvin Hamlisch.

Given the circumstances of the events of the past few days, they had no idea what to expect. Frankly they were pleasantly surprised the concert had not been cancelled altogether. More than ten thousand were holding tickets like our parents. Two hundred showed up.

No one could blame the ninety-eight hundred who didn't. It was not only cold and damp that night. There was also a sense of impending doom everywhere. The collective fear was palpable. People were afraid to gather in groups anywhere, afraid they could be targets like the people in the buildings with the machines that fly. In addition, both performers had been lucky to get from where they had been the day before—Hamlisch in Iowa and Eder in New York City—to Philadelphia.

When they returned late that night, Mommy and Daddy couldn't stop talking about what they and everyone there, the performers included, had experienced together. It really must have been extraordinary. So much so that Mommy and Daddy still talk about it occasionally all these years later. As do other friends of theirs who happened to be there that night.

As do the two performers who have both referred to it in concerts and interviews over the years. In fact, not long ago, Mommy was standing alone at the top of the stairs in the New York City train station, waiting for her train to bring her back to us after a business trip. When she looked up, she saw that someone else was now waiting for the same train: Marvin Hamlisch. Quietly Mommy said to him, *"My husband and I were at the Mann Center that night, just after 9/11. We were there when you and Linda Eder performed . . . "*

Mr. Hamlisch immediately looked up at her and just as quietly said, *"It was quite the night . . . I will never forget it. We were so glad to do what we could to make people feel better and we ended up feeling better ourselves just being there with you.* THANK YOU."

The night of that concert was a night like the week that led up to it and the time that followed—full of emotion.

When the world as we'd always known stood still . . . and changed forever.

When the thousands of those like my brother Lucky and me would never understand why *their* loved ones didn't come home from work that day.

When, ever since, Mommy and Daddy have kept us ever closer to them and are even more convinced that every moment we have together is a gift, one never to be taken for granted.

Every day to be lived: one day at a time.

CYCLES OF LIFE: MY BROTHER'S KEEPER

There's a song that Daddy plays for me quite often I've come to enjoy and appreciate. It's called *"Cycles,"* by someone named Frank Sinatra. Its melody is so touching. And as for its lyrics, as much as I will never fully understand all its words, with Daddy and I being so kinetically connected, it's not been difficult at all to glean its meaning from him.

I knew well before the day my brother Lucky would no longer be with us, that one of life's cycles would be one of my biggest challenges. And for a very good reason. You see, as tough as it would be for me, I knew for my parents it would be worse, much worse.

For unlike my own natural instincts which help me deal with the inevitability of the cycles of life with a certain degree of equanimity, I knew that for Mommy and Daddy the loss of a loved one like Lucky would open deep, deep caverns of sadness. Those which only a very, very, very long period of time and healing could eventually fill.

For me, however, the cycles of life are something quite different.

A loss brings with it memories that are not just sad, but also sweet and warm, and comforting too. For instance in the case of my brother, I knew I'd always be reminded of all the time he and I spent together, more than a decade in traditional terms, 70 plus years by our counting. Memories of the toys we played with. His eternal residual scent on the beds, blankets, carpets, and baskets we once lay on side by side. And all the places we explored and the times we had that were so much fun, and which brought us all so much happiness, love, joy, and affection.

If only my parents had been given the gift of my ability to focus this way. Always on the day to day . . . on today. And only on the "bestest" of what was yesterday.

I suppose now that's one of the reasons, for as long as I can remember, I've viewed a big part of my role—my job—as being to help them do that. To help them fill the deep emotional craters inevitably opened up by the last of life's natural cycles.

· · ·

Well before his final day with us, the second to last day of January 2004, I had a pretty good sense Lucky's health was waning. The signs were there. When we would go for our daily walks, his once insatiable appetite for, love of, and unlimited energy to scamper up and down the hills that are part of the campus of the private school near our "housis" were no longer a part of his makeup. For him instead, those joys of life had become a struggle. Something he still really looked forward to, but a struggle nonetheless.

He hurt.

His whole body hurt from the pains and the aches of arthritis that accompanies so many of us growing older.

And his eyes—once so beautifully clear brown and full of the mischief of life's surprises he never failed to appreciate on our walks (like the "squirrely deerzies" and the other animals and the magnificent fall colors he'd look out at across the lake near our home up north)—his beautiful soft eyes were now totally clouded.

At best he could see shadows, but even those were very vague.

And because he could no longer see, *we* no longer got to enjoy the exquisite wonderment that used to overtake his beautiful sweet face, with every sighting of one of the wide species of large and small exotic birds behind both of our "housis." Or the geckoes we would always stare at together. Or the golfers we'd see passing by while we stood guard as our parents swam in the pool in the back of our Florida "housis" he absolutely treasured. And I still do.

He had grown deaf, too.

Perhaps it was age. Or maybe it was congenital. Whatever it was, it hurt all of us. To see him trying so hard to strain to hear what we were saying. No longer able to take in the soaring sounds of melodies with which our parents would fill—and still do—our two "housis."

And how much I know he missed Mommy's soft and tender welcome to him each and every morning: *"Hi there, Sweetness."* And Daddy's resonant, *"Good morning, Mr. Wack Wack . . . did you have the 'bestest' sleep?"*

Still, despite all that, even though we knew full well he could no longer hear any of what we had to say, to the very end, my parents and I never stopped talking to him, as if he could.

. . .

As I said, I figured out Lucky's health situation a lot sooner than my parents did.

It's just basic instinct.

Yet as the final months evolved, maybe a half year or so (my parents' time), I could tell Mommy and Daddy began to come to terms with the notion that my brother was going through one final phase, one last inexorable downward spiral in his health. From which there would eventually be no resolution.

It was during that time, on at least four occasions, they asked our Doctor Uncle Greg, *"How do you think Lucky is doing? Do you think it's getting to that time?"*

And each time, Uncle Greg, I think realizing that there would be no turning back from a *final* decision regarding my brother's declining health, he'd patiently listen to my parents' questions with his typical compassion and affection. All the while, gently stroking my brother's flanks and his bowed head and almost pure white muzzle.

And to my parents' queries Uncle Greg would never give a direct answer.

I think I know why.

It was too hard for him to just come right out and say things to our parents he probably knew deep in his heart of hearts he could have just as well said at any time over the last few months. But which, for him, not surprisingly, wasn't that easy. You see, while Uncle Greg might have been our doctor for many years, the problem for him was shared by so many others from around the world who had come to know my brother Lucky over almost one hundred and five years (my time) of his life.

Uncle Greg simply adored him. It was almost impossible not to.

For when it came right down to it, if you want to know what Lucky was all about right up to the very end, all you have to do is look up in the dictionary the expression *"joie de vie."* And there you'll see my brother Lucky's face.

As you will too when you similarly look up the phrase *"a sweet and gentle soul."*

He was truly the "bestest" in life: a joy to be around, and an ever quiet but very discernibly sweet presence in the lives of all who had come to know him.

. . .

My parents tried everything they could. To not just prolong my brother's life, but to do so with empathy, by assuring some semblance of quality of life they thought he'd still appreciate.

We shortened his walks to alleviate the discomfort.

He was lifted onto the bed and the sofas so he would not have to strain. And when that proved too difficult, on the floors in the various rooms he loved to stay in with us, my parents made his baskets as comfortable as that of any five star hotel bed. Where not only he, but I too would sleep snuggled by his side.

This meant that for some time I didn't sleep in my parents' bed as I had been long accustomed to.

Admittedly, we could have lifted my brother onto the bed. But that would have not have worked. The challenge for us, you see, was that for months, he had to go to the "batroom" in the middle of the night. No one was quite sure how he'd deal with getting off our parents' bed in the dark in the middle of the night if need be. So to make sure he did not feel isolated or alone, and to give him peace of mind, I just decided on my own to sleep in a basket beside him as he slept peacefully in his bed . . . Both of us now, on the floor at the foot of Mommy and Daddy's bed. Together.

From there, I'd be best positioned to know when he had to go outside. And when he did, I'd wake up and shake my head loud enough for Daddy to hear all the jangling stuff hanging from my collars. And Daddy would get up, gently guiding Lucky by his collar to the top of the stairs, and then immediately proceed to get in front of him so my brother wouldn't fall down accidentally, and then lead my brother safely down to the first floor. Where Lucky could sense where he was. And that's where my brother would take over. He'd guide Daddy out to the garage and from there to the door that opens to our fenced-in dog run where Lucky could do whatever he needed to do.

. . .

For almost a year (my parents time), as my brother's age had slowly but inexorably taken its toll on his health, each member of our family instinctively understood there was a role for each of us to play.

Mine was self-evident.

As Lucky's sight progressively declined and then virtually disappeared along with his ability to hear, my parents did not have to ask or prompt me.

I simply decided on my own one day that my brother needed a *"seeing eye dog"* to help guide him around. And I proudly served in that capacity until the afternoon he left us forever.

My decision to do so was a *"no-brainer."*

You see, when we were young and I was recovering from my radical double hip dysplasia surgery, along with Mommy, my then new brother Lucky had been the wind beneath my wings for the duration. When I most needed it, he'd come over and gently "nuzzie" me with a kiss on my nose and my muzzle and around my ears. He'd look straight into my eyes, and with that telltale little wag of his tail, he'd let me know he was looking forward to the day when my new hips would be fused strong enough for us to play together. To romp together. To explore together.

His unspoken message was consistent: I just needed to be patient. And allow nature to do its work in healing my body.

It was one thing to hear that same persistent message from my mother and father several times a day. And then again one more time, just before Mommy and I went to sleep in the den every night, while my brother Lucky and sister Samantha slept upstairs in bed with Daddy. It was another thing, however, quite different and even more reassuring, to hear it from one of my sibling peers.

That's why now, many years later, it was my turn to do the same for him: *To be my brother's keeper.*

It was not a difficult task, just as it was not a difficult decision. Frankly, it came as naturally to me as did Daddy's becoming a full-time caregiver for Mommy when she got real sick from cancer in 1994.

One does it unquestioningly, he explained to those who asked. It's what true love is all about.

Daddy's right.

But for me, to help my brother went far beyond that.

For it was, in fact, just one more reaffirmation of the gratitude I've always felt for my life being spared all those years before, when Mommy and I had found each other at the adoption agency. It was my way to once again thank, in a very concrete way, the people who are my father and mother today for not bailing out on me, as others did when they found out my hips needed to be replaced. Had they not kept me and helped me, the truth is, my prognosis was not only not particularly positive—in fact, my life span would likely have been at most only a few more months (my parents' time).

So you see, being given the opportunity to help my brother when he most needed it was another answer to one of life's truly vexing questions I have occasionally reflected on over the years: *Why had I been given a second lease on life, just as my mother was given hers from her cancer shortly thereafter?*

. . .

My job as my brother's keeper was straightforward: To watch over him; to guide him; to comfort him. In other words, to give him the sense of security he needed.

By his being able to feel me by his side, wherever we were; wherever we were going; whatever we were doing.

My job was to be by his side: hip-to-hip, flank-to-flank, haunches-to-haunches, always together.

Without trying to be preachy about it, here's how I looked at it.

In a day and age when there is so much of a *"dispose if otherwise inconvenient"* attitude, being my brother's keeper was not only my responsibility. It was also my duty and my job. And it was all about love.

I not only did my job very well—I would very happily do it again if ever called upon to do so. As that man said about the horse Seabiscuit who became famous in the 1930s for winning races, *"You don't give up or discard something just because it might be a bit broken down."*

Oh yes, one other thing.

Just as Daddy said after he took care of Mommy during the worst of her illness, taking care of my brother Lucky turned out to be the "bestest" job I ever had.

. . .

In the fall of 2003, about two months before we left for Jupiter, I stopped lying beside my brother when we'd go to sleep at night. It was when I knew it was time to begin to focus most of my attention and effort on the two people I knew Lucky's eventual passing would hurt terribly. Instinct told me to begin that transition. Even if our parents did not realize that time with Lucky was running as short as it was. For them, instead it was more like the feeling of a dark cloud hanging over our family, every hour of every day for days at a time.

That's just one reason why I knew they needed for me to be close to them.

Here's another. While I obviously knew he was still with us in body, intuitively I had the growing sense there was a part of my brother's soul and spirit that had already begun its own transition to his seat on our family bench. To be with our grandfather (Mommy's father) who was with his trusty companion, Brandy, and the latter's older brother, Tracey. And my siblings, Smokey and Samantha, and my ancestral half-sister (Daddy's beloved first daughter), Shenka, all of whom were keeping Mommy's father company.

. . .

I know one thing: Wherever that place is, it's a wonderful world. The same name as the name of a song that will not only forever remind us of Lucky but whose words most accurately depict his legacy and how he lived his life.

. . .

That being said, what my parents wanted more than anything else was to get all of us to our "beachis housis" in Jupiter where they thought Lucky might have an opportunity to do better than he would in the damp and cold of the oncoming Pennsylvania winter.

And so after figuring out the not inconsiderable mechanics of how they would maneuver my brother down from our soft "beds" in the back of the car whenever we needed to stretch our legs, go to the "batroom," and get some fresh air en route the 1,107 miles between our two "housis," Mommy and Daddy and Lucky and I finally left for Jupiter.

In my heart of hearts, I sensed it would be Lucky's final drive.

I sort of think my parents felt the same way. But none of us dwelled on the thought. Instead we simply did what we had to do to make the trip as comfortable and as enjoyable for him as had been all the other drives we had taken just like this one.

As usual, my mother did the formal navigating while Daddy drove.

I could sense the sadness within both, but particularly my father. For this was the first ever trip to Florida when our Lucky was not able to navigate us by looking out the window, snuggled onto Daddy's left or right shoulder, to ensure we were going in the right direction. It was the first trip during which Daddy never once got to feel the usual quiet cadence of my brother's anticipatory breathing, and the softness of his muzzle next to the left side of Daddy's neck—as the latter drove and Lucky helped guide us, in trusting silence, during all of our previous trips.

Instead Lucky slept most of the two days on the road.

Daddy missed my brother's assistance.

But deep down, I had the feeling throughout the ride that with all we had gone through over the past nine years (my parents' time) with my mother's illness and now with Lucky, my father was just grateful we were all together in that moment. Which told me that, while it had taken quite awhile, both our parents had finally learned to *truly* live in the moment, something they now say they learned from living with us.

. . .

We overnighted as usual at the motel we always stayed in Florence, South Carolina. We like it there much more than the other one nearby where we had stayed the first couple of trips. It's cleaner, less noisy, and there are more places for Lucky and me (and now just me) to use when it's time to go outside after dinner, before going to bed, and then before and after breakfast the next morning.

From the time we pulled into the parking lot around 7:30 that evening, until we left about 8:30 the next morning, the sights and smells were familiar to me. And I made sure to do what I could to pass my comfort along to my brother. Who it seemed could at least sense where we were—one day closer to one of his most favorite places in the world, our "housis" Serenity2 in Jupiter, Florida.

While no hotel room will ever be a match for either of our "housis," that evening we were as always quite comfortable.

We ate our dinner, and then lay quietly as we watched our parents eat theirs. And then after dinner, as always, Mommy and Daddy read their newspapers, after which they watched the box with pictures and voices while Lucky and I relaxed. Indeed the only difference between this visit to Florence and the others we had experienced over the years was the prevailing silence between our parents.

They were sad, I could tell. They knew but did not want to admit to each other or to verbalize out loud what my brother and I had already accepted: This would be Lucky's last visit to Florence.

Mommy slept by my side in one bed. Daddy did the same with my brother in the other.

I slept well as did Lucky. The drive is tiring on my body, and sleep that night was deep.

Unfortunately though, Daddy, however, had a very difficult time getting any real rest. He could not get his brain to turn off. Almost hourly, he'd look up to see how his beloved pal Lucky was doing beside him. Through silent tears, he'd kiss his muzzle, and gently stroke his head and flanks.

To reciprocate, my brother would look back to where he could feel the affection of my father's familiar touch. And with his telltale slightest wag at the very tip of his tail, Lucky told our father that the two of them, as always, were totally in sync with each other.

They were as close as close can be. As they would always be.

My brother and I always knew our parents' love for us is infinite. That's why our trust in knowing they would do what's best for us has never been a question.

. . .

As I think back on that trip, there are two other images I know my parents and I will never forget. One, only my father and I saw firsthand. The other, all of us got to witness.

. . .

As dusk's twilight turned to darkness the next evening, we finally got to our exit of a very busy I-95 and Donald Ross Blvd. As the crow flies, it's only a few miles from our "housis" in Jupiter. Thankfully, it's far enough away so that we never hear its traffic. Yet close enough so that by the time we'd get to that exit, Lucky and I could always tell we were almost home.

That's when as if by rote, we'd get up from our car den. Go over to the windows. And take in the smell of the salt ocean air that came in from somewhere east of us in the not too far distance.

That smell always, *always* made us so happy. It still does for me.

That evening was no different. We did as we always did when we got to this point in our two-day trip. We signaled to our parents and to each other we knew where we were.

As usual I did it vocally. Surprisingly perhaps, Lucky did it too . . . in his own way. That he did at all made it even more memorable.

Simply put, by somehow calling on the energy needed after a long and draining drive of more than eighteen plus hours, Lucky, like me, did as he had always done at the junction of I-95 and Donald Ross Blvd. Despite his failing health, despite his inability to hear, despite his inability to see, and despite most significantly his failing sense of smell, he got up, went over to the partially rolled down window behind my father, put his nose outside, and took in the surroundings.

And then he turned, smiling, towards Mommy sitting on the passenger side across from Daddy and wagged his tail—and then gave first Mommy and then Daddy and then me a kiss!

It was another extraordinary moment of my brother and "bestest" pal simply being Lucky. It was one wonderfully poignant moment in time when everything, even if only for a short time, seemed quite normal.

We were so happy to be almost there. At our winter "housis" nearby our beloved "wild beachis," where we knew our parents would be soon taking us. To the late afternoon daily walks in the community we had come to think of as being ours and were happy to share with the other residents. The one place where Mommy's health always seemed to be just a little better. And where, when there, our father's bad back did not ache as much.

Our two wagging tails signaled our obvious joy—which in turn brought out huge smiles and not a few tears of happiness and amazement from both Mommy and Daddy.

For a moment, at least, it was as if the dark cloud of sadness had lifted.

. . .

The last few miles as always, were idiosyncratically Mommy and Daddy.

We stopped to pick up the local newspapers at the Publix where we always shop in Jupiter. Next our parents debated—they would say discussed although to me it always sounded like a debate—whether they should order in dinner from a restaurant, or call our friend Aunt Sandy at the clubhouse dining room down the street from our home and ask if she could prepare our usual night of arrival meal: a Caesar salad with chicken.

They decided, like they always do, to call Aunt Sandy.

Then we stopped at the entrance of our community to say hello to my friends the security guards waiting for us in their "gatehousis."

When Daddy rolled down the window on my side of the car, I let them know, *"It's nice to see you again . . . Where have you been? . . . It's okay, we're here now . . . We have things under control . . . I'll see you tomorrow afternoon when I stop by the guard booth tomorrow for my daily cup of water when we're taking our walk."* That day I was frankly really excited, maybe even a little bit impatient, to get to our "housis," so I spoke a lot faster and louder than I usually do.

Our parents and the guards seemed to get a kick out of it.

From the guard booth to our "housis" is approximately one mile. The road we drive on to get there is simply beautiful: surrounded on both sides by golf fairways, tees, and greens, water hazards, and lots of different Squirrelly Birdies. And beautiful trees.

I had forgotten how wonderful the smells are. Even Lucky's nose went into high gear. Somehow he was picking up the same sensations.

Two minutes later, we pulled into our driveway.

It's fair to say Mommy and Daddy have this part of the trip down to a "T." Mommy went into the "housis" to turn off the alarm, start the air-conditioning, and turn on the lights inside and outside. She found a lock and went around the side of our home to put it on the door of our fenced dog run—so that we'd be safe and secure when we needed to use it.

When Daddy pulled the car into the garage which Mommy had by now opened, I saw our other car was already there. I was ecstatic to see that our Uncle Jim Stewart had already arrived safely with all our belongings—our parents' and ours too. All that Mommy always packs when we go to Florida.

Uncle Jim has become a true friend of our family over the years. He is so much like all my parents' real friends: genuine, honest, candid, and totally without airs. He and we have seen each other through good and sad times on both sides. He remains today very, very special to me, just as he always was to my brother too.

Mommy started to unpack the car we rode in, as soon as Daddy opened the door to allow us out.

I jumped.

My brother was gently lifted by Daddy.

And with that behind us, I didn't wait—I "flew" into the "housis."

How much I adore its feeling. At once open and casual and friendly and elegant. And it's all on one floor—there are no stairs.

I ran everywhere.

I looked around for my personal favorite places.

The sofa in the den I love to lay on.

Our parents' bed that we had all shared, some time ago.

The place in the kitchen where my meals are served, my bowl awaiting me.

The carpet in the living room, which helps serve as my hub as I keep an eye on things, no matter where each of my parents and Lucky might be in the house.

The far left corner of the counter which separates the family room from the kitchen, where my parents often sit and have dinner together especially when there's no one visiting us and where, by the way, they keep many of our "monkees." Which weren't there yet, but knowing our parents and Uncle Jim, I was pretty sure they would be soon enough. They *never* forget to bring them.

As I completed my annual tour, the feeling was overwhelming: *freedom!* That's what this "housis" means to me.

Free from the cold, and the damp, and the stairs we have to navigate up north. Free to lay out on our lovely screened "porchis" out back, where my mere presence ensures no golfer passing by just outside of our rear fence gets too close to Mommy as she swims her laps daily in our pool.

I was so excited to be back!

So much so that I don't know how long it was before I realized my brother had not accompanied me on this systematic if frenetic tour, as he had traditionally done in the past.

Not this time.

No, this time, Lucky decided to take his time. To fulfill this ritual of ours, on his own terms, at his own pace: more tentatively, more deliberately, lingering here or there a little bit longer than usual, taking it all in.

And in so doing, he gave Daddy (and me) one lasting memory of him that neither of us will ever, ever, ever forget.

. . .

It began simply enough.

After giving Lucky that helping hand from the car, Daddy actually followed me as I started my formal "housis" inspection.

Wherever I ran went, Daddy went in to check to see if maybe I had unintentionally left things a bit messy. He wanted to be sure that when Mommy did her tour, she saw the place exactly in the same condition I had.

So by the time I had finished the run of the "housis," and had been waiting with my tail wagging in anticipation of soon being served dinner, Daddy had not only been into each room, but had also pressed the buttons that controlled the hurricane shutters outside on the "porchis" and turned on the lights out back, even the one in the pool.

And seeing everything was functioning as it should, he turned around to head back to the kitchen to feed us. Only to be happily interrupted by something he and I saw that even today fourteen years later (my time), we still recall, each in our own way. And when we do, it is with gratitude, amazement, and awe.

. . .

My brother was just completing his own welcome-home tour. Which in and of itself was quite interesting. For what exactly he got out of it I really can't say. I simply don't know. You see, as I've said earlier, by this time, Lucky was almost totally blind. Uncle Greg and the eye specialist said, at best, he could only pick out shadows—and even those would be fuzzy. And he was not only blind, he was also deaf. If you stood right behind him and clapped your hands, he had no idea you were there.

Besides being blind and deaf, his sense of smell had been in quick decline too. So much so that for the past few weeks at least, our parents had had to put his dinner down on the floor literally right in front of him before he had any sense it was there.

On top of all this, he also was very stiff. I'm sure his arthritis had not been helped much by our just completed eighteen-hour drive.

All of this is terribly sad of course. But my brother Lucky had a great attitude about it all. He never complained. As always, he epitomized strength through stoicism and his life philosophy of truly enjoying each moment.

. . .

Yet I could tell, like me, he too was very happy to be back in Florida.

Lucky went over to the sliding glass door that covers the width of the living room leading to the balcony. He couldn't see it. His nose however could touch it. And when he did, he satisfied himself that everything was where it should have been. After which, without any hesitation, he proceeded to take a full 360-degree look around while taking a very deep breath.

And then just like you and I do when we feel that strange combination of elation and relief about something that is important to us, my brother—deaf, arthritic, blind, and old—leapt incredibly high into the air accompanied by the deepest shout of sheer joy we ever heard from him, finishing off with an enthusiastic Lucky-wag of his tail.

Daddy and I looked at each other . . . and then, in tandem, back at my brother. Who now stood totally still in the area between the living room and the family room.

The sheer joy on his smiling countenance must have matched the shock of elation on my father's face and mine.

To this day, it is that one shout of joy and that one sight of my brother's smiling face that are forever embedded in my memory bank of lifetime best memories. And I know Daddy will never forget it either. I'm just happy he got to witness it too. We're just both sorry Mommy wasn't there to see it.

Daddy walked over to my brother, bent down, and gave him a kiss on his nose. *"You know where we are, don't you, Mr. Wack Wack. You really know where we are. You're really happy, aren't you?"* he quietly said while tenderly stroking his head and his flanks. While Lucky's tongue took care of the tears of amazement, gratitude, and great joy running down our father's face.

. . .

Less than a week later (our parents' time), Daddy told Mommy, *"It's time . . . for him, for Princess, and for us. It's not fair for anyone if we keep doing what we're doing. Big Guy deserves better. He has given us everything and more all of his life. We owe him the dignity to know we know when he can't do what he wants to do anymore."*

How much our parents loved my brother and me!

How hard they had tried to find some sense of normalcy for them, and for us, ever since we'd settled into our Florida routine.

How quickly they had worn down, physically and emotionally, in so short a time as they attempted to give me their attention they felt I had been missing for months, while also attempting to do whatever they could for Lucky under what were very trying circumstances.

The truth was brutal. Also harsh and real and difficult to accept. My brother—once so bouncy and vibrant and alert—he was now slowed and bowed.

For him, every day was now a struggle. To awake and get up from his deep sleep. To find the route out the garage door so as to go to the "batroom" in our dog run, without tripping over the step. To being able to make it outside before he couldn't hold it in anymore. And to do so cleanly, without stepping onto my own *"leave-behinds,"* which he once navigated around and over with such agility.

Now, if I had gone out there before him, he would come back embarrassed, having been unable to avoid what I had left behind. Because he couldn't smell or see.

On those occasions, when he couldn't find his way back inside by himself, sometimes Daddy would say, *"Prinny, please go get your brother."* I was happy to help when I could.

Sometimes I was successful. But unlike up north where our dog run is twice as big if not more, and I was always able to find a clear path when leading my brother out, in Jupiter that was not so easy on this trip. So when I could not get Lucky's attention, I asked Daddy for his help, and he'd have to get on his knees and reach out from the dog run door to try to find a way to grab onto Lucky's collar.

That wasn't all.

No matter what Lucky ate, he had trouble with it. Sometimes it literally passed right through him. There was one time, for instance, on one of our walks, he got so sick he honestly scared our father. For what he saw come out of Lucky was so bad . . . and there was just so much of it, Daddy had to use about 10 water bottles to clean up the sidewalk. And when Lucky did the same thing the next day in the middle of the street, right down from the "housis," it frightened all of us even more.

That wasn't all.

Sometimes he'd cough up remnants of his meal and Mommy and Daddy had to clean that up.

And on three separate occasions right after eating, he followed Daddy towards the door that is the gateway to the garage and the dog run. But then, unable to recognize it was only two feet away, two of those times, Lucky ended up urinating right in front of the dog run door. And on the third, he never got as far as the garage. And our parents had to clean up that mess in the hallway and throw the carpet into the washing machine.

They never said a word . . . they just loved him.

Honestly it was hard on everyone.

Moreover, Lucky, I intuitively sensed, did not want these to be our final memories of him. This was not a fate he or we would have wished on anyone. He had always been so good, so impeccably clean, and so immaculately groomed.

Still, as much as I recognized this to be the case, I also knew Mommy and Daddy needed to come to that realization on their own. Thank goodness less than a week later (my parents' time), they finally did.

. . .

It took many calls, at least one of which caused our parents a great deal of anger and frustration. Which also resulted in a pledge I overheard Daddy make to Mommy and me: *"If it comes down to having no other options, I'll drive Lucky home myself while Prinny and you stay here. At least there we know we can trust (Uncle) Greg will do right by Lucky. At least we know he'll do it not just for the money but because he loves and respects Lucky."*

My parents' moods by then ranged from anger to desperation to despair to incredible sadness.

As my Mommy put it so eloquently sometime later, *"I had always prayed all of us would have said good night to each other like we always do every night and God would have allowed Mr. Sweetness to peacefully pass on in his sleep and not have to wake up the next morning."*

No such luck.

While I could see how terribly difficult it was for my father to see his canine soul mate suffer the indignities of the aged, I knew how even more difficult it was for him to have to acknowledge the looming reality of an eventual first day of the rest of all of our lives without Lucky's gentle presence.

On top of all this, both parents understandably but wrongly worried how my brother's absence would affect me. If only there had been some way I could have convinced them their concerns weren't warranted.

Let me say it directly: I knew all along I would do fine.

Simply put, everyone knew my brother had been the absolute love of my life. We had been blessed with many happy joyous years together. We adored each other, were committed to each other, and loved each other more than life itself. However, he and I also shared the common gift of acceptance of the inevitability of life's cycles. As such he and I knew it was now time for me to take whatever *I* had left in love, energy, and time, and share it unabated and fully with our parents.

I knew that Lucky knew that I knew that my time as my brother's keeper needed to be redirected. To help fill the massive hole in each of our parents' hearts that would soon accompany my brother's peaceful departure for our family bench in Heaven.

. . .

Finding someone to help us, however, would prove to be one of our most vexing challenges.

WE SAID GOOD-BYE TODAY

Lucky's last day with us was like so many of all the days he spent as a member of our family: quiet, comfortable, serene, completely within himself, totally trusting and loving.

Two days before the last day of January of 2004, Mommy and Daddy talked to Uncle Doctor Greg in Pennsylvania by telephone.

When for the first time they themselves described really candidly without the usual speculative *"Well, maybe it means . . . "* attempts on their part to soften what they saw of my brother's symptoms, I couldn't hear for myself the response they got back. But I did see its effect.

My parents' silence was deafening.

Later it became clear why. In describing the conversation with Uncle Greg—*"His demeanor (was) gentle yet very direct,"*—Daddy summed up his message equally directly.

"If you're asking me what's happening with Lucky, and what you should think about doing, let's just say it's not going to get any better."

There was no way around what they had been told by the one person my brother and I and our parents trusted most to tell us what we needed to know, when we needed to know it.

His place had finally been arranged for Lucky on our family bench in Heaven.

Though they weren't surprised, Mommy and Daddy were devastated by the stunning reality of what would turn out to be Uncle Greg's final diagnosis of my brother.

. . .

No words will ever aptly describe the indelible sadness marked on my father's face. It was what it was.

It was officially time to say good-bye to *his* canine soul mate, and the one and only of *my* own kind I have ever adored—whom both of us loved more than life itself.

I can't tell you how much Mommy and I could feel the intensity of Daddy's sadness. If only we could have taken some of it away from him, maybe his heart wouldn't have had to hurt so much. But the truth was, at that moment, we couldn't. Because the love Mommy and I shared for Lucky was as deep as Daddy's. Our own sense of impending permanent loss hurt us just as deeply.

So in some ways, it was good to see that Daddy did what he had always done when times were really bad: He immediately went into what he called *"my emotional autopilot."*

In so doing, I knew he would find productive ways to keep himself busy and his mind occupied.

The fact is I had seen him do it before.

It was immediately after he received the phone call from Mommy's doctor regarding her cancer. It turned out to be a state of mind he didn't get out of until he was convinced she was fully on the way to recovery . . . at least twenty-five or thirty years later (my time).

It must have helped.

Mommy credits him for helping to *"save my life."* I just took it on faith it wouldn't take four plus years (my parents' time) this time.

. . .

As soon as the call with Uncle Greg ended, Daddy made a promise to Mommy and me that *"if we can't find someone who will help us do this for 'Big Guy' (Lucky) with the dignity he deserves and the compassion like (Uncle) Greg, I'll drive him up north and ask (Uncle) Greg to come over to the house to do it. I know he'll do the right thing."*

My mother and I both agreed but hoped it would not be necessary.

. . .

Daddy placed a call to our friend Uncle Jim Stewart to see if he had anyone he could recommend. But the office he told us to call was closed. So Daddy left a message.

Then he called the doctor on Indiantown Road near Military Trail in Jupiter, a woman doctor who apparently treated a neighbor of ours down the street. I always found it disconcerting that this neighbor—we really had never become friends but noted each other's presence when we'd pass each other twice a day on our walks—kept having to go back to that doctor so frequently, his mother said she *"figured that we had paid for the vet's mortgage."*

And the two times I did go over there, I am sure my parents could sense my own lack of enthusiasm for the place. And the people. I was ready to leave as soon as we'd walk in. The office gave me the creeps. It didn't help that they'd take my collar, lead me behind a wet smelly crowded corridor, and stuff me into a cage too small for my size by at least half. And this would happen *after* having to deal with the person at the reception area, someone best described in two words: very moody.

One time, it was in the afternoon. The other, it was first thing in the morning. So you know it had nothing to do with the time of day.

I'll be candid with you here. It seems to me that those who work in those kinds of places should understand that patients like me are already uptight by the time we get there. As such, they might wish to consider how much more welcoming it is to be met with a smile and a kind gentle word of hello, like they do at Uncle Greg's.

That was not my experience at this place!

Although to be fair, I also know I am not the easiest of patients for anyone but Uncle Greg, especially when it has to do with cutting my nails.

Daddy calls them *"fingertails."* I'm sure he thinks that I won't know we are talking about my toenails. He's wrong!

However, the two times I was at this Jupiter doctor's office, I thought it best to keep my reservations about the place to myself, and thus, it's possible neither of my parents knew I had some real concerns when Daddy called over there to see if they could possibly assist with Lucky.

The person who answered the phone told us someone would call back right away.

• • •

By the next morning, my parents were hurting, frustrated, angry, and at their wits end.

No one had returned their calls, despite the urgency of their messages. As a result, Mommy and Daddy had no idea at all who they could trust to do what they already knew was going to be a difficult thing.

All in all, it wasn't a good atmosphere at home.

I'm just grateful that Lucky's deafness and blindness allowed him to be oblivious of what was going on around him. He had enough to deal with.

He had had a bad night. His dinner had disagreed with him, and so he kept mostly to himself before falling asleep in his basket while our parents and I tried to lose ourselves in the mindlessness of the box with pictures and voices. Until we too fell into a deep sleep, from which I found myself being woken up in the middle of the night.

It was Lucky!

He was telling me he had to go out—right now! We needed to hurry!

So I shook my collar as hard and as loud as I could until Daddy finally heard me, waking up to take Lucky out to the dog run through the garage.

Unfortunately my brother couldn't make it on time.

I could feel his embarrassment, his sense of shame, after he'd returned to the bedroom, while our parents cleaned up what he'd left behind.

As odd as it may appear, two incongruous thoughts crossed my mind right at that moment:

Incontinence is clearly not one of God's nicer gifts of life for anyone.

And God bless all the caregivers who do what they have to do for their loved ones.

· · ·

A few hours later, Daddy started the round of calls all over again.

This time, someone working at the doctor's office, someone I did not like, told Daddy we should have never been told someone would call us back. According to this person, they had no idea who we were. They didn't have any records of my having ever been there. She also said we needed to understand that the doctor was extremely busy, so the promise that had been made the day before by the same person who had promised a call back was *"a mistake. I have no idea why you were told that."*

On this one occasion, *that* mistake of a *"promise"* was no trivial matter.

You see, my parents had been assured that the doctor would do what she had to do for my brother, and would do so in the familiar comfortable surroundings of our "housis," which he loved so dearly.

Instead, now my parents were being told that this was not the case at all. The doctor would not do it at our "housis"—but would be happy to have Lucky come to her office where she *"would be happy to fit you in for double our usual price because we have no records of your ever having been here before . . . and because it's our busy season."*

I will never ever forget the icy cold quiet anger in my father's voice as he hung up the phone.

I knew there was no way he would ever again allow those people to treat Lucky, or me for that matter. To us, this doctor and her office epitomize the antithesis of medicine as a calling.

So you can only imagine my parents' mutual outrage a few months later when we received from that same doctor a notice supposedly for late payment of an itemized bill for services she had *never* rendered for my brother Lucky the day my father had called them.

Unbelievable as it may seem, their invoice covered every single item for every service that was indeed eventually carried out on behalf of my brother. BUT NOT BY THEM.

Instead it was carried out *by another doctor of another totally unrelated medical practice located in a different town altogether!*

For days afterwards, I couldn't help myself being dragged down by negative thoughts. I couldn't stop thinking that this must have been some sort of attempted fraudulent business practice. One that's predicated on the hope that one out of every ten patients would pay a bill in haste without ever studying its legitimacy. And if caught, the doctor would try to explain it away as some administrative error.

I had my suspicions. The truth is I still do. As do my parents.

Particularly after several calls were made by them to the offending office, requesting a written acknowledgement that the doctor's invoice was in error—which to this day their office has refused to do. And particularly when they tried to justify their refusal to do so on the basis of their assertion that *"the paperwork for such a thing is too expensive."*

I recall Daddy's reaction very well. He promised Mommy and me, *"They will find themselves written about sometime."*

(Whatever that means, knowing my father as I do, I am sure they will be).

. . .

Early Friday morning, my mother received a call from one of the first doctor's offices we had called two days before. I don't know exactly what went on during the call as Lucky and I were being fed by Daddy at the time. All I know is that Mommy whispered to Daddy something like, *"I think we've found someone who will help us."* And with that they both got on their knees and gave my brother affectionate kisses on his nose. In return for which he looked up to where he thought they were kneeling and gave each a kiss.

He was wagging his tail. Mommy and Daddy were crying.

. . .

By 11:00 a.m., Lucky and my parents were waiting to meet someone in a nondescript-looking doctor's office located in a tiny strip shopping center in Tequesta, Florida, about ten minutes from our "housis."

The name of the doctor they met was named Allison. She did not own the veterinary practice; she just worked there.

Either way, I will forever think of her as my brother's guardian angel. And my parents and I will always cherish her personal goodness, integrity, infinite compassion, and consummate professional expertise.

In the months that followed, I would often hear recounted the whole story of the incredible rapport Aunt Allison immediately struck up with my brother. The gentle kindness and respect and compassion she showed him. All of which I got to see for myself later that day.

. . .

As always when he was out with our parents, my brother was well behaved: quiet, composed, the picture of discipline.

I understood why.

From the first day of that chance meeting between Lucky and Daddy through the years to the very end, my brother's trust in our parents never wavered. For him, they represented the sense of security he had been seeking in vain, ever since being terribly abused as a baby who was beaten badly and chained to a fence for days with no food or water. They had given him the loving shelter, the positive reinforcement, the opportunity to fulfill his life potential. For which he reciprocated in kind, every single day of his life, by *"just being Lucky."*

In hindsight, my intuition tells me that is what Aunt Allison saw that morning when they all met in her office. She saw the unconditional love and mutual respect all around. She shared in the warm embrace of loving affection that ran right through my parents to my brother.

She knelt beside him, doing all the things we were accustomed to Uncle Greg doing: checking Lucky's heartbeat, taking his blood pressure, looking deeply into his clouded eyes that could no longer see and the ears that could no longer hear. And she told my parents what they already suspected.

"You know the only reason I asked you to bring Lucky here was for all of us to meet each other. In one sense, it really is not necessary. I could do what needs to be done without ever having to get to know him. But I have never felt that to be the right way."

You see, according to Aunt Allison, too many people see the doctor as *"a way out"* for the elderly like my brother—or for those of any age whose only sin is to have become *"inconveniences"* in the lives of the families that have adopted them. Being old, or no longer wanted, or inconvenient often means *"discardable."* So they call up any doctor and say *"It's time."*

For those families, Aunt Allison has neither the time nor the desire to do their bidding. If anything, she has only loathing. For what they are doing is shameful.

It *was* time for Lucky, however. And Aunt Allison could see that for herself. She also told our parents she could literally *feel* the love they had for him—and his love for them.

She listened intently as Mommy and Daddy shared with her their stories about both of us, *"our canine children."*

About Smokey, their wedding gift to one another, who they simply willed it so that he wouldn't die from parvo.

About Samantha, who only wanted a home and a family to love and got the chance to prove to her father she was neither slow nor retarded but rather very smart, even if she marched to the beat of her own drum.

And about me. How I saved our "housis" from a fire. How I had a job to do, and so I became Mommy's cancer companion and guard dog because she needed me to do that, and then took over as my brother's guide dog after he became blind.

When they talked about Lucky, Aunt Allison saw for herself how proud my parents were of what he was about and who he had matured into over the years. From the emaciated mangy quivering mass of fear my father found, he had evolved into a tall, dark, handsome, polite, athletic, smart, loyal, congenial, and caring sweet soul who filled our family life with such unmitigated joy.

The terrible hurt and ever deepening sadness in Daddy's eyes spoke legions to Aunt Allison of how hard this last act of love and faith and kinship for my brother was going to be for both of our parents.

Daddy tried his best but couldn't succeed hiding his tears, even as Lucky's empty eyes and that look of immutable trust on his face for the people he loved so much moved rhythmically, back and forth from Daddy to Aunt Allison to Mommy and back.

The more they spoke of him, the more they shed their tears of loving respect for their son. And the more they did that, the more Aunt Allison could not help but be swept up in the emotion that filled the examining room. Until, inevitably perhaps, she too could no longer withhold her own tears.

"I am not ashamed to say this is hard on me too," she admitted. *"For those of us who really care, it never gets any easier to say good-bye."*

Looking directly down at my brother, she held his whole face in her hands and added, *"It's especially true in the case of someone as good as you are, Lucky. I can see why your parents say you have been their 'bestest' little boy."*

It hadn't taken long. My brother had met and made another convert. He had turned a complete stranger into a trusting friend without trying. That was his real gift in life. It's one too few are blessed with. It truly is a gift of nature.

Turning to my parents, Aunt Allison quietly promised she'd *"be happy to come out to your home . . . that's where you and he will be most comfortable, I know. There, there will be no rush. You can take all the time you need then to say a final good-bye."*

. . .

On the way back, Lucky sat in his usual spot in the back seat of the car. He was neither antsy nor worked up. If anything he seemed quite content, even serene.

It was the first time in a very long time all three—Mommy, Daddy, and my brother—seemed to be at peace.

I for one will forever be grateful to my parents for working their tails off to find someone such as Aunt Allison who understands us, just like Uncle Greg.

. . .

It was Daddy's idea to take us to our favorite "beachis."

"It's the last time the four of us will be a full family together, and it will allow all of us something wonderful to remember before Allison gets here at four o'clock," he explained.

Mommy was in full agreement. I wasn't surprised. She has always known the right thing to do. Somehow she just knows what the perfect antidote is under trying circumstances.

By 12:40 p.m., we were on our way.

Lucky immediately sensed the excitement I felt as soon as Mommy took out our usual paraphernalia for when it was time to go for a "beachis" walk. He got excited too! You could tell from the way he jumped in his own classic way: up and backwards at the same time with a full double twist turn of the body and three shakes of his head up and down! The type of thing you see horses do when they are excited.

You should know it's a habit I've picked up too. To let my parents know when something they've suggested sounds particularly appealing to me.

When we got to the big intersection before the bridge that crosses over to Jupiter Island, we made a left turn onto highway US 1. I knew exactly where we were and where we were going. We were in Tequesta, ironically right near where Lucky and our parents had just met with Aunt Allison, and we were heading to a place we absolutely adored.

A place that is all about nature. A place where there's no housing whatsoever of any kind. Just seven and half miles of white sand, dunes, pelicans, shells, very few people, the roar of the surf, and the occasional spinner sharks, large turtles, playful dolphins, every so often a manatee just offshore to catch your attention, and lots and lots of wonderful clear, clean smells.

Officially it's called Hobe Sound Nature Preserve Beach.

Lucky and I always referred to it as "wild beachis."

I stuck my head out the window to follow its scent ten miles north, two miles east. On this occasion, Lucky did the same. Just as he had always done over the years, when he could still see, and hear, and fully smell the smells.

Whatever gave him cause to put his nose up to the top of the partially turned-down window (which Daddy had opened to a level where Lucky could take in the smells, but without getting hurt), the sight of him doing so made both our parents feel good despite their obvious sadness.

Two miles from our destination neither of us could sit down.

As always, we switched places in the back seat. All the while, our voices (mine louder and more insistent; my brother's, an almost silent whimper) told our parents we knew exactly where we were. While imploring Daddy to ignore the 25-mile-an-hour speed limit of those final few miles.

If only for one more moment again, everything seemed so normal like it had always been.

What we didn't know at the time was that something utterly inexplicable was about to play itself out. So unique that if this were fiction, it would be rejected as implausibly mystical. Something so unique, it remains to this very day one of the single most remarkable events of my life.

• • •

From the parking lot, we took our traditional route to the "beachis."

For Lucky and me, walking up the steep wooden steps to a deck and down other steps out to the "beachis" had never been our preference. From the very first time we ever went to "wild beachis," our parents always understood that to do so would be very uncomfortable on our feet. It would be very hot. And there were also nails sticking out that could do damage to the pads on our paws. So instead, they had found for us a really interesting "back route" that had no stairs. Only a narrow path comprised of sand and tropical type plants on both sides, full of the smells of many kinds of creatures who were very obviously hiding along the way. The irony is we never saw too many, though we could sure hear them scurrying away as we made our way past them.

Thankfully for Mommy and Daddy, the snakes referred to on the sign at the path's entrance never came out to say hello. Had they, I'm not sure how we—especially our parents—would have responded. Since I had from my earliest days heard them say they loved all kinds of nature, but didn't feel the same way about bats, spiders, and snakes.

One thing I did see with my own eyes, the first time we traversed that path was someone my parents named "Mr. Armadillo."

Him, I liked a lot.

I guess he may have not felt the same way about me. For as soon as he saw me casually meander over to say hello, he dove down a large deep hole in the ground just off to the right of the path that he had apparently built well in advance for just such circumstances. And unfortunately, he has never appeared again.

What a shame . . . I would have liked to get to know him better.

He was really interesting-looking. He had a strange colored skin that from a distance looked like he was wearing a shell. Unlike me or my siblings who were born with really nice faces and attractive noses, this guy (I assumed he was a guy) had a really long narrow snout that ran ahead of him as he moved along looking for things to smell in the ground. He had short legs and beady eyes.

I assume he was the shy retiring type. For as I said, on the day I spotted him I tried to engage him in a conversation. But he never responded. Of course I refused to give up right away. So when I saw him scoot down his hole, I kept trying to establish verbal contact with him. But he still shied away.

To this day, whenever we go to "wild beachis," I try to look up "Mr. Armadillo" to see how he's doing. But as I said, I haven't seen him around. Though I have seen some of his brothers and sisters on occasion along the highway (sometimes squashed) when we drive down to Jupiter.

. . .

Lucky never saw "Mr. Armadillo." Even if he had, I strongly doubt he would have been half as interested as I was.

You see, "wild beachis" to my brother was not about meeting others. That is, unless they were introduced by our parents. Instead it was about the clean smell of the ocean air, the vibrating sound of the pounding surf, and the enjoyable tingling he used to get from the feel of warm sand under his feet.

To Lucky, visiting "wild beachis" was always a very special occasion. It meant something both adventurous and serene, a time for exploring down near the water and up towards the dunes.

And most important to him, it meant he'd be doing it with our father.

As the two of them would get to the top of the path, just as it opens up to the full expanse of the beach, they never failed to be awestruck by the utterly breathtaking scene of sound and view they'd suddenly come across: the pounding turquoise surf straight ahead and the almost pristine, totally untouched, undeveloped white sandy beach that went as far as either could see.

I have heard since our first visit that "wild beachis" is a nature preserve, operated by the Federal Government, and it runs right to the edge of the Port St. Lucie Inlet, which you can barely see in the far distance. To be candid with you, even if no one had ever said it was a nature preserve, I would have known anyway. The giveaway: the plethora of different squirrelies, the pelicans and ducks and geesees and turtles and dolphins and sharks (spinning just offshore) and even the occasional manatee.

I just hope whoever owns this place appreciates its magnificence and doesn't begin to do what has been done too often at so many "beachis" by allowing buildings to be constructed.

· · ·

Whenever Daddy would say, *"Are you ready to walk Mr. Wack Wack?"*—Lucky would invariably react exactly the same way each time every time.

He'd leap into the air almost vertically, almost as if he were clicking his heels in joy.

He'd look back at Daddy with that smile of his and proceed to take my father on their favorite journey together. A half mile or so to the left, then pivot fully around and proceed again in the opposite direction for about a mile or so.

How much they were in sync. Father and his canine son. Canine and his human soul mate. Daddy lost in his thoughts, my brother focused on his sights and smells.

Every once and a while, my brother would stop. Take a deep breath and exhale, after which he'd give Daddy a look that said, *"Okay, Dad, I'm ready to continue."*

My mother and I would watch them from a distance. She had a special name for it: *"a boy and his dog."* And then she'd bend down to gently pet me.

And quietly remind me once again of our own little private secret she had long ago previously shared with me, *"You and your brother are magic."*

On occasion at "wild beachis," Mommy and I liked to do our own thing.

We get as close to the ocean's edge as possible and look for shells.

I'm not particularly adept at spotting the kind of shells she likes, but I do my best to help out by moving in concert with her as she moves down the "beachis." For me, there are few better feelings in life than doing something collaborative with my mother.

Although I never tire of the thrill hearing my father call out: *"Prinny, it's **your** turn now. Would you like to go for our Olympic marathon run?"*

At "wild beachis," those words have always meant one thing to me.

It means running off together down the "beachis" for something considerably less than marathon distance, of course, to protect my surgically repaired hips. It also means the two of us having a fun run, just far enough for me to show off my natural athletic skills for all those who stop to watch us.

For Daddy and me, it has always been our own very special *"one moment in time,"* just like the song of that name, that brings out the widest smiles of pride and joy and happiness from Mommy and Lucky.

Daddy has a pet name for these special occasions: *Daddy-Doggy time.* A name he first used when he'd go for long walks with my brother Smokey. Or for when the two of them would sit and listen to the music they so much loved together. It's also the name he long ago gave to the special private one-on-one moments he carved out every night with Lucky. Lying on the sofa together listening to music, playing "trow-ball" together in the hall-way, and even when Lucky used to look over Daddy's shoulder in the car to ensure we were going in the right direction. Most recently, it's also meant something different: Lucky flaking out in the basket beside Daddy's desk while he's working. Just the two of them in the special emotional space they shared.

Having said that, there's absolutely no place anywhere either of us enjoyed *Daddy-Doggy time* more than when at "wild beachis."

Where, even the end of every visit had a routine we looked forward to. A walk back via the same path. Car windows turned down to allow the wonderful ocean breezes to cool us a bit. Followed by air-conditioning to completely cool things down, followed by the "bestest" tasting previously frozen bottled water in the world from our favorite hiking doggy-dish. Followed by a fantastic deep sleep and sweet dreams, happily replaying the sights and scents and thrills we'd just experienced.

• • •

Of course, on this, what would be my brother's last visit to "wild beachis," my parents and I agreed fully that we would approach it a little differently.

First and foremost, we viewed it as *"Lucky's time."* Whatever he decided he wanted to do on this walk, we'd do our very best to oblige.

My brother felt safe and secure as Daddy held him close while they made their way slowly down the familiar path we always followed from the parking lot to the "beachis."

And when they got to that spot at the end of the path that opened up to that dramatic combination of the sound of the roaring surf and that wonderful sight of vast stretch of white sand, it was the feel of the sand under Lucky's feet that told him what his ears could no longer hear. What his eyes could no longer see. What his sense of smell could no longer tell him.

They had arrived at "wild beachis."

Lucky stopped right in his tracks.

He took in a longer than usual deep breath of the rather cool—for "wild beachis"—fresh air, and then gave an even more pronounced exhale.

He looked back at where he thought Daddy would likely be standing and watching. He was right; our father was doing both. With a palpable degree of pride that you know, at that very moment, extended right through the leash that bonded father and son.

What Daddy saw is a sight still so strongly embedded in his memory it remains like a portrait on the walls of his memory bank a year and a half later (my parents' time).

First it was the incredible smile of sheer joy that took over the full length and breadth of my brother's muzzle, so white now it made you forget it had at one time been so dark.

Then it was something so familiar and yet now so totally unexpected. Lucky did what he had always done when he got to that same spot. He leapt with joy, almost vertically, high up into the air!

And then, as soon as he came down from his flight of exuberance he turned, walked right back to where he sensed Daddy stood holding the other end of the leash, picked his head up as high as his arthritis would allow, and gave his human soul mate a thank you kiss on Daddy's tear-stained face.

I immediately recognized this for what it was.

My brother was saying for one last time *"the boy and his dog"* were in sync.

They may have started out as two very different versions of God's creation, but they were bound by a love so deep, and a mutual respect for each other so strong, it knew no boundaries.

It hadn't all come about as quickly as one might have thought. It had, in fact, taken some time, for Daddy needed to heal from the devastating loss of our late older brother Smokey, who first had touched Daddy's life so profoundly. He needed time for his heart to open up, to let Lucky in. To fill the emptiness of Smokey's love and carve out new space of Lucky's own. Where, together, they eventually created new memories of unconditional love.

I stayed with Mommy as Daddy and Lucky turned left to begin their final exploration together of "wild beachis." During which time something soon occurred which to this day still has an enormous impact on my father's psyche.

How huge of an effect?

Well at the risk of going on a little too much, let me put it into some perspective.

First, as was the case with Lucky and me, my father's earliest years had some serious challenges to overcome.

As a young child, our daddy could not walk. So as I understand it, his doctor placed a metal bar between his feet to help build up their strength so he could learn to walk and run. It was a condition he did not learn he had until the age of fourteen.

He also learned to speak later than most children. It turned out he had a hearing problem. That too was fixed somehow.

As a young man, he had an accident in an airplane that severely damaged his back. It took a long time, but fortunately the last doctor to treat him for it fixed him up, just like my hip doctor fixed me when I was young.

Turning to the "strange but true": When my Aunt Joanne (Daddy's much younger sister) was born, my father told his brother (my Uncle Lonny) the exact moment it happened. What makes this remarkable is that Daddy did this ten minutes *before* he got the call from his father (my grandfather) to say the baby had been born—exactly ten minutes before!

And when my brother Smokey was still young, my father had a very severe allergic reaction to exactly what it was, no one yet knows. And when Daddy woke up hours later in the hospital room to accurately describe to the lady doctor everything he had "observed" while lying on the gurney, she responded, *"That can't be possible. You were unconscious at the time. You had the most severe form of an anaphylactic reaction. You were gone."*

As a physician, she said she found it difficult to accept that Daddy saw what he said he saw because according to her, Daddy had gone to a place she called *"the other side."* Perhaps though you can see things there others can't, unless they've been there too. Since she also said everything my father described in full detail was accurate.

Daddy also inherited my brother Smokey's uncanny ability to predict earthquakes. As incredulous as that may seem to others, Lucky, Mommy and I witnessed it firsthand on several occasions. This is a talent, of sorts, now passed on to me.

And then one morning, just a few years ago, Daddy completely freaked out Mommy when he suddenly told her he had *"a really weird sad feeling that Princess Diana is going to die tonight."* She was killed in Paris later that evening.

It reminded her of the time, years before I was born, when he similarly freaked out the thousands of people who used to listen regularly to his radio talk show in Minneapolis as he recounted to them the true story of how, *"I was shaving this morning, when I suddenly had the strangest thought that 'I hope the Pope will be okay today. I have this strange feeling someone is going to try to shoot him today.'"* An hour and a half later, somebody did!

Still, after all these rather extraordinary life experiences, it would be something that happened on "wild beachis" that day, on that final walk with Lucky, and then the next day, and finally the day after the next day, which have superseded everything else in terms of their spiritual impact on my father. And reaffirmed for both my parents what they have quietly believed for some time: that for them, Lucky and I have been their own private angels from God.

· · ·

I trust by now I have successfully conveyed to you just how much my brother loved my father. That he had spent his life doing all he could to thank Daddy for saving his life. That he viewed his daddy-doggy relationship as being bound with his Daddy, together as one and forever in spirit.

This final walk of theirs was no different.

Lucky may have no longer been able to see or hear and could no longer depend on his sense of smell to tell him where he was going, yet he had not an iota of fear whatsoever of where he was being led. As long as it was Daddy doing the leading.

He always knew he was safe in his father's love.

And so, in a sequence they had followed as long as either could recall, Daddy first took Lucky up to the dunes near the top of the "beachis," then down to the ocean itself.

How happy that made my brother!

How much he loved the feel of the ocean water on his paws!

They repeated it three times, my brother's sparkling smile widening with each trip.

Finally they turned back up away from the surf. It was time to return to where in the distance Mommy and I had been watching this extraordinary partnership of human and canine do something they so absolutely treasured doing together.

. . .

Suddenly my brother seemed stuck!

He seemed literally enveloped by a hill of sand, almost as if it were an immovable object.

We saw him try to go around it . . . to no avail.

He tried to actually climb it . . . unable to get the traction they needed, his legs sort of seemed to spin almost in midair.

The more he tried, the less he was able to move.

It was like one of those old war movies Daddy and I enjoy watching late at night when neither of us can sleep. When we'd see a tank get stuck in the sand or mud. The more it tries to get out of its quandary, the worse it spins—going nowhere.

Lucky turned his head towards Daddy. My brother, the one we all called our "sentinel," because over the years we'd become so accustomed to him walking ahead on lookout to keep his parents and siblings safe from things threatening or unfamiliar upfront, was himself now in trouble.

He needed a helping hand.

Daddy bent down. Gave him a gentle pat on his head and assured him it was okay. Help was here.

And then without commotion or fuss, he gave a slight lift to my brother's legs, first the front, then the back. And Lucky got over the hump that had stood in his way.

They both stopped to think about what had just occurred. It was a single act that said everything that needed to be said about their daddy-doggy relationship. Tail wagging, Lucky proceeded to slowly turn his whole body all the way around to face Daddy head on. He looked up to where he thought my father was standing. And then standing as high up as his arthritic hind legs would allow, he leaned forward to give his human "bestest" friend a grateful kiss. It's nothing but a guess on my part, but there's a strong likelihood my brother may have mistook the wetness streaming down our father's face for perspiration.

Either way, at that moment, I knew precisely what Lucky was thinking. For I have thought the exact same thing all through my life whenever I'm out with Mommy.

"It's okay. All is clear. We're both safe."

· · ·

Before leaving "wild beachis," Mommy came up with one more really good suggestion. It was that we carry on as we had always done.

So Daddy and I did our usual "beachis Olympic Marathon."

After which we posed for family pictures, all of us together, taken by a very nice older couple walking by. There's one of Lucky and me with each of our parents. Then Lucky alone with Mommy. And then Lucky and me walking for the very last time ever, together with Daddy.

They serve as poignant reminders of a gentle soul—a loyal and proud son, an extraordinary friend, and the world's "bestest" brother. And all the wonderful times we were privileged to share together as a family at "wild beachis."

• • •

Once again back at home, Lucky walked out to the lanai to recover from our outing. He was happy, pooped from the exertion. And although almost immediately fast asleep, his tail kept wagging.

I recall wondering at the time if he was dreaming about our friend "Mr. Armadillo." Whom I had as usual looked for, on behalf of both of us, but didn't see that afternoon.

• • •

If Lucky was surprised to find Daddy lying beside him when he awoke a few minutes later, he didn't mention it. But he didn't have to tell us he was really happy about it. His tail said it all, especially when he felt Daddy's kiss on his muzzle, and the soft massaging of his haunches.

As always, Lucky reciprocated in kind with his tongue, showering Daddy's face with the softest of kisses.

The more he did so, the more Daddy tried but could not staunch his tears that were now flowing like a quiet brook.

All I could hear was his broken voiced whisper saying how brave and good my brother had always been. How much he had added to our lives. How proud all of us were of the adult he had grown up to be. How much he would be missed by us. But how much love and comfort and joy he would find in the embrace of his beloved grandfather he would soon meet for the first time in heaven and his sister whom he had adored so much before my arrival and would soon see again, along with his older brother whom he had hero-worshipped as a youngster.

I tried my best to help Mommy be brave.

I stayed close by her side near the table where she sat watching from her favorite chair. She, too, was too heartbroken to hide her tears.

I nuzzled as close as I could to her, to let her know how much I loved her and how much I knew she was hurting inside. And to tell her in my own way, how hard I would work afterwards to help fill the terrible void we were all going to experience, each in our own way.

Mommy walked over to where my brother and Daddy both lay on the floor. She bent down to give Daddy a long kiss. They had long known what was about to happen, but it didn't lessen its impact.

"You have been a wonderful Daddy to our little boy," she whispered. *"He knows how much I love him too, doesn't he?"*

"More than you will ever know," my father replied. *"You know, Boulie, what keeps running through my mind is what you said to Mr. Snarf the day we first brought him home: that we looked forward to the day he would feel comfortable enough to share with us all of his secrets and to tell us his whole story . . . He really has, hasn't he?"*

"You remember when he used to be so terrified of everything back then?" Mommy replied. *"Who would believe that today? He's become such a brave Little Mr. Hazzamazzaboobo. I am so proud of him!"*

They kissed again. Their hearts may have been broken. But in their heart of hearts they were at peace, knowing they were doing the right thing by my brother.

And with that knowledge Mommy then bent down to give Lucky perhaps his most favorite expression of affection.

She gently bit the area of his muzzle, just as his birth mother would have surely done for him, and mine did for me when we were still a part of those packs.

For reasons she's never fully explained since, Mommy decided right there and then she'd be remiss not to take a final picture of her *"boy and his dog"* together. It was also right there and then a couple of things would juxtapose almost as if by fate or accident, although my parents think it's much more than either.

. . .

As Mommy retrieved her digital camera, I decided it was time for me to say my own personal good-bye: a "thank you" to my brother for giving me the gift of a once-in-a-lifetime friendship and love.

Together we had met, matured, explored, played, loved, eaten, slept, worked, and grown older. We had seen each other through thick and thin, as well as all those happy times at "wild beachis" down south, at the lake at the school near our home up north, in addition to the more trying circumstances such as the fire, Mommy's illness, and the ones he and I had too.

I thought if I went over to where my brother lay, I could also comfort Daddy a bit. I wanted him to know we would get through this saddest phase of the life of a loved one. That it would take time . . . and it would hurt. But that we would do so as a family, comforting each other with our love.

Finally for both my brother and my father, I wanted to convey my messages for each that would leave no doubt whatsoever that I loved both of them more than life itself.

I did so with a kiss.

I kissed my brother on his muzzle; I kissed Daddy on his face.

I had never done either before.

I have never done it since.

Simply put, I just knew it was the right thing to do.

I was just following my mother's example. She has always known the right thing to do.

I can't speak for my brother, but I know for a fact my father was utterly emotionally overwhelmed by what I did.

I have seen it for myself many times, ever since Daddy first saw the rather dramatic photographs *and* an actual video Mommy happened to take with her camera. That not only captured my actions of that afternoon, but more importantly will forever serve as a permanent record of the look of sheer contentment and joy on Lucky's face.

For he was where he liked to be most whenever and wherever we were together: comfortably surrounded, in the loving embrace of his whole family.

Just as he would soon be with our other loved ones he'd be joining to help keep our family bench warm for the rest of us in Heaven.

· · ·

Around 3:45 p.m., I met Dr. Aunt Allison and an associate of hers.

She bent down to tell me she had heard all about me from my parents—that I was *"some remarkable girl. You know Princess, they're right . . . you really are so very beautiful."*

I took an instant liking to her. It wasn't just about what she said, but how she said it. The kindness of her tone, with a gentle earnestness much like Lucky has.

Along with Mommy who had been the first to greet them at the front door, I led Aunt Allison and her assistant out to the back "porchis" where Lucky and Daddy still lay close together, side by side.

Where it immediately became obvious that Aunt Allison must have made the same impression on my brother when they had met hours before, as she had now done with me.

For when she bent down to give Lucky a pat, he immediately got up, wagged his tail, and proceeded to give her an affectionate kiss on the nose.

· · ·

I lay down quietly, nearby on the porch as Lucky received a sedative to keep him calm. It was so like him. He was so quiet, so composed. There was a genuine serenity to him as he lay in my father arms. He knew he was safe.

I was just relieved he couldn't hear my parents' tender crying.

I heard Aunt Allison ask us where Lucky would best like to be at the moment he went to Heaven.

Mommy and Daddy and I agreed immediately. It would be lying down in my parents' embrace on our favorite bench on earth. The one we had long ago named the *"Harry and Gladys Bench."* The one that Mommy had given to Daddy as her housewarming gift to him when they moved into our beloved *"beachis housis."*

For us it has always had a very personal spiritual meaning and does even more so today.

And that is where we said our final good-bye. First Mommy and Daddy . . . and then me.

In allowing me the opportunity to pay my respects, I will forever be grateful to my parents for treating me with such understanding, respect, and love.

For it allowed me to sense for myself that my canine soul mate was no longer in pain, no longer hurting. He was somewhere else. An even better place, one where he once again knew the unlimited energy and strength and the sense of wonder of his younger years as a member of his family. Where he could once again see and hear and smell the smells of his wildest nature.

Lucky was at peace.

He was already keeping the seats immediately next to him on our family bench warm for the rest of us . . .

Our Last "Beachis" Walk
Lucky, Daddy and Me

THE DAY AFTER

I now understand why it's said that a "beachis" never looks exactly alike two minutes—forget about two hours or two days—in succession. It's all about nature: the shifting sands caused by the flow of the tides; the impact of rainfall and wind; the tracks left behind by those who visit; and the restoration of it by its caretakers.

• • •

I found this out for myself at "wild beachis," when my father and I went back there alone for a private visit the day after Lucky left us to go to wait for all of us at our family bench in Heaven.

Candidly I don't recall whose idea it was. But both Daddy and I felt equally compelled to do so. Despite—or maybe it was in fact due to the enormous sense of sadness that hung over our "housis" like a dense fog. Either way, we both felt we needed to be there, to close the loop of life perhaps. Or better yet, maybe it was something we simply had to do, so that each of us could more easily come to terms with one of the saddest realities of life: the loss of a true loved one.

Whatever it was, all we knew is we needed to do it.

My mother had seconded the idea. She told Daddy she thought *"it might do you some good. At least it will be a good way for you to show Princess that our life with her will go on. That she should never think her brother did something bad and that's why he is no longer with us. That what we did, we did out of love."*

Mommy probably didn't know it, but what she said struck a huge chord within me. For the first time ever, I fully recognized that neither of my parents understood I *didn't* need to be convinced that all would be okay. That I had fully supported what they had done, and in no way had any misgivings whatsoever. The fact is I had already instinctively known this had been the case all along. Moreover, what Mommy's comments did communicate to me is that I had to quickly find a way to *show* her and Daddy that they didn't have to worry about me. For as much as I adored our Lucky, I was fine, and I would be fine.

To prove the point, however, I instinctively knew would take something quite dramatic—yet natural—to convince them beyond a doubt that they would not have to worry about me.

. . .

As soon as Daddy and I arrived at "wild beachis," it was obvious everything that had been the way it had been when we were there the day before—it all had changed. The texture and layout of its sands had been completely rearranged by the near–gale force winds and heavy rains that had kept me sleepless most of the previous night. Although for one of the first times in my life, the roaring sounds and bright lights of the accompanying thunderstorm didn't frighten me at all.

I simply figured it was just Heaven's version of fireworks with the Boston Pops Orchestra welcoming my brother, just like the many fireworks concerts Lucky and I and our parents watched together every July 4th.

In any event, when we got to the spot where Mr. Armadillo's path meets the top of "wild beachis," Daddy and I stopped to take in the view. Neither of us could get over how radically different it looked from the previous day, when the sky had been blue and the seas only a bit noisy. On this day, the day after, the sky had the feel of a storm and the seas seemed foreboding, rough, and angry.

Still as always, I loved what I saw.

I called out loudly to tell one and all we were there.

I looked up at Daddy. He was smiling despite what seemed to be tears trailing down his cheeks.

I knew full well who he was thinking about. We both were . . .

I leaned my head against the side of his leg to let him know we would be fine. He petted me and bent down to give my muzzle a nibble.

And then without further fanfare we turned left, to the north, as he and my brother always did when beginning their walks at "wild beachis."

. . .

About ten minutes north from where we had set out, I found myself at a spot in the dunes that drew my attention in a big way. There was something familiar about it . . . something reminiscent.

I asked Daddy to give my leash a bit of slack. I felt compelled to check it out.

At once it felt both very new and strange. It even had the feel of some sort of challenge to overcome. I can't explain it any better than that.

At the same time, however, it seemed to give off a scent that I recognized, but couldn't exactly fully identify. It had a sense of comfort to it. Yet if you had insisted right at that moment for me to explain what I meant, I would have been hard-pressed to do so.

I looked back up at Daddy who had been watching me quite intently. Almost as if *he* knew where we were and what we had just found.

I bent my head down to get one more full scent of the spot . . . and then began to pull Daddy a bit as I began to pore over every inch of its immediate surrounding borders. It just seemed so very familiar . . .

That's when it hit me; I suddenly got it!!!

I don't know why it took so long, but it did. No worries. *"Don't sweat the small stuff,"* I always say, because if you spend too much time analyzing why something was or wasn't, you never get to truly enjoy what is.

I now knew **exactly** what it was and where we were! Now, all I needed to do was to let Daddy in on my discovery.

I wagged my tail . . . bent real close and took a deep breath right above the wet sand, after which I turned back again to look at Daddy who was still looking at me.

So I turned my attention back fully to where I had been focused.

. . .

Was it a minute later? Who knows? It might have been. Or it could just have been fifteen seconds (my parents' time).

Whatever it was, with a wag of my tail, and realizing that Daddy had given my leash a fair amount of slack, without warning, in one motion, I suddenly pulled on it as hard as I could and leaped higher than I had ever leaped before. High! High! Way up high into the sky! Over the sand hill immediately in front of where Daddy and I stood.

As I turned to get Daddy's attention, I found myself *yelling* excitedly, almost involuntarily, even a bit frantically to be heard against the roar of the wind and the surf.

There had been no reason to though. For as soon as I saw him, I realized from the smile and tears on his face that he already knew exactly what I had just come to know myself.

This was the exact same spot where the day before Daddy had lifted up my brother to help him get over the last obstacle he would ever encounter at "wild beachis."

I recognized Daddy's smile and tears as the awe and sheer wonder he was feeling at this very moment.

Daddy really looks forward to those walks at Coral Cove.

For him, it's all about the focus required of him to peer through the incoming waves for the right shells, something he enjoys almost as much as he likes the exercise. On occasion though, he just goes there to think. No more. No less.

Which was the reason, on the day after the day after Lucky left us, that Daddy decided to go to Coral Cove . . . alone.

Candidly, both Mommy and I thought it would do him some good, just as our going to "wild beachis" the previous day had been good for both Daddy and me. We knew it was more than Daddy's broken heart that needed healing.

His spirit did.

He needed to come to terms with the emotional vacuum created by Lucky's leaving us the day before the day before.

And while it would obviously take time, we knew he would need some help from both of us.

That being said, I was confident that between our being there when he'd need us, and doing things like going to the "wild beachis," there would be a point someday when my father's memories of my brother would be more sweet than sad, and that he and we would all be okay.

. . .

When Daddy finally got home almost four hours later, he told Mommy and me that even had he wanted to look for shells, for a few hours there were none to be found. The surf was not only far too rough. It was also high tide—when shelling is never the best.

So Daddy just walked . . . and walked . . . and walked . . . and walked.

He said it made him feel *"both totally alone and yet completely embraced. As if someone's arms were around my shoulder like what Irwin Gelernt did when you (Mommy) had just come out of surgery at Mount Sinai Hospital."*

Daddy told Mommy and me he *"felt Lucky on my shoulder like when we rode in the car together and he navigated. He was beside me the whole time. I can't explain it . . . I just know it was real. His presence was visceral."*

He told us it made him smile.

It also made him cry.

But he never doubted Lucky's presence over his left shoulder for even a second.

· · ·

Shortly before turning back northbound for the last time to head to where he had parked the car, my father told Mommy and me that he *"did something I haven't done since that day at Mt. Sinai Hospital when you had your big surgery. There I prayed to God to take care of you (Mommy), to keep you safe and not frightened. And most important, whatever happened, to let you know how much I loved you. We had had a great life together, and I wanted God to thank you on my behalf for the wonderful journey. And that I knew in my heart of hearts, ever since my near-death thing, that we'd be together again, even if it turned out you were not meant to come out of surgery."*

· · ·

You see, at the time of his walk at Coral Cove, something happened that reminded my father of the moment on the day in New York City when he'd been waiting for Mommy's surgeon to come out to tell him how her massive surgery had gone. Daddy had just returned from the chapel to the reception area where he had set himself up hours before to wait for Mommy's surgery to end.

Dr. Gelernt came out. He put his arms around Daddy's shoulders and said, *"Bobbie did very well . . . We got it all . . . It will be tough . . . It will take a long time for her to recover from the surgery—it was massive, but you will have your life back together."*

It was the vivid memory of that exact moment that stopped my father right in his tracks at Coral Cove the day after the day after. He looked out at the ocean.

Where the seas had been incredibly rough and noisy not more than two minutes before, it was now calm, docile, and lake-like, gently lapping at his feet.

To memorialize this moment, Daddy bent down to look for a shell, any shell. And where there had been none for so long that afternoon due to the snarling waters, there were now quite a few. Though having been broken or at least half-broken, likely a result of their involuntary rides in along the roiling waves, none appealed to him.

He thought about what had happened over the past forty-eight hours: about the bond he and my brother had formed over almost a decade and a half (my parents' time) that had come to the end, by the force of time. About the sense of comfort Daddy had within him, a sense of certainty that Lucky and he and indeed all of us would all be reunited someday.

Still, he felt emotionally torn about everything that had happened. Still a bit ambivalent about whether he and Mommy had done all the right things, the right way, at the right time for Lucky.

I knew what he was feeling. It was the inevitable residual sense of guilt any parent would feel about whether enough had been done, not just then, but over the previous few months.

"Lucky," he thought to himself while looking out over the ocean, *"My Mr. Wack Wack, I know you're out there. And I know you're okay. But if you can hear me, please Lord, ask Lucky to give me a sign, just any sign at all that he* **is** *okay, and happy, and I promise to never doubt again."*

He waited for a second or two and looked down at his feet.

He saw nothing.

He looked north and south.

He saw nothing.

And heard nothing, not even a wisp of the wind.

In his heart, he knew he should not have asked. Thought of it as an indicator of spiritual weakness: You either believed or you didn't. But you shouldn't ever ask. It's too narcissistic—too selfish.

That's why he later said he apologized in his inner thoughts. To whom I can't be sure. But he told us he couldn't recall doing this for a very long time. Maybe as far back when he was a young athlete in summer camp and desperately wanted to strike out a batter during what seemed at the time to be a game of life-and-death importance. When, after striking the guy out, my father felt he should make a private apology to *"no one in particular"* and made a promise to himself he would never do that again. A promise my father kept, right up to the time of Mommy's surgery and then that walk at Coral Cove the day after the day after.

• • •

He did one other thing.

Just before turning around to head north back up the "beachis" to retrieve the car still waiting for him in the parking lot, and to finally come home to Mommy and me, Daddy decided to say something in the form of a personal prayer of love for my brother Lucky.

A prayer, in which, he asked for nothing but simply said what was in his heart: *"Be safe, my Mr. Snarf . . . be at peace . . . be where you don't hurt anymore . . . That's all your mother, sister, and I ask for . . . Know you are and will always be in our hearts."*

And with that said, my father started walking, lost in thought.

• • •

To this day, Daddy is not sure just what it was that made him do a "180" a few minutes later. But whatever it was, as he later described it to Mommy and me, it obviously had an enormous effect then and still does, in some ways even more so.

"It was like there was this sudden sound of surging surf. You know the kind that seems to start way out in the ocean, gathers momentum, and then crashes high up into the beach, way beyond where you thought it would hit. Well, that's what it sounded like . . . "

Except for one thing: There'd been no crashing surf! In fact, there had been no real surf whatsoever. Which is why Daddy turned back around to the south again, to where he *thought* the noise may have come from and peered as far as he could down the "beachis," along the shoreline.

There was nothing.

So he looked the other way. Northwards, in the direction he had been heading.

Again, there was nothing.

Then, *something* told him to look down, immediately right in front of him. And that's when he saw something that *"just blew me away,"* as he's described it ever since.

It was a shell: the most interesting, perfectly smooth, impeccably polished, unusually shaped, absolutely most unique shell he had ever seen.

And the color! If a shell can ever be described as the color "brindle," then this shell was that color with symmetrical spots almost as if they had been painted as an afterthought. Daddy is color blind but he knows what brindle is: Brindle is how Mommy first described the parts of my brother Lucky that she always found so striking.

My father picked it up as gently as he could. He wondered where it had come from. It hadn't been there just a few seconds before . . . Before he had heard that incredibly loud noise, the source of which to this day he has never been able to determine. But in fact, he's never really had to. He's known it from the second he saw it and put it in his hands. He knew right there and then, just as he knows today more than fourteen years later (my time), that the shell, which now sits so proudly on Mommy's shelf, was Lucky's way of answering Daddy's prayerful plea a few moments before.

"It's okay, Dad . . . I'm really okay . . . I'm happy . . . I'm free . . . I am no longer in pain . . . I can see . . . I can hear . . . I can smell the smells again of my wild nature . . . and I know we'll see each other soon . . .

In the meantime, you go on with what you have to do. You have your job to do: Take care of our Magic Girl, Princess, and my 'bestest' Mommy and tell them exactly what happened and what I am saying to you . . . Tell them both I love all of you . . . And always will forever and a day . . . And tell them not to worry. Everyone's here: our Samantha and Smokey, and your Shenka, and Mommy's Brandy and Tracey—everyone! We're here taking care of Grandpa, helping him keep our family bench warm for when we'll all be together again."

Today, when my father recalls what Lucky told him at Coral Cove "beachis" that day after the day after, he still tears up. But it also makes him smile.

For he knows the brother with whom I shared my own most unforgettable love story is once again healthy and happy and at peace. It's all my parents and I could have ever wished for him.

Being Lucky is all he ever wanted to be.

UP HIGH UNDER THE TREE

When I think of my most favorite spot where Lucky, Mommy, Daddy, and I used to regularly visit together, I am reminded of a scene from a picture with moving parts and voices we'd all watch together.

It's called *"Out of Africa."* It has wonderful soaring melody to match the majesty of its scenery.

When that particular picture with moving parts and voices would appear, Mommy and Daddy would usually sit on our sofa or lie on our bed holding hands, while Lucky and I would lie together side by side, affectionately crossing one another's paws.

There's a scene at the end I truly love: There on a hill overlooking a giant plain filled with all kinds of nature, we see one lion walking into the picture frame to join up with a mate. There are no airs about it—just two "bestest" soul mates like Lucky and me lying down together to take in the spectacular vista.

My family has a spot just like it.

A specific spot with its own spectacular view that I will forever treasure. Where Lucky and I would regularly take our parents whenever we and they could—a special place that's up a hill and under the tree on the bucolic campus of the private school not far from our "housis." Where for over twenty years (my parents' time), ever since my parents and Smokey and Samantha moved into our country "housis," all of my siblings and I have walked and romped and played, and reveled in its beauty. The particular spot is small and very private despite its openness, just like the place the lions enjoy. Usually Mommy and Daddy would suggest we go there at the end of each visit to the nearby campus. Sometimes Lucky and I would let them know that we wanted to go there.

For we instinctively knew once we got there its impact on each of us would always be the same—extraordinary.

There's an amazing view of our friends, the black "cowzys"—my parents call them cattle—grazing on the hills in the distance, and the extraordinary sight of our "deerzie" friends prancing and dancing and eating not far from us, in the field across the street and immediately below our perch up high under the tree.

It's also where, no matter the weather, my parents would stand holding hands, or on occasion sit on the grass hugging us tight. Almost always in complete mutual silence, taking in the whispers of the wind that never ever fail to flow through this favorite spot of theirs and ours.

It's where for my parents the presence of their firstborn, Smokey, and their second, Samantha, has never ever faded. And never will. And where too, for Lucky and me, the comforting effects of their long-ago scent always remained strong. From our very first visit together to my last, quite recently with Mommy and Daddy.

It's also where I have no doubt Mommy and Daddy will tightly hug all of those who will follow me. Where, long after I've left for our family bench in Heaven, I know they will explain how special this spot will be to them as it has been for all of us. That place up high up on a hill and under "our" tree at Westtown School that has meant so much to us.

WE CAN DO BETTER

Right in the midst of recounting my story, I fell very ill . . . very, very, very ill.

In fact, if it hadn't been for the quick actions on the part of my parents and the above-the-call responsiveness of my doctor Uncle Greg in Pennsylvania—we were in Florida at the time—I could easily have died.

For many reasons, I am obviously very happy they did what they did. One of the most important reasons is that had they not done so, I would not have been able to finish up recounting the love story that defined the relationship between my brother and me, and between my parents and us. And I would not have some pretty revealing thoughts to share with you based on this experience.

It turned out to be a very rough week to say the least.

Over a seven-day period (my parents' time) I went from feeling fine, to a bit punkish, to suddenly without notice being totally incapable to holding my stomach "in check." Up to then my stomach had been gurgling for some time, but I always thought this was normal for me. But not that day.

Suffice it to say it's a good thing I have a dog run to go out to right outside the garage. If not, my parents would have had to be taking me outside every twenty minutes or so for a long period of time. In any event, they were still forced to hose down my run as soon as I did what I had to do. Because they knew that I would have to go out again twenty minutes later—or less—because I was just that sick.

We think now it was a serious case of colitis. Perhaps brought on by some sort of putrid-smelling poison sprayed either into the plants or lakes in the community in which we live here at the "beachis housis."

I don't know why they do that. I'm sure they have good reasons to do so. However, I have to believe they don't know how deadly it is to residents like me. It would be hard to believe they do it on purpose. At least I hope not.

Whatever . . .

My parents had noticed the awful smell a few days before. I say that because I heard them comment about it when we took our daily walks. But because at the time I was focused on other things—all of nature's many forms and smells so abundantly represented on our daily path—it didn't really register with me. So I didn't give much thought to their concerns.

Ironically it was Mommy who first began to feel the effects of whatever eventually hit me. *She* suddenly came down with a dreadful headache and stomachache followed by back spasms that literally debilitated her. And worse, she found herself having to go to the "batroom" constantly. Which for her is not easy after the massive cancer surgery she underwent when I was young.

One night was particularly bad.

Daddy had to help Mommy very carefully get up from the floor where she had literally crumpled when getting out of bed. Because of the severity of her spasms, it took almost two hours for him to do so.

After we got over that not-so-mini crisis, Daddy made sure Mommy took the meds needed to relax her back. And over the next couple of days, her back pain, stomachache, and headaches all began to dissipate. But not before she had endured terrible pain. So much so that for a while there I was really scared Mommy was really sick again, like she had been for four or five years (my parents' time) when cancer hit.

And I don't have to tell you how alarmed Daddy was. I could see the tension in his face. I could sense the growing concern building inside him.

. . .

It wasn't two days (my parents' time) after Mommy got better that Daddy and I both got sick, almost simultaneously.

Basically within twenty-four hours, Daddy went from feeling well enough to do one of his one-and-half-hour workouts in the gym, to having back spasms that literally forced him to his knees. Not just once or twice. *I mean all the time* . . . and with no warning.

And then just like Mommy, my father's stomach got so sick he began to think there might be something seriously wrong with him. But because Mommy was still weak from recovering he didn't want to scare her. So he didn't even mention it.

He didn't have to though.

I could read it on his face. So I tried to comfort him, staying close by him almost like the shadow I had been to Mommy years ago when she needed me by her side.

It was also my way of trying to give Daddy a "heads-up" that things were about to go downhill very quickly. And did they ever!

You see, whatever was wrong with Daddy suddenly went from really bad, to terrible, to an out-and-out crisis of major proportions.

With a headache he would later describe as being of *"epic proportions"*—beyond any migraine he had ever experienced at any time in his life. A constant pounding—stemming from his upper spine, through his neck, into the base of his head, all the way to his eyes, that would not go away for over sixty hours (my parents' time).

As is my nature, I tried to do what I could to comfort him, although I was now feeling pretty sick myself.

Nevertheless, I made sure he knew I would be there for him. I stayed real close by him as he lay in bed, especially when in the midst of it all Mommy had to leave for two days (my parents' time) to visit her Mommy up north where another crisis was happening.

. . .

Yes, I know some will say that all of these things that hit my parents and me might have been purely coincidental. But as I have said before, Lucky and I never believed in coincidences. *In our view, there is a reason for everything.* And so there must be for what happened to my parents and me, particularly over such a short period of time.

For what it's worth, here are some of my thoughts on that.

First, the poison—one that's potentially lethal to all kinds of nature that was being spread at the time to kill nearby golfing fairways and greens and lawns where we usually walked—should be thoroughly investigated. Because if it isn't, someday others will become sick, maybe even sicker, and who knows one or two might even die.

Come on!

Look, this time it was me and my parents. And we learned later it also made some of my other canine cousins in the neighborhood equally sick. It could just as easily been the lives of babies and older people who also walk along the same paths every day being put at risk.

How much forethought and effort would have it taken to at least warn everyone there was this poison being spread on the ground to kill the grass so that it could grow back stronger? To protect all of God's creatures from being put at unnecessary risk . . .

Forgive me if I sound upset. But I am. For it seems to me that what happened to us and others in our neighborhood need not have.

As Daddy always says, we *can* do better.

Second, the whole experience was just one more reminder of how extraordinary a person is my Uncle Greg, my doctor up north.

He is plain and simple just one of God's medical gifts to nature. He is compassionate and caring. And he refuses to put money before the welfare of his patients.

I say that because the same cannot be said for some of the Florida doctors my parents contacted on my behalf during this crisis. I trust you will forgive my candor, but the actions of those doctors are shameful.

If you think I'm being harsh, picture the following and then decide for yourself.

At one doctor's office Mommy called where I had visited previously for one of my routine checkups not more than a month or so before (my parents' time), the nurse said we could come in. However, she also immediately went on to say that we needed to know *right up front* they would likely do a full workup on me, *then* put me through a comprehensive series of scans and the like, and *after* they had done all these things, they would in all likelihood then ship me off to a nearby, separate "emergency" clinic.

And this was before my mother had had the chance to explain to the nurse what my symptoms were!

This, as you may know, was not the only time we had experienced such a travesty in medical care for those like me.

There was that other doctor who first said she was too busy to help my brother when he needed to find a way to join up at our family bench with our grandfather and late siblings in Heaven. On that sad occasion, she said that she was *not* so busy that she wouldn't "help"—and would agree to do so *if* my parents would agree up front to pay twice the normal price (*"because this is the busy season"*). And then she had the audacity to send my parents a warning for late payment of an invoice for her "services" —which you know by now that Mommy and Daddy had Aunt Doctor Allison provide instead.

And then when my parents politely requested a letter for their records from the doctor who sent the false invoice to acknowledge in it that she had never actually cared for Lucky, that doctor refused to do so on the basis *"it's too much paperwork . . . "*

Who are these people!

How dare they put themselves up as caring providers of medicine for God's creatures like me!

Let me be direct: I think it's an outrage.

I don't know whose authority it should come under—local, county, or state—but there needs to be some real oversight. Some regulatory body to protect consumers of health care delivery for those like Lucky and me and others like us, just as there is for those like my parents.

And in the event there *is* such an authority, then they should *do* their job properly to protect those who cannot protect themselves.

Simply put, what my parents experienced with Lucky and me is galling—or worse.

You see, in my view, it is only common sense that if it happened to us, it's happened to others. The odds are strong we can't be the *only* intended victims of such unconscionable behavior. By those who have presumably committed to do their best—but don't.

Again, please forgive my candor here, but their kind of behavior is offensive and irresponsible, if not just out and out criminally corrupt. Especially from trained professionals who presumably pledged to uphold the principles of some veterinarian form of the Hippocratic Oath to serve those like me—that kind of behavior is nothing more than hypocritical and predatory.

The salient point here is, I think many if not most people who care for their loved ones like my parents care for me may not know there is another way.

They have no other doctors with whom to compare and contrast these money-grubbing types. So thinking they are doing the right thing, they put their loved ones like me through these exhausting, incredibly expensive, and very possibly unnecessary, even harmful tests. Or they pay for bills sent for care their loved ones never received, from those who just figure that no one will notice.

Daddy's right: We *can* do better.

Fortunately, my parents and I have Uncle Greg as a benchmark.

He didn't *start* by *talking* about tests.

He listened carefully to what my parents were describing to him in a phone call and asked a lot of questions. What he heard clearly concerned him. But the more he asked, the more he learned. And the more he learned, the more he was able to advise Mommy and Daddy what to do. He suggested something to calm my stomach down and strongly recommended my parents do their best to ensure I did not become totally dehydrated.

He was candid but compassionate and thorough in every conversation with my parents.

And only at the very end of his conversation did he mention that if what he recommended did not work, maybe then tests might be in order for something more serious—like cancer, which was the starting point on the part of the other doctor's office.

But Uncle Greg's first instinct was that he thought it might be something other than cancer. His other first instinct was *not* how to milk my crisis for as much money as possible by prescribing unnecessary tests.

He called in two medical prescriptions to a pharmacy near his office, not far from our "country housis," which in turn transferred his prescription to another pharmacy just down the street from our "beachis housis" in Jupiter, Florida.

He also did one other thing: He told my parents to dramatically alter my diet.

First cottage cheese only, then cottage cheese and hamburger meat that had been boiled and completely drained of all its natural fat.

He suggested they try to get me to eat some rice as well—the only recommendation of his I refused to abide by. Despite that it would have helped me, I don't like rice!

And he also told my parents to watch carefully over me. To observe me closely, to do what they could to encourage me to drink water, and if that didn't work, to even try giving me a human drink with a funny name called Gatorade to replenish the electrolytes I was losing every twenty minutes, each and every time I had to go to the "batroom."

. . .

I didn't get better overnight. It took a little over a week (my parents' time). And it was hard.

But I did recover.

And as I recount all these events, it's fair to say I'm still a little weak, of course. But I am getting stronger every hour. Sufficiently so that I am okay enough to go for my daily walks.

My tail is back doing what it has always done when I feel good—wagging.

My eyes are clear and my appetite is great —I love this new menu!!

And while I am still a little fatigued from the meds which I will have to continue for a few more days, I am back doing my job of watching over our household.

Two other things you might be interested knowing.

First, *if* I had gone to the doctor's office where they apparently do tests first and then ask questions afterwards, Uncle Greg says not a single one of those expensive diagnostics would have done any good. They cannot detect colitis, even the most severe form that I had.

Second, to show you the kind of person my doctor Uncle Greg Hahn is, when my mother weeks later picked up from his office the bill for some supplies I need on an ongoing basis, she noticed there was *no* charge for all the hours he had spent on the phone throughout my ordeal. *He* did not think it was called for because there had been no formal office visit!

To my mother's credit, she did just as I would have expected of her—just as my parents always expected of Lucky and me—to do the right thing. She insisted on being charged just as if there had been office visits.

In our view, it's all about doing the decent thing, doing the right thing.

No patient should ever try to take unfair advantage of his or her doctor.

Just as no Florida doctor (I am leaving out the names right now,—but if you call and ask, we will be more than happy to tell you who some of them are from my very personal experience) should ever try to take unfair advantage of his or her patient—animal or human!

Understandably, my parents and I came away from all of this grateful, if chastened. In a sense, it was just one more "wake-up call" of life as Mommy and Daddy would say:

> *To never take anything for granted.*
> *To always take life one day at a time.*
> *To cherish each other every moment of every hour of every day we have left together.*

SEPTEMBER 5: I'M HAPPY TODAY

I'm happy today. And relieved . . . content . . . relaxed . . . and at home. And I know why.

Daddy came home yesterday. He's been gone all week . . . on another business trip. Just like the several other trips he has had to take since July 5th to be exact. Quite remindful of all the almost weekly trips he used to take for several years when Samantha, Lucky, and I were still young. When—much as we tried to hide it so as not to upset Mommy—we missed him terribly.

It's been a really long time since Daddy has had to be away from us, with so much consistent travel. With some exception, it goes all the way back to the time when Mommy got cancer. He stopped immediately, and really did not travel at all for at least four or five years (up to 35 years my time), while we and he took care of Mommy until she got better.

I guess in all that badness about cancer, his being home all of the time for so long was something good that came out—in addition, of course, to Mommy getting better. Another good thing came out as well: When Daddy has had to travel, he now does something he really did not do previously. More often than not, he asks to speak to each of us by the box that rings which Mommy puts up to our ears. He started to do that before Lucky said good-bye to us. And he has consistently done so with me ever since.

That way he knows I know that he is safe and will be returning to our "housis" soon.

. . .

In any event, something happened on July 5th, right after one of our favorite holidays, that changed Daddy's daily pattern. One which, as I said, had for some time really focused on taking care of all of us and doing something else he enjoys: writing.

He started doing a consulting job for a former client of my parents, a very large financial services company in Boston. As he and Mommy explained it, they got a call they could not refuse. From a former client who was high up in another financial services company. She had left the original company, done nothing for quite awhile apparently, and finally was able to land a job with a new employer.

It was she who called Daddy.

"We need help," she told Daddy. *"Our CEO needs someone like you to help us do what you did for (her former employer)."* Ironically she did not know that her new boss' boss' boss had been a client of my parents many years before. For whom the work done by Mommy in particular helped to make him a legend in his company and in the industry.

So that is what Daddy has done for the past few months. He has enjoyed the new challenge, detested the travel, and hidden his discomfort with what he's learned about the culture of the company based on his intense interaction throughout the organization.

I am not surprised.

For my father has changed dramatically over the years of my lifetime.

Whereas when he and I first laid eyes on each other, I could see he was really intense and seemingly somewhat distant from me and Lucky and Samantha, focused no doubt more on his career and on his work than on the "softer side," the latter which surfaced more after Mommy's cancer.

Daddy's life focus today is totally different. His priorities are different. What makes him smile, what makes him happy today, is different.

My father, it's fair to say, became a poster child for learning to *"stop to smell the roses."*

All he wants is for Mommy to be healthy and happy, and for each of us to fulfill our life potential in any way we wish to.

Nonetheless, Mommy suggested for Daddy to *"go for it . . . You'll find out whether you still like what we used to do with them, although I honestly don't think you will. You'll get tired of it again. You'll get frustrated by all the corporate politics, people caring about their careers more than caring about their loved ones, and their obsession with making money . . . but go for it . . . because if you don't, you will regret not having done so . . . And I know one thing I'm confident of: You'll not get caught up in all that—you are way beyond that."*

While not exactly pushing Daddy to take on this new assignment, I'm pretty sure I know why Mommy encouraged him to do so. It was no secret in our "housis" that the period between the time we said good-bye to Lucky till July 5, 2005 has been really tough on my father. He has never really gotten over the memory of our last hours with my brother.

They were as close as a Daddy and canine son could be.

Lucky's sweetness and openness and trust and affection and joie de vie had brought out even more of that softer side in my father. And now with the reality of Lucky being gone, Daddy kept swaying between privately wondering whether he had held onto Lucky too long before making that life-changing decision for all of us or was simply having difficulty reconciling the cavernous hole Lucky's departure had left in my father's broken heart.

Mommy knew the symptoms. She had seen it before—after Smokey died.

That's why I agreed with Mommy that Daddy needed a change in his daily working environment, no matter how short or long in duration. It would be a positive distraction which over time would take Daddy's focus off of my late brother, and onto matters of unknown new challenges.

. . .

The three months (my parents' time) between the first day he met with the CEO and his senior staff and yesterday (the end of the first phase of the project) have really gone by in a heartbeat.

It's been challenging and different and strange for Mommy and me as we have had to spend a good part of the summer alone with each other.

I also know it's been challenging and different and strange for Daddy too . . . and lonely for all of us.

The reality is he'd really gotten used to spending his days with Mommy and me ever since Lucky said good-bye. It was almost as if he thought the more he did so, the better he could protect Mommy and me from any dangers or more unexpected surprises of sadness. He saw that as his job, just like I see it as my job.

The good news is the first phase is over. And whatever Daddy has to do for that company will require less travel, or at least it will be travel that he can better control. He's proved his worth—and not just to the client. He's proved as well to Mommy and me and him that we are a family, a threesome now who know how to make the best of things even when we are not terribly enamored by the opportunity presented. To us, these are but necessary intervals which lead upon successful completion to what we really cherish: time together.

And we are about to have more of that.

THE LATTER YEARS

MOMMY'S STUNNING ACHIEVEMENT

I could not be happier right this minute. Nor could I be prouder of my parents, especially my mother.

It started with what Mommy told Daddy last night—something very, very special. Yesterday was *"one of the very happiest days"* of her life.

And today I heard her repeat the same thing, although in a different way on the little box she speaks into that she carries around to talk to him.

She said: *"Rufe, do you remember the time I was really sick and we didn't know if I'd survive the surgery, and I said to you that you will never do anything more important in your life."*

I knew, of course, right away what she was referring to.

That time in my life when I was still very young.

That time in the life of my family none of us would ever forget.

That time when my mother was really, really sick and Daddy was taking care of her full time.

That time when none of us dared to allow ourselves to think about anything beyond what would be happening in the next hour—forget about the next day or week or month or year.

For that was the time when, as far as we knew, it seemed more likely than not that we would be saying good-bye to Mommy for good.

But that was then and this is now.

Mommy had just returned to our Florida "housis" from New York City. And from the moment she walked into the "housis," I could sense something very different—something beyond just good. Something I'd describe as a palpable pride and happiness that literally exuded from her. And a long-sought peace of mind she'd found from deep within her.

I knew she had been comforted while she'd been away with the knowledge that my Uncle Richard, the security guard in our development, would take good care of me. Especially since this had been by far the longest stretch of time I would be alone without one or the other of my parents, ever since Lucky went to the Rainbow Bridge.

Yet I could tell what she was feeling was much more than just comfort about this significant milestone in my life, and in our Mommy-daughter relationship. Yes, it was much more.

You see, my parents had gone to New York City to celebrate something I was unable to fully understand at the time, but very much could discern from my mother's demeanor before they left just how special the occasion would be.

It was to celebrate the thirtieth anniversary (my parents' time) of Mommy's MBA program graduation. The latter being an accomplishment of hers I knew made her so proud.

Now two mornings after that anniversary celebration, she was talking to Daddy as he was waiting at an airport in New York and about to fly to Boston. Where I knew he had a job to do for a few days. And after which he was scheduled to rejoin Mommy and me at the "beachis housis."

Mommy was obviously incredibly happy. I could tell that from the tears of joy streaming down her face.

"Rufie," she told my father, *"I just want you to know, that was one of the most important things you ever did . . . "*

At that moment, I admit I did not immediately understand what she was talking about. But clearly Daddy did. And I knew that upon his return, I'd hear everything that happened in detail, and be better able then to share both his and my mother's great pride and happiness.

The truth is that for my parents their trip turned out to be not just a huge milestone but rather a real turning point in their life journey together.

Trying to put something complex as simply as possible, I would sum it up this way.

Mommy now knew for sure she was totally and completely better. That she has come *all* the way back from the throes of cancer, which for our family and for her especially was a really bad time.

She's also beaten cancer in more ways than just defeating a disease from which we had originally been told she would not survive. But also surviving all of our traumas of her illness, losing an inordinate number of family and friends from the same disease and others since then, and getting beyond "the fire"—which almost destroyed the "housis" my brothers and sister had grown up in.

In other words, Mommy came to terms over the weekend with something even more personal—something even more important.

That all was okay and that she was okay. And that most importantly, she and Daddy had been right all along. There had been a reason for everything she had had to go through to get to this juncture in her life.

By now, I think you realize she and my father have shared a life partnership that everyone always described as more than special. A once-in-a-lifetime relationship, like the one Lucky and I enjoyed, comprised of affection, love, and mutual respect for one another and for us, their children.

That being said, I wish I had been there when all of this played itself out at the reunion. Where Mommy not only got to visit with other women she had gone to school with two hundred and ten years ago (by my calculation). But she also got to hear firsthand at that reunion that no matter what she may have somehow allowed herself to believe differently, she was—is—in fact an extraordinary human being who has lived a remarkable, accomplished, and interestingly different type of life journey.

And she got to share what she heard that day with the one person who had known it even longer than I have: my father. Who it turned out was the only male there, invited to be there to serve as a Master of Ceremonies for that event. Which as you know by now is something he truly loves to do—and is as natural to him as my job is to me of taking care of my mother.

For Daddy, it must have been something quite unique and very special. Just being there, he got an insight into what it's like when scores of we females get together to share our own "war stories." And when they did, he and Mommy privately sought out each other's eyes, for they knew this was one very special occasion, a truly magic life event Mommy never dreamed she would ever have lived to experience.

I understand exactly what they must have been feeling: Lucky and I had shared those same types of special moments. Moments that needed no words. Moments we knew we'd forever remember no matter where our family's life journey of love took us.

At the end of the day, neither Daddy nor I was surprised by what Mommy discovered for herself at the reunion. She just needed to hear it for herself.

In fact, from our perspective, the only thing that was extraordinary (and certainly well deserved) was that she *finally* got to be recognized for the person she is and how she has lived her life. Throughout which her natural instincts have always been to give of herself. To help others, being the *"wind beneath the wings"* of her family and friends.

Let me say again how much I would have enjoyed being there!

To see all those at the reunion, who according to Daddy *"were pure and simply blown away by what they heard. It was like something out of the movies. It's a true life story that should be turned into a feel-good movie."*

You see, it turns out that my brothers and sisters weren't the first to be rescued by my mother. The fact is the brother and sisters of one of her classmates also were—many years before. When my mother was still an MBA student at that school.

When she felt morally compelled to privately call upon—to implore—Dr. Edward Mortola, the president of her university to find the money to help her Vietnamese classmate's family escape, literally, from their war-torn country in its final days as it was "falling"—the horrors being played out on television screens around the world for all to see—including her friend.

To help that family to begin a new life in the United States. And her friend to gain her own personal and professional guardian angel—the Pace University President—as she began her ultimately successful business career after graduation . . . at the same time taking on the awesome responsibility of raising her younger refugee siblings to their maturity.

And that's exactly what happened as result of Mommy's extraordinary action of compassion.

What makes this story even more extraordinary is that in the thirty plus years (my parents' time) in between, with the exception of Daddy, Mommy never told anyone else what she had done.

Not even her classmate, her very close friend, Niem Dang.

Not until the day of the reunion when Mommy learned from Niem, that the university president had, in fact, followed through as he promised Mommy he would, on that day she pleaded with him, some 30 years (my parents' time) ago. Niem never knew why, or how he happened to come to help her. She just knew he had.

Our mommy never sought attention or credit.

She simply thought at the time it was the right thing to do—even if no one else dared to do so. She acted out of conviction. The moral sense that Mommy's friend and her friend's family deserved to live as a family. Just like I and my brothers and sisters were able to when our parents took us out of our orphanages.

So you can just imagine the tears of emotion that flowed among the audience when Daddy introduced Mommy's classmate's *sister*—the sister who is now a respected physician—to everyone on that day of the 30th year MBA celebration. That sister who was a young girl 30 years earlier

(210 years earlier, my time) and had been rescued and raised by her sister Niem, thanks to our mommy's quiet intervention.

The sight of both sisters in that room together almost three decades later (my parents' time) spoke for itself: *My* mother had done something truly remarkable—truly "bestest" as she always encouraged us to do no matter what.

She had literally saved the lives of others. Just as she eventually did, years later, for my siblings and me.

I cannot tell you how happy I am she was recognized for her courage and savvy even at such an early age. And how proud I am to call her my mother!

THE DAY AT THE *PALM BEACH POST*

B y now you know I have inherited from my Anatolian Shepherd canine ancestry the commitment to our job, dedication to those we serve, and the sense of modesty with which we do both.

Our nature is to what we do and how we do it. We are not in it for recognition or adulation.

That having been said, as you might imagine, I am very proud of Mommy's feature story about me. The one that was published in the *Palm Beach Post*, the original draft of which you may have seen at the beginning of this memoir. Of which I have heard many others say how succinctly and beautifully my mother captured—in words and pictures—who I am, why I am the way I am, my dedication to my job, and especially my loving relationship with my family.

What she did not get the chance to tell you about though was the day we went to the newspaper to meet Aunt Anne, the editor who made the decision to publish Mommy's article, along with her newspaper colleague, the photographer. Who it seems fell in love with the subject of their work (me) just as I came to cherish their friendship, courtesies, and total sense of professionalism, as they turned *this* Princess into "Queen for a Day."

It was in fact, and will always be to me, one of the most fun, most interesting, most different, most exacting, most exhausting, most happy, and very, very "bestest" most magical days of my life. Even if it started off with a bit of an unexpected surprise.

The surprise occurred when we arrived at the newspaper offices. Mommy, Daddy, and I were stopped in our tracks by someone dressed in a uniform like my Uncle Richard the security guard wears. And we were ordered to leave the building immediately!

Although I now understand, better than I did at the time, why he did that: It seems those like me were not allowed there. In fact, no one like me had ever been allowed to enter before. So looking back on that moment, it's hard to criticize someone when he was just following the rules.

On the other hand, it did not get things off to the "bestest" of starts for what eventually turned out to be one of the most memorable experiences in my life.

Here's why.

First and foremost, meeting Aunt Anne (Rogers) was like meeting someone who could just as easily been Mommy's lifelong "bestest" friend. The chemistry between them from the moment they met was wonderful to observe, like the chemistry Lucky and I had from the moment we met. It was clear Mommy's story about me had touched a nerve in my new "bestest" aunt.

She not only loves and appreciates those like me. But even better is that she knows all about Anatolian Shepherds—she is the only person I know who does, other than my parents. Years before, she had actually even written a news story about my cousin Anatolians and in her research, she met and fell in love with one JUST like me.

It was obvious to me that Aunt Anne couldn't keep her eyes off of me. Nor could she hide the smile she had on her face till the moment we said good-bye to each other a few hours later.

Second, once I got comfortable with all the bright lights shining in my eyes as first I, and then Mommy and I, and then Daddy, Mommy, and I together posed for pictures, I really enjoyed being the focus of my friend the photographer's attention. It seemed like every time someone said *"smile"* or *"cheese"* or *"Prinny look here"*—there would be a quick flash of light and a click, and then everyone would tell me how good I was being

—and how pretty I was. And Mommy or Aunt Anne or Daddy would pat my head or lightly caress my fur.

What girl wouldn't have enjoyed all that attention?

And every once in a while, between clicks, Mommy and I would give a quick glance at each another. Just to let the other know this was really fun. And for me to be sure she was comfortable lying on the floor beside me. For I knew it could not have been the "bestest" of positions for her after all her surgeries. But I also could tell the experience we were having together, along with Daddy beside us, made up for much of the physical discomfort of the moment.

. . .

The more we posed, the more we were asked to do more posing. And the more we did that, the warmer and then hotter it got under the glare of the bright lights.

Still I would not have ever thought about complaining. Not for a second.

For as close as my parents and I had become after Lucky's departure for our family bench, it would be hard to imagine anything after this once-in-a-lifetime event that might ever be able to bring the three of us any closer in every way possible—physically, emotionally, and spiritually—than we were that afternoon.

And watching Aunt Anne watching us with her twinkling appreciative eyes and her terrific smile made the whole thing truly magical.

. . .

Finally, after the hundred clicks or so by my unofficial count (though it turns out there were about 130), the formal part of our visit ended, and I was allowed to enjoy some personal downtime time while Mommy and Daddy signed some papers.

So, being curious as always, I took full advantage of the opportunity to explore every part of the office we were in.

I decided to drop by and introduce myself to reporters and editors who were working at the type of computer desk similar to the one where Daddy's been helping me with my memoir. However, as I sensed instinctively my sudden presence might be a bit of disconcerting, I made certain to announce I meant no harm by shaking the chains around my neck as hard as I could. Just as I do whenever I need to grab my parents' attention.

The technique must have worked: *Everyone* responded to me with a smile and reached out to give me a hug or a pat or both. And one person whose name I never learned was even nice enough to give me a treat. Which wasn't necessary, of course, but by no means did it go unappreciated.

I loved the feel of the place: It had lots of corners and nooks and crannies to explore. Any sense of formality was covered up by all kinds of papers sitting on desks and on the floor, while pictures of families including those like me, although of different breeds, hung from walls or were placed lovingly in picture frames for everyone to see.

There was also a great smell, especially of food that people were kind enough to think about offering me—and even kinder to not give me for health purposes.

Wherever I went, everyone I met during my exploration seemed happy to meet me, welcoming me as they did with soft-spoken *hellos* and thoughtful observations about my appearance.

Some it seemed must have actually been expecting me, as each asked in different ways, rhetorically I assumed, whether I was the one—"*the MAGIC Girl who took care of her mother with cancer and then her brother*"—who would soon be in Aunt Anne's section of the paper.

I let each of them know with "nuzzies" that yes, it was in fact me about whom Mommy had written.

As busy as I am sure they were that afternoon, absolutely no one made me feel unwelcome or unwanted. In fact, they could not have been nicer!

And then when I finally returned to where Aunt Anne works, it felt just like my den, crowded with all kinds of stuff, and made even more personal with the photo she showed us of her canine she absolutely loved and finally had to say good-bye to, presumably to go to his family bench in Heaven.

It's struck me then, there's just something about Aunt Anne that tells me we have made a very special connection. She is someone whose friendship and affection I will always cherish.

And why, I suppose, when it was time to leave that afternoon, it was so hard for all of us—the photographer, Aunt Anne, Mommy, Daddy, and me—to say good-bye.

However awkwardly it may have started, it turned out to be an afternoon of firsts. The drive to the Palm Beach Post. The trips up and down the elevator. The lights and camera and clicks of the photo shoot itself. The "after-party" exploration of the rest of the offices. The privilege of meeting all kinds of journalists, reporters, photographers, and editors.

And even the security people at the reception desk who graced us on the way out with the warmest of smiles and "bestest" wishes.

For my parents and me, it put a wonderful cap on what had been a totally memorable experience—a truly magical afternoon we would all always remember.

Postscript:

My wonderful day resulted in something truly special. At 7 a.m. on a Saturday morning several weeks later, after we had driven back to our "housis" up North, the phone rang. My Aunt Sandy from Florida was calling to tell us that the *Palm Beach Post* had just published Mommy's essay—and it was surrounded by beautiful photos taken by the *Post* photographer that wonderful day of our visit, and also some that Mommy and Daddy had taken that the newspaper had used.

It was nearly a whole page! My story was now there for all to see, and as we learned, I was now the most famous "Magic Girl" in Palm Beach County!

DADDY DOGGY TIME

I t's almost summer, 2006.

I'm in what my parents refer to as our Television Room—my den. I know it as the room with the box of moving pictures and voices. Whatever its name, it is my favorite room in the "housis," and I am doing one of my favorite things ever: lying on the sofa beside Daddy, enjoying *Daddy-Doggy* time with him. Just like the times he used to spend with my brothers Smokey and Lucky.

It's something that's been very special and taken on even more pleasure for me as I've gotten older. So I thought I'd describe it in some detail using tonight as an example.

. . .

I probably shouldn't tell you this, but we're downstairs because Mommy and Daddy got into a spat about something both of them hate: computers. Mommy thought Daddy's computer has a virus, and he needed to know. He had just gotten home, was tired, and did not care to know about viruses. Or anything else. So a special dinner they had made plans to have together that night got canceled.

Mommy went upstairs to check the computer, while Daddy and I decided to spend quality time together.

I know it will turn out that Mommy's worry was warranted—but will not prove to have been necessary. Either way, sometimes it's best for the three of us to go our separate ways for awhile, particularly after a tense week.

246

. . .

As soon as we lay down side-by-side together, I could tell Daddy was wondering what they have to do to turn the feeling of sadness and doom that's increasingly enveloping our "housis," into something positive. It's wearing on him and Mommy too.

I'm not naive. I recognize that feeling has to do with me. That for my parents, it seems almost as if every hour of every day is a countdown to a time the three of us don't want to talk aloud about, but we all know is coming sometime. We just don't know when.

I can appreciate why they feel that way. It's hard not to. I may not always understand the exact words. But I sure do pick up on the tone and the look in their eyes, each and every time someone we meet somewhere on our nightly walks says the same thing upon learning of my advancing age: "*Oh . . . I feel so bad for you. How hard that's going to be.*"

We heard it again a couple of times on our walk today.

So I'm not terribly surprised Daddy's feeling a bit introspective. And that Mommy and he bickered over the computer, something trivial but of common contempt. It was their way of not having to deal with what's really on their mind: me.

It's during times like these, when we are together, Daddy puts on a song that he adores listening to. As do I.

It's called *"I Want to Live"* by a man named John Denver. We both love its melody, and Daddy has always praised its lyrics. Taken together, it is truly beautiful—profound in its simplicity. Yearning yet inspiring; melancholy yet optimistic; retrospectively thoughtful, yet optimistic about the future.

I know it makes my father think, especially about my brothers Smokey and Lucky and all of those who have preceded me.

I agree with its message.

I believe we can make this a better place. There is so much natural beauty to appreciate. And unnecessary, inexplicable sadness and cruelty that need not be.

Just a few days ago, my parents were reading of a family litter of those like me who had been buried against their will under the earth by someone intent on committing murder of a mother and her babies. For no reason other than someone thought it would be "fun."

And there was the case Daddy can't get out of his mind about a baby human being thrown onto a highway from a bridge—for who knows what reason.

And the mother who killed her children because she thought someone was speaking in her ear telling her to do so.

And how many times have we heard about puppy mills in the name of breeding those like me, but which are really torture chambers for those whose "purpose" has run out?

So I have to believe we can make this a better place for all of us who are good. Until we eventually go to an even "bestest" place. Where my family has a bench which my siblings and grandfather are keeping warm for us. Where John Denver's *"I Want to Live"* is reality, not just a plea.

Listening to music like this is my favorite part of *Daddy Doggy* time together with my father. It's been this way for a very long time.

And it always will be until it's our turn to say good-bye.

CHRISTMAS EVE: TIME'S WINDING DOWN

Mommy gave me a kiss, "nuzzied" my face, and kissed me on the nose tonight while tenderly tucking me in on my sofa in my den. And as we always did, we wished each other *"Sleep well, sweet dreams."*

It was about an hour later, after they had shut down the box with pictures and voices they had been watching in the living room, when I heard she and Daddy tiptoe back into the den, where they stood as still as they could, watching me breathe I guess.

She, of course, would not have known it, but I overheard Mommy whisper, *"Our beautiful girl's asleep. She's tired. I think time is winding down for her."*

Daddy didn't answer. There was no need.

He knew as always that Mommy was right.

My time *is* winding down.

I'm fifteen years old now (my parents' time).

Although, I'm still alert when I need to be.

For instance on the walks with my parents they and I have come to treasure.

Also whenever there's that smell in the air outside on the deck that was there the day of the fire.

And whenever I know Mommy needs me to do any job she needs me to do, such as when Daddy's away and Mommy needs someone to warn her of strangers and such things.

Otherwise, most of the time, I try to sleep. For frankly, at my age, I tend to tire more easily. I feel no pressure to do otherwise.

I have taken to heart what Daddy said to me after the fire and after Mommy came home to recuperate and did so with me by her side: *"Princess, you have nothing else to prove."*

I'm good at what I do. And they know I will continue to do what I have to do till my last breath. For it is who I am—what I'm all about. And why I conserve my energy to be ready when needed.

Having said all that, as my time does wind down, I do worry quite a bit about how my parents will fare emotionally when I am no longer around. Whenever it's my time for me to go to the family bench in Heaven which Lucky and everyone else are keeping warm for me and eventually for my parents.

So unbeknownst to my parents, I am doing what I can to help with the transition. I've started making arrangements to ensure they will find someone to take up from where I let go—just as Smokey did when he handed over to me the torch of the family Alpha dog.

Like I said, it's something I've not spoken about. Nor will I telegraph my intentions.

No need to.

It's just part of my job.

And when the time is right, it will be the very last thing I do . . .

BARBARO: A KINDRED SPIRIT

January 29, 2007

Today is a landmark for those like me with four legs and those like my parents with two.

For early this morning, someone my parents greatly cared about, and spoke of with the same tone of affection and respect as they always have about me, decided it was time to say good-bye to all of his admirers around the world.

His name was Barbaro.

He was my friend in kindred spirit.

He will forever remain in all of our hearts: a once-in-a-lifetime creature.

From the box with pictures and voices, to the phone calls that kept ringing at our home, to the newspaper and Internet features my parents could not get enough of, the only way I'd be able to aptly describe today is one of profound subdued sadness.

And pride . . . and relief . . . and admiration . . . and awe . . . and wonder . . . and gratitude . . . and wistful hopes raised and dashed . . . and all the other good things one might say about one who was a once-in-a-lifetime creature.

. . .

Mommy and Daddy and I had watched the Barbaro story going all the way back to last May, when he won the Kentucky Derby.

He was nothing less than a spectacular athlete.

Even more than that was his unusual demeanor: a quiet but obvious confidence, an intelligence that was clear to all those who observed him. You couldn't help but notice that he had the innate ability to forge an indelible trust with his jockey and his trainer and eventually with his doctor and everyone else he knew was trying to help him.

This wasn't something only I observed about him. *Everyone* did.

From the television announcers to the analysts to the doctors who took care of him to the jockeys who rode him and competed against him—and their trainers and owners.

They all seemed to characterize him the same way: He was a once-in-a-lifetime.

I agree fully.

A few weeks after the Kentucky Derby, I was watching the racing program again with Mommy and Daddy when all of a sudden, we all noticed something indescribably terrible happen.

It was Barbaro.

He was running. But it became clear to me just before the announcers confirmed it, that he was doing so on three legs—with his fourth being carried at a distorted angle, clearly broken.

I could see his pain and his fear. That same immediate sense of panic I have felt when I knew something terrible was happening to me, but which I could not immediately identify.

Such as the time my legs folded unnaturally under me when Daddy played "trow-ball" with me for the first time, which told my parents that I needed my hips replaced. And the two times I had to have the drastic cancer surgery. And of course the time we had the fire.

However, I could also see right away something my parents and their type could not: that Barbaro understood—as I had—that *he* had to do everything he could, as quickly as possible, to overcome that instinctive fear and panic so as to allow others to help him as much as they could.

And that's exactly what he did to everyone's amazement, and to my relief as his peer and friend in kindred spirit. By trusting his jockey to dramatically slow down from a gallop to a trot. And then with little transition to a stop, Barbaro then stood as calmly as possible, against all his natural instincts—to be comforted quietly as he and his partner, Edgar Prado, waited patiently for the doctors and a big machine with wheels to take him to the hospital.

That would prove to be only the beginning of a public drama that played itself out almost every day and every night over the ensuing months.

We all watched his situation unfold. His will to survive, if not to compete anymore. His sense of dignity and enormous pride and yet preternatural willingness to give up control to others whose passion and job it was to do whatever they could to help him.

It was an extraordinary spectacle of collaboration between those like my parents (humans) and nature—like Barbaro (and me). A few memories, of which, will stay with me more than most, and among those, one more than any other.

Simply stated, I will never forget my parents' reaction when they and I watched a news report which chronicled how Barbaro would somehow instinctively know when he should raise his leg so that the doctors and nurses could change his dressing, while recovering from surgery.

"That's exactly what Prinny does," Mommy said in recognition, almost in awe. Daddy nodded in agreement as they both looked directly at me, and I back at them with a reciprocal slight bow of my head.

None of us had to say anything more. We all understood.

. . .

Over the summer and fall and into early winter, millions followed Barbaro's story of courage and stoic heroism. No one wanted more than me for him to have a miracle ending, just as we had all counted on one for Mommy when she was so ill.

Unfortunately, for Barbaro, it was not meant to be.

He tried his very, very "bestest."

He was brave and strong when others might have been willing to give up.

His courage and optimistic way about him gave everyone around him the courage and optimism and will to forge on. Even when it may have seemed too hard, and they thought they were too tired, or were on the precipice of losing hope.

Even when he and they knew that for Barbaro, life had become something I have heard my parents refer to as *"ever increasingly smaller concentric circles."* Something I instinctively accept as a phase of life, one I saw firsthand as my beloved Lucky grew older. And a phase of my own life that my parents and I fully recognize I entered some time ago.

"Ever increasingly smaller concentric circles" is such an apt and poignant description. A phrase my parents first read in an article about someone we have never met, but for whom Mommy, Daddy, and I have enormous empathy and respect.

It turns out there's a man who lives not so far from us who rescues healthy horses like my friends Chippy and Baby, along with a small pony who is a bit different. The latter whom he treats with the exact same passion and love as for any other member of his human and equine family.

I know this because every night, at exactly 11 p.m., the two—the man and the small pony—go out together, and they walk around in what the man says have become *"ever increasingly smaller concentric circles."* But they do this the way they do this because for whatever reason, it works best for the pony at that time of day, every day, in that exact same way. Just the two of them—the small pony and the man.

Why?

Well, it's because the pony's human caregiver knows doing this the same way every day brings a ray of deserved happiness to his pony who is not only small, but also happens to be autistic, deaf, and blind. Doing this the same way every day allows his small autistic, deaf, and blind pony to enjoy all he can from the life he's been granted, albeit one of *"ever increasingly smaller concentric circles."*

Just as it was for Barbaro. For whom walking was very difficult at best and running no longer an option. For whom life meant now waking up every morning in a stall that was comfortable but still meant being surrounded by four walls, waiting for old bandages to be removed and new ones put on. For whom there were the rarest of opportunities to walk outside, breathe in fresh air, and munch on grass that had been a given in his life up to the moment of his accident.

Yes, as the days turned into weeks that turned into months, for Barbaro, life had become a matter of *"ever increasingly smaller concentric circles."*

Still, he was never bitter. He never complained. He knew what he meant to those who loved him most: his human parents the Jacksons, who did exactly what my parents have done for me during my times of medical crisis—everything they possibly could. No matter what the cost .... No matter what others might think .... No matter how much the ending hurt them.

Mrs. Jackson summed it up in a way that told me she and my parents and I might have been close friends, had we ever met: *"Grief is the price we pay for loving."*

Barbaro had a wonderful doctor just like I have had. *My* uncle Dr. Greg Hahn is to me as *Barbaro's* Dr. Dean Richardson was to him. Of them it's fair to say that as much as they might try to hide their emotions about how they feel about us, Barbaro understood as do I the reality.

We have had a very special place in their hearts.

That's why Daddy understands why I not only want—but feel the need to do something different—perhaps unexpected, at this juncture of my memoir.

I want to take a moment here to say on behalf of all my four-legged peers, large and small, who observed what they did for my friend Barbaro:

Thank you, Dr. Richardson and Mr. and Mrs. Jackson for showing the whole world the definition of caring and compassion.

. . .

It was for this reason Mommy and Daddy went out to the nearby hospital where Barbaro said good-bye early this morning. I knew they would because I knew they could not not do so. For they intuitively understand the pain and hurt and sadness everyone connected with Barbaro feels today, and will feel for some time. I am proud my parents did what they did.

And even happier they made a donation for research in Barbaro's name. The memory of which they will forever have with two wristbands dedicated to Barbaro they brought home for me to smell.

For my parents, I know saying good-bye to Barbaro hits home really hard. For his persona and mine are so similar; our instincts are so alike.

I can feel their emotions today. I know what they are thinking even if they do not talk about it directly with me, nor even mention it to each other.

I know they can only imagine what the Jacksons and Dr. Richardson and everyone else close to Barbaro are feeling today, because they sense only too well that day is coming for the three of us, in the not too distant future.

When it will be my time to say good-bye, and to join my grandfather and all of my siblings who are keeping our family bench warm in Heaven.

Where I am absolutely sure they have made another—much larger—visitor's seat available for my friend in kindred spirit, Barbaro. And where in due course all of us will be together, running and romping, galloping and playing with each other totally free, and free of pain.

I *know* this, in part, because I know my beloved Lucky, Mr. Congeniality, is already there getting things ready.

You see, I have not forgotten he said *his* final good-bye exactly three years ago tomorrow (my parents' time).

MARCH 27: REALITY CHECK

I've seen it in Mommy and Daddy's eyes. Probably because they have seen the same in mine: This is very, very likely to be my last trip to Serenity 2, our "housis" in Jupiter, Florida.

It's clear I've been really slowing down since we got here a few weeks ago. In many ways, this visit already feels like we've been here a bit longer than it has actually been because I have really had my "moments"—some not very positive signs of what may very well be on its way.

Let me explain.

While I still look forward to the private moments with my parents in the morning, when Daddy and I have our muffins and coffee, and while I still look forward to our walks in the afternoon throughout our neighborhood as we stop to look for golf balls in the bushes (we've found upwards of 350 or so over the past year), and while I look forward to my meals at breakfast and dinner, it's obvious not everything is working right.

In short, I have had a few accidents at home.

Yesterday was the worst.

It happened when Mommy was talking outside to someone from our neighborhood about hurricane shutters. All I know is I could sense Mommy's growing frustration as I overheard the conversation as I lay beside Daddy's desk as he worked at the computer. Mommy was trying to tell the person what our only priority was—the only thing that mattered:

to protect our "housis" in a hurricane. And by doing so, likely those of our neighbors too.

It was the start of what turned out to be a difficult day for the three of us.

Having lain quietly by Daddy's side for a while, I got up. However, instead of just turning around to lie on my other side as I usually did, for whatever reason and without warning, I found myself thinking to myself I'd be unable to reach the dog run outside our garage. So I simply squatted and made a mess just outside the room where we were working.

I don't know why I did what I did when I did it. Not then and not the second time as well not too long afterwards. And not the third time which was after Mommy and Daddy had taken me outside to go to the "batroom", which I didn't feel like I really needed to do, so I didn't do anything when they took me out. Whereupon immediately after we'd walked back into the "housis," I proceeded to make another mess in the middle of the hallway.

Anyone who knows me would tell you I had never done anything remotely close to what I did. Frankly I was scared. I looked up at Mommy, asking with my eyes what was wrong. Why was I doing what I was doing? Why couldn't I control myself?

I couldn't hide the embarrassment—nor the shame I was feeling.

I also saw the look of concern in both of my parents' eyes morph into a quiet panic. They knew me as well as anyone has ever known anyone of my type. They knew that I would never have done this under any circumstances unless something was terribly, terribly wrong.

I knew what they were thinking. Who could blame them?

Was this the end? Had my age and all the health challenges I have endured during my lifetime finally caught up with me?

Truthfully, I was thinking the same. But if my parents were not ready to give up on me, I wasn't either.

So I made a commitment to myself I would do everything possible to hold it in if I could. And when I could no longer do so, I'd give loud notice I needed to go out. And in the meantime trusted Mommy and Daddy would find someone to help us—fast! As they have always done.

• • •

Well, that long and tiring half a day turned into an even more tiring and exhausting full one.

In between taking me outside about a half a dozen times or so at the slightest hint I had to do so, my parents found a nice doctor to help me. My Aunt Anne (Rogers), the lady who printed the story Mommy wrote about me in the *Palm Beach Post* gave us Dr. Aunt Celia's name.

She had an office quite far away. But she was kind enough to say she'd see me as quickly as we could get to her office. So we left immediately.

Where she worked was not like my Uncle Greg's office up north. It's different—not as spacious or new as some. But Aunt Celia is very nice and from the minute we met, she seemed very caring and yet appropriately dispassionate, businesslike and supportive. Those are comforting qualities to find in a new doctor.

Also, while we were there, she and Uncle Greg collaborated on the phone and decided on medicine for me and a whole new type of menu for breakfast and dinner going forward. That they trusted each other to work together on my behalf gave me great comfort about their plan of action.

Not surprisingly, Mommy and Daddy were relieved if a bit stunned by the sudden and vast turn of events.

The bad news, we learned, was I now suffer from a condition that forces me to eat differently than I ever have eaten before (every meal will consist of cooked, totally skinless boneless fat-free chicken and freshly microwaved frozen vegetables). But the good news is really good: I have no cancer, which was our biggest concern after my two previous bouts with cancer. I love my new food!

I could see on their faces and hear in their tone of voice as we drove back to Serenity 2 from Aunt Celia's that for my parents, this had been a terrible emotional ordeal. A cruel reality check of sorts.

The notion that *we live on borrowed time* (as goes the title of another favorite melody Daddy introduced me to some time ago—you can read the words near the beginning of this memoir) has once again been dramatically reinforced.

. . .

Still, in as much as I am not quite ready to leave for our family bench being kept warm by Lucky and everyone else, I still have my job to do. And I plan to do so as long as I possibly can. Or at least until we get back to our "country housis" up north. And that won't be for some time to come.

So, in the meantime, as one of Daddy's favorite prayers goes, the one he created for our family when Mommy was very sick with cancer: "*We will in gratitude take what's been granted to us . . . one day at a time . . . till all the days run out and become forever and a day.*"

MOMMY'S DAY

This will be my last full day I'll ever be in Serenity 2. That's my thinking right now. Whether I'm right or wrong is really not that important. Nor is it a matter of particular urgency. But assuming it is my last day, I thought this to be as good a time as any to chronicle it for posterity.

All I know is I love this place.

Each and every room (other than the guest bedroom) has become my room.

And while I am comfortable in all of them, and they all feel like my own, my favorites are our den, which is a combination of office/study/library. And the family room just outside the kitchen. And the "porchis" (locals call it a lanai), which overlooks the pool and the golf course where as you know I am always on guard protecting Mommy from the golfers when they get too close to our fence.

From the very moment Lucky and I first arrived here with our parents, I have simply adored the openness of Serenity 2. The coolness of its floors. The comfort of its soft carpeting. The dramatic yet serene view overlooking the pool, the golf course, and the canal beyond both.

Even though I can no longer leap onto the bed to join our parents as Lucky and I used to do early on, I love sleeping on the deep carpet of our master bedroom, and occasionally still find myself drawn to the basket Mommy and Daddy placed for me next to the bed.

How much I feel good here! How much I love this place as my muscles and bones don't ache nearly as much as they do up north when it's cold. It makes it so much easier to do my job.

In short, Serenity 2 feels as much a den to me in the winter, as our country "housis" up north feels like my den in the summer.

Both are really nice.

They are just really different.

. . .

It's an extra special day today: MOMMY'S DAY.

So as I have every year, I asked Daddy to translate my thoughts into words in a personal letter to Mommy in which I told her how much I love her and how much I have loved being her "dogter."

Here is how we expressed it:

"Mommy,

You are always and will always be my snarf mother . . . I do not know what I did to deserve someone with your gift of love, compassion, understanding, and ability to listen to me and my brothers and sister . . . You are the 'bestest'—and I will always be your 'bestest' too . . .

To me, Mother's Day is every day with you . . . and I try to live that way for you . . . and please know that sometime soon you will have the 'bestest' Mother's Day gift I will ever be able to give you—this memoir I've dedicated to you.

I love you forever and a day,

Princess Sheba Spirit of the Mushy-kins . . . and always in spirit my siblings and your canine children, Smokey Max Brooks Pomerantz, Samantha Blackie Brooks Pomerantz, and Little Mister Hazzamazzabooboo Sweetness H.G. Lucky Brooks Pomerantz"

Perhaps it's because of it being Mommy's Day or perhaps for their own reasons, I get the impression that my parents view this day quite like the way I do: as something much more special than usual. Almost as if each of us is given only a finite number of these days to celebrate together with our own Mommies. Almost as if the passing of each day feels a bit like sand passing through an hourglass. And as it does, its memory becomes something to be even more cherished and held on to.

. . .

Since Mommy is almost finished packing for the trip up north, she took time to take a really good picture of me. Having Daddy whistle to me so as to grab my attention for the right pose made it really special.

Although between you and me, it really wasn't necessary. I would have turned on command for Mommy. But as I said, it made the whole effort more memorable doing it the way we did.

Later, Daddy and I sat poolside as we listened to Judy Collins' beautiful song *"I Can't Cry Hard Enough."*

It has such profound meaning: about letting go . . . like when you let go of a kite. It's about her son.

For Daddy and me, it is about our beloved Lucky.

Indeed, whenever I hear Daddy listen to that song, it makes me feel good inside. For it reminds me that I am not the only one who is keeping the spirit of my brother close. It was nice to see Daddy was smiling as we listened to the words. Usually they make him tear up. Or at least that's been the case ever since Lucky had to leave. Today, though, it brought him smiles, and because it did, it made me smile too.

It's a good thing.

For I know he knows that I know that while we both try to hide it from each other so as not to make each other sad, both of us in our own way really miss Lucky. I can only guess how much Daddy does. But I know it has to be a lot—since I know how much and how often I think about my brother. Particularly in this "housis," the one we always looked forward so much to visiting together and could not wait to get to once the cold weather would set in up north.

I can see Daddy is thinking deeply about the words to our song. It says a lot that its theme of living every day as if it were the last is in fact how I have lived my life—and taught Mommy and Daddy to do so too.

. . .

It's been a really good Mommy's Day. Mommy got to swim. She's a bit more relaxed knowing everything is almost packed. I can see and am so happy she's gotten toned by her swimming while we have been at Serenity 2 this winter. Swimming does her good, both physically and mentally.

Daddy and I are so proud of her. I can only wish I had gained that skill set (swimming) when I was much younger. I never did. Which is one reason why, at my age, I'm happy to stick to my slow daily walks, even as they've gotten shorter, but no less enjoyable, the older I get.

. . .

It's been thundering on and off late in the afternoon.

But just before it started, I had a bath. It felt so good on my body. It got rid of the itchiness my dry skin generates in this hot weather. It must have looked really good too, for each time I get a bath, it never gets tiring hearing my parents and others refer to my fur *"looking and feeling like* **velvet***."* **Velvet** being the name, you may recall, first given to me at the orphanage.

I suppose that's why I have forever been grateful that Mommy and Daddy always wanted me to remember that name, even after they formally changed it to my present name: Princess Sheba Spirit.

Then right after my bath, Uncle Jim Stewart came by to say hello to me and to work out any details he and my parents needed to finalize before we left, and before he drives the other car up north a day or two afterwards. I have liked him very much for as long as we have known each other. He's a good man who deeply loves his two adoptees like me, just much smaller breeds. Another reason I think Uncle Jim and I connect so well is because a few years ago, just like I did with Lucky, he too had to say good-bye. To someone who was to Uncle Jim, what Mommy is to Daddy. I am so happy he's found happiness once again.

On each of our journeys north, both Uncle Jim and we will be carrying very special items.

One is a portrait of me that Mommy and Daddy specially commissioned that is simply beautiful. I am so proud of it. The light captures my coloring perfectly; the details of my fur which reflect who I am and the twinkle in my eyes and smile on my face which reflects the enduring love I will always have for my family.

The other is a set of two paintings Uncle Jim will be carrying in his car, which I know will put smiles on the faces of my Uncle Len and his parents who very recently went through with their Hogan what we went through when we said good-bye to our Lucky.

My parents had the same lady, Aunt Leslie, who did my portrait, do his. She did two of him. They are both beautiful. I know seeing Hogan's face will help raise their spirits. Just as the words do for Daddy and I when we hear the beautiful hymn, *"You Raise Me Up."*

The fact is whenever we hear it played or sung, particularly by someone called Josh Groban, a real-life picture comes to mind.

Of Lucky raised up on his back haunches, holding onto Daddy's hands with his forepaws. It is my favorite vision of them together. I only wish we had another one of him when he, like my sister Samantha, would crawl up on Daddy's chest in bed and bathe him in kisses. It is in fact one of Daddy's favorite memories of the relationship he and my brother enjoyed. They trusted each other because they understood each other. They loved each other as much as any human and canine could love one another.

I know—I have the same relationship with Mommy.

· · ·

Most of this Mommy's Day, I've spent a fair amount of time thinking about my life. How much has happened over my lifetime, not just to me but in the world.

As corny as it may sound, here's what I've concluded.

I am so grateful I spotted and picked out Mommy at the orphanage. It's been a wonderful ride. It's been a wonderful world. I've learned so much, experienced so much, received so much love and attention and affection and compassion from my parents and others I've met along the way. And in return I have done whatever I could to give back—to reciprocate in kind—in those ways I can do best.

I've also been thinking about the long drive north, about which I already know for sure two things.

One is, it's going to be tough on me.

The other is, at some point during our drive up north, when the sound of *"You Raise Me Up"* reverberates throughout the car, I am sure Mommy and I will see Daddy's right hand subconsciously reach across to a spot on his left shoulder; where Lucky used to lay his head as he helped navigate our trips up and down I-95.

I know what he'll be thinking right at that moment: about the wonderful feel and breath and sweetness that personified my brother's presence in all of our lives.

And I know tears of genuine gratitude will accompany Daddy's shy smile of his that I love so much.

Finally, I also know that on what is likely to be the last long drive I will ever take, I will find my own special way to express to my parents something from my heart. Something I want them to always remember when they think of all my siblings, and Lucky and me.

Thank you, Mommy and Daddy, for raising all of us up to be the best we could ever be . . .

MEMORIAL DAY WEEKEND

I think Mommy and Daddy realize, as I do, that the sands of my lifetime are running out more quickly now.

I am not sad about it, not at all. Just tired and worn down by age and candidly the hurt and pain that come from the grind of a lifetime of duty. Doing what I was born to do: my job as my mother's guardian.

Soon enough, it will continue but take another form: as her forever Guardian Angel.

There's a peaceful quiet in our home—one of relief and gratitude that we were able to get back safely to our summer country "housis" up north.

It's rather amazing that it's only been twelve days (my parents' time) since we drove through the gates of our Jupiter Community on our way north. After saying good-bye to my Uncle Jerry who runs the security company for which my Uncle Richard the security guard works, and making one very quick right hand turn, then another, and finally another, leading to the main road for the long drive home.

I could tell from Uncle Jerry's eyes that deep down, he had a sense this would be the last time we'd see each other in this lifetime. Just as it was obvious, throughout what turned out to be a very long and even uncomfortable trip for someone of my age, that Mommy and Daddy shared the same sentiment. One they never openly discussed, however, during our two-day drive. Fearful, I guess, that I might understand.

I love my parents for their thoughtfulness. But they should have known better. They needn't have tried to secret away their fears. For if asked, I would have been happy to tell them I not only thought it had been my last visit to Jupiter—I knew it.

. . .

The morning we left, we got started later than we normally do. So understandably there was an initial concern, if unspoken, we all shared that we might not make it to our favorite hotel in Florence, South Carolina. The place Lucky and I, and then I alone have always recognized even before we'd arrive there. It turned out to be a false alarm though; Daddy got us there in time. And lucky for us, we even got a renovated room to stay in.

As usual, upon our arrival, we followed our normal routine: Mommy unpacked while Daddy fed me. And then he went out and got dinner for Mommy and him from OUTBACK, and then my parents read and watched the box with pictures and voices while I slept off my dinner cuddled beside my pals Periwinkle and Lionmonkee and Fluffy—who as usual were with me on this trip.

And then when it was time to go to sleep, Daddy took me out to do my El Crapo, after which I had my biscuits and water. And then Mommy and I lay together in one bed until I decided to sleep on the floor, while Daddy tried to rest his aching back in the other bed.

I dreamt good dreams that night. This one was about waking up in my favorite place in my parents' room up north, surrounded by all my "bestest" friends such as Periwinkle, and Kiss Kiss and Fluffy, and Blueberrymonkee, and Lionmonkee, and Polarsnarf.

In my dream, I was reminded of the fresh smells of the crisp, cool, northern spring air— which I have always adored. It is so different than Florida, although to be fair, I have loved it at that place too.

No wonder my first thought upon awaking the next morning was how fortunate I've been to have a family that loves me so very much that they have given me two comfortable "housis'."

. . .

Since we've been home, so much has happened in twelve days it's been hard to keep up.

Daddy has had to travel out of town twice.

The swimming pool had that strange cover taken off.

Mommy took me to see my Uncle Dr. Greg, and he did that stuff to me I really don't like. But I know he means well, and besides it's his job. And I was glad to see him again and know he is nearby.

Within hours of our arrival, we unpacked our travel car and did the same with the second car as soon as it too arrived with all our belongings from Jupiter a few days later.

Aunt Sue came to help Mommy to clean the "housis," and her demeanor towards me seemed to be different from before: more caring . . . more tender . . . a little more attentive.

And after our first spring lawn cutting, our front and back lawns had the look of velvet, the neatness of a golf fairway, and the feel of a park with small rolling hills.

On my first walk up the street, I saw Chippy and Baby, my horsey friends across the street. They have permanent company: newcomers Bakey and Shakie as we had named them, not knowing their real names.

As soon as they saw me, Chippy and Baby literally jumped up with long welcoming whinnies of *"Hello!!! How are you? . . . I haven't seen you in a long time."* So we made plans, in our own way, to catch up.

As I did too with my "bestest" young Collie friend, Paris, and our mutual German Shepherd friend, Snoopy, who lives right across from Paris. They too seemed very excited to see me after all these months. I hadn't realized how much I missed all of their company.

A couple of days later, I spotted my old pal Sinbad, the Samoyed, lying on the ground outside his "housis" next to ours. He was asleep, so I decided not to wake him up. I've heard through the grapevine he's slowed up considerably, lost much of his hearing, and his eyes are not so good either.

I can relate.

It's been unusually warm since we arrived, which is a very good thing. First, because as warm as it is, it still isn't as hot as it is in Jupiter at this time of year. There it can be so hot and so humid it can get a bit difficult to breathe for someone like me. Second, the sun and the warmth feel so good on my shoulders and my haunches; they help take away a bit of my arthritic pain. Third, because when it's warm, it means I get a bath. And as you know, I have come to love the baths Mommy gives me. They take away my itchiness. Cool me off. And honestly, I love my mother's tender touch, her whispers of affection, and the ensuing walks with her or Daddy around the yard as I dry off.

In fact, it's been warm enough that when my parents and I finally had some downtime together, I got to see them put their toes in the cold water of the pool as early as they have ever done. That alone told me summer would soon be upon us.

. . .

This has been about the bestest Memorial Day holiday weekend I can recall.

Last night, Uncle Brian, my sitter and favorite pal (other than my Daddy), and Lucky's too before he left us, came over for a wonderful barbeque. He and my parents always seem relaxed with each other. There's genuine affection there. I may have already mentioned this: Uncle Brian calls them his "Adopted Godparents." And they think of him proudly almost as a surrogate son— whose late mother would be so happy and relieved he has elders to look out for him when he needs it, to advise him when he asks for it, and to give him the personal space he deserves.

The three of them had planned to attend a fun spectacle my parents have come to think of almost as their own holiday tradition: a nearby major fireworks performance that's synched with music and dancing fountains. I've not seen it personally, but I hear only great things about it. And so they planned to introduce the music, dancing fountains, and fireworks experience at Longwood Gardens to Uncle Brian.

Unfortunately, shortly after they got there along with 10,000 others, they were told it was canceled due to lightning and thunder. I wasn't surprised. I had tried my "bestest" to warn them even before they left that this might occur. I had picked up on the potential change of weather several hours before when it was 80 degrees, sunny, with not a cloud in the sky.

Instead they were forced to drive back to the "housis" and arrived just as the worst of the storm hit. Which was a good thing since the storm lasted a very long time, and I would have been worried about their safety.

Later that night, they found out the fireworks did actually take place very late, well after midnight, after the thunderstorm subsided. They were okay with it though. It was much more fun staying close together, listening to music, reading, and for me, having my fur stroked.

. . .

The last day of the weekend was truly wonderful—not too hot, not too cold. Just a perfect sunny afternoon for a bath my parents gave me which felt soooo good.

The neighborhood had been quiet all weekend: Seems like everyone was away. This meant very few cars while we went on our nightly walks, and lots of silence—broken only by "squirrelly birdies" singing, an occasional snort from my horsey friends, and Snoopy's usual barking up a storm.

I missed seeing Paris in her usual place outside her "housis" once the holiday began Friday evening. My parents seemed to understand what I was feeling. So they explained that Paris and her family had taken a few days to vacation just like we had at our "beachis housis." When I heard that, I felt better. I'm happy for all of them. They are a very nice family. And I know how much they enjoy the special trips they take together.

All in all, the holiday was remarkable for its simplicity. No airs. No commitments. Lots of time to rest and relax and think and recharge my batteries for what I anticipate will be a challenging few months doing my job for Mommy, as Daddy travels doing his job for all of us.

. . .

The morning after Memorial Day weekend, I slept in late . . . enjoyed a poppy seed muffin with coffee with Daddy, after which he and I went upstairs to work—a conference call for him, and me doing my job of guarding him.

That's when something happened I cannot explain even now, wished it had not happened, and sense it may foretell something of what the future might hold in store: I did an El Crapo right there in the carpeted office.

To be fair, maybe it might not have happened if Daddy had interrupted his call to take me out right after I'd finished my breakfast. On the other hand, again to be just as fair, I usually do not have to go out right after eating. And when I do need to go out, I usually can communicate it to my parents. Something I didn't—couldn't—do on this occasion.

Why did I do what I did? Why didn't I tell Daddy I had to do what I had to do?

Simply put: because I never knew I had to go. My body did not tell me it needed the break. Instead, I just got up from the spot where I was lying guarding my father and, without any notice, went to the "batroom" right there in the office.

I could see Daddy's shock—and his obvious concern.

I could also tell he wanted to find a way for me not to be embarrassed. He had already seen the sheepishness in my own eyes, and my bowed head.

I think he knew right away this act was not one out of typical "batroom" necessity, or defiance, or rebellion, or anything more than what its real cause was.

The aging process! I didn't even know I had done what I had done, until I looked down and saw what I did. Now I fully understood what I had heard my Grandma Beazie talk about so often, about what sometimes happens as we get older.

My father cleaned up the carpet . . . then bent down to gently pat me on my head with words of loving and compassion and understanding I will remember forever and a day.

"It's okay, Magic Girl. I know you didn't mean to do it. And you and I know what it means. Lucky is waiting for you. But as long as you want to, I'd like you to hold on, for as long as you are able to. I have one more job for you: to take care of Mommy while I'm away. And when I get back for good, you'll let us know when the time is right. Always know we love you . . . forever and a day."

Looking right into his eyes I let him know I understood, and would do my "bestest" as always. In return, Daddy gave me a bite on my lips and a kiss on my muzzle as I "nuzzied" him.

After which, we went downstairs to tell Mommy what had happened.

THIRTY YEARS MINUS ONE DAY
(MY PARENTS' TIME)

This is a very special day, one to take a step back and reflect. July 4, 2007, the day I originally had thought would be a good time and place to end this book: 210 years minus one day (my time) since my parents met for the very first time in 1977, totally by accident.

It was a fluke of happenstance really. So much like other flukes of chance and happenstances of life we all have had. And then look back on years later in gratitude, if not awe.

Clearly, if not for that event, I would not have had the very special journey that has been my life story. About which I have tried my best to share in bits and pieces with you in this memoir.

Here's the way I look at it.

If Mommy and Daddy had not made eye contact thirty years ago tomorrow (my parents' time) at 10:30 in the morning—through the window of my mother's boss' office at a company I heard them call AVON, in New York City, and then when they met again that evening— I would not have had the opportunity to pick Mommy out of the pack of other potential parents at the Chester County SPCA on our meeting day. And my desire to live might not have been extended—or even allowed for that matter—much longer than a few more days.

And if my parents had not been destined to meet thirty years ago tomorrow (my parents' time), the fact is that Lucky and I would not have had our love story.

And, some other "housis" I might have been living in could have burned to the ground, with me inside of it.

And I would never have escaped from the cold to Serenity 2 in Florida every year, nor stayed at nice hotels along the way, nor seen the changing of the scenery as we have done year after year.

And I would never have been able to visit the place in Canada where my father grew up, nor visited my grandparents' "housis" there, nor stayed in a beautiful hotel where I was treated like royalty, nor had the chance to meet, for the first time, one of my nicest aunts—Aunt Linda.

And I would never have been able to be treated by extraordinary doctors like my Uncle Dr. Greg Hahn and others like him such as my Aunt Dr. Celia, and my cancer doctor, and my hip replacement doctor, all of whom have helped save my life along the way.

And I would never have been able to use the very special place my grandfather built for my siblings and me to conveniently use just outside our garage whenever any of us has needed to go to the "batroom."

Not only that, my neighbor, Paris, the young collie, who according to her family is so afraid of everyone but me . . . she and I would not have had the opportunity to say hello every night.

And Snoopy the young and brash German Shepherd with whom I exchange views most nights about things that are important to us—we would not have been able be able to do so.

And my old friend Sinbad and I would never have been able to hook up, even as infrequently as we have this spring and summer.

And all four of my horsey friends (okay, two are ponies but they view themselves no different than do the horses) and I would never have been able to connect.

And most importantly, if my parents had not met when they did, Mommy might likely have not survived from cancer, based on everything she has told me and others.

In short, if my parents had not met three decades ago tomorrow (my parents' time), I would not have been able to fulfill my potential, doing what I do best, doing what I was born to do: my job.

A job I have continued to strive to carry out even as recently as last night when my parents took me over to my Uncle Len's "housis" to meet his older parents. Where all of them needed an emotional pick-me-up, as they had had to say good-bye to their beloved Hogan, a distant cousin of mine I had never met. But about whom I could certainly sense everywhere throughout their "housis" last night.

I'm happy we went. It turned out to be a very special evening for everyone.

Uncle Len's family used the opportunity to thank me personally for inspiring my parents to have two magnificent portraits commissioned of Hogan. Both of which hang up in a perfect place: on a wall as you come up to the top of the stairs of their second floor. Where, as Uncle Len's mother told Daddy and me, *"I can say good morning and good night to him every day . . . funny isn't it?"*

For a second, I thought about saying, *"No, Mrs. Gorney, it's not funny . . . or strange. It's rather understandable and perfect."* And about telling her that I say the same thing to Lucky, in the room where I go to sleep every night, and wake up every morning. And also each and every time I gaze at the cover of his box in which his spirit rests. On which is written a promise, that *"all of us will see each other again soon at the Rainbow Bridge."*

The place where I know he . . . and my sister . . . and brothers . . . and step-sisters . . . and step-brothers . . . and my grandfather are keeping our family bench warm until we are all together again.

As I know we will be.

In any event that's what I thought about saying to Mrs. Gorney. However, I decided not to. For sometimes some things are best left unsaid. Sometimes actions speak louder than words.

Instead I walked over to her and gave her a gentle "nuzzie" against the side of her hip.

The kindness in her eyes looking back down at me told me I had done exactly the right thing.

Perhaps it was the silence that filled the space among the three of us standing there. Or maybe it was the tender hurt in Mrs. Gorney's eyes.

Whatever it was, at that exact moment, for reasons I cannot explain— perhaps they don't require explanation—I decided to change a long held decision I'd previously made: *I have decided not to end my journal just yet.* Something in me tells me this is not the right time. But when that time does arrive, I will be the first to know it.

In the interim, it will give me more time to reflect on the implications of some new quite random thoughts that have been increasingly coming to mind.

The sum of which I'd characterize accordingly.

As I have grown older, I have also grown the wiser about everything. This has been enabled in part or in whole by something my parents have done their very "bestest" to impart onto me and my late siblings. From the day each of us joined our family. And undoubtedly will be the case for those siblings who will follow me.

The first thing is to not have fear of the unknown. To not be afraid to explore all that life offers, once you have been offered the gift of life, as each of us was by our parents.

The second is to never stop learning. Never allow your curiosity to waver about all that's around you—the sights, and smells, new experiences, and new acquaintances.

The third is to never be afraid to ask questions. As I still continue to do in my own manner, most often wordlessly. If you listen hard enough, you can "see" what I am asking. The point I am trying to make is that after more than one hundred and five years (my time), if anything, I have more questions to ask, more answers to find, more knowledge to soak up.

About myself, about life, about loyalty, about love, about friendship, about leadership, about honesty and integrity, about what this world has become, and seems to be turning into.

It seems the more questions I ask, the more questions I have. For which satisfactory answers seem harder and harder to find.

You see from what I have been able to ascertain from the box with pictures and voices which my parents and I watch almost every night, there is an incredible amount of violence and hatred and rudeness and anger and hypocrisy and nihilism and self-centeredness and self-promotion and hubris.

People are talking past one another, instead of conversing with and listening to each other, their intent seemingly to impress but not necessarily communicate.

And I ask myself, why does it have to be so? I honestly don't understand the point of it all.

Aren't we all in this together? Shouldn't we be?

I say that because I have always been touched by the words of someone I never met, but the words of whose song early on really spoke to my parents. And hence I have tried to live by them.

His name's John Lennon; his song is *"Imagine."* And all I would suggest is everyone should take a little time to listen to that song and take it to heart. If we all did so, I can only imagine the kind of place we would all share. What a wonderful world it would be, as Lucky's favorite song suggests.

I suppose it's fair to say, at this stage of my life, having finally reached the status of a DOG (Distinguished Old Gal), these are the kinds of things I find myself spending more and more time thinking about. And will continue to do so. Until I know it's the right time for me to stop.

I hope you don't mind.

STILL DOING MY JOB

From the moment my parents came downstairs, on August 12, 2007, they could tell something was off. It was about me. They could see that. They just couldn't tell why.

I wish I could have made sense of it. But as hard as I tried, I couldn't. I suppose now —now that I know what it was all about— I will be better able to tell them the next time.

Simply put, I could not get comfortable with myself. No matter whether I stood or sat. No matter whether I tried to lie down or walked around. Whatever I did, I kept feeling like something big was going to happen.

Compounding what was going on inside of me, I could literally feel the fear, sense the concern, and just about touch the angst in both Mommy and Daddy.

The more uneasiness I exhibited, the more uneasy they were.

I could tell they thought that something was very wrong. That maybe it was my health that was in question again.

It wasn't. Not this time.

It was something totally and completely different. A new feeling that was igniting a reaction in me that I could not control.

Now that it's over, my only wish is that it could have happened sooner to spare my parents the worry.

280

Now I know that if and when it happens again, I can give them a "heads-up" so to speak. I can tell them that *"a Smokeyism is about to occur . . . so brace yourselves."* The fact is the spirit of my late brother is alive and well inside of me. A phenomenon I'd actually known of for ages, but I hadn't allowed it to come to the surface very often—and not for a good long time.

. . .

On this particular morning, in my own way, I made sure both my parents recognized that whatever they were planning to do the rest of the day, they had to stick close to me. I accomplished it by running nonstop, back and forth, as often and as fast as I could between their respective private studies.

Until I could feel both of them following me up the stairs to our office.

There I first tried lying down in my usual place near Daddy's desk.

When that didn't work, I next tried hiding underneath Mommy's desk and then Daddy's, where both write on their respective computers.

That was equally unsuccessful.

By now feeling really out of sorts, I became a sort of whirling dervish—constantly standing up and lying down, jumping to my feet and sitting down, all the while moving around with an intensity I had seldom shown since the fire.

My panting was heavy. So much so my parents were becoming increasingly concerned that I might be having a heart attack. A concern I did not share. For I knew I wasn't. In fact, this wasn't about me at all.

The problem, however, was finding the right way, any way, to explain exactly what was happening and why I was reacting the way I was, for as long as I was.

Then it happened: a sound much like an explosion!

So loud, so strong, so powerful I guess that it startled all of us. Not just my parents and me but others like them and me who live nearby. Like us, everyone else came running out of their own "housis." Within seconds, everyone was talking and looking and wondering what had happened.

All any of us knew was that there had been a huge noise and all of our power went out. Again, I tried my best, if in vain, to communicate what they should all be looking for.

I guess that next time, I will know how to do so more effectively. I'd better. For it could have been as serious for anyone of us, as it turned out to be for one unfortunate family further up the street.

It had been an electrical transformer blowing up outside their "housis," no more than a few hundred yards away, just down and across the road from us. An explosion that was bad and could have been far worse.

For as I understand now, while it blew out their power (and ours), and caused that family's computers and washing machines to explode too, it might have caused even more damage—had the fire that was started by the explosion gotten out of hand.

Fortunately, instead, as it blew up, it sort of flamed out. So their "housis" was spared. And no one was hurt.

The buildup to the about-to-be explosion is what I had been trying to communicate. Though it may have seemed to Mommy and Daddy more like a case of over-anxiety on my part about something which they could not understand, and I could not effectively articulate at the time.

I wish I'd been able to. My instincts were telling me that something big, something bad was happening!

Even though there were no outward signals to warn my parents or our neighbors. And even though the forces responsible for the eventual explosion were unleashed only when everyone's computers were turned on and washing machines operated.

For good reason, my parents and all the neighbors were a bit stunned by what had occurred, but even more relieved that no one was hurt.

When we got back into our "housis," I could hear the pride in Daddy's voice.

"She was telling us what was about to happen—just like Smokey used to. She was trying to warn us to get out of the house. She is such a good girl . . . . After all these years, she's still teaching us . . . She never fails to find new ways to surprise us . . . She's still doing her job."

"She really is amazing . . . You know she will always be our Magic Girl," Mommy quietly agreed, gently stroking my flanks as we sat together in the den.

I was pleased that they were pleased.

And then, suddenly feeling that kind of fatigue that hits you when all the tension dissipates from all the commotion that leads up to what could have been a potentially disastrous situation, I lay down and went to sleep.

THE DAY AFTER LABOR DAY

It's the day after Labor Day.

In about an hour or so, we're expecting a visit from a very close family friend. Someone I have referred to quite a bit. Someone I have come to trust and respect and hold dear. Someone who has played a big role, not only in my life, but in the lives of my whole family.

From everything that's happened, been said, and not said over the past few days, however, I'm pretty confident that this will not be just some casual *"drop by the house."*

That's why Daddy and I have decided to use the time between now and then as propitiously as possible. To chronicle all the events—at least those that are important to me—that have happened over the past few days, a time which no doubt will forever have enormous meaning for my parents and me.

. . .

WEDNESDAY, August 29, 2007

It all started when Daddy got back late Wednesday evening from what would eventually turn out to be the last of a series of his trips to help the careers of some people I've never met. But about whom I had heard a lot, as each time Daddy would share with both Mommy and me what had been going on during the many trips to places with the names of Boston and Providence.

The one thing, however, I recall most vividly about this particular trip is the warm "nuzzie" I gave him just before he left two mornings before.

284

When, as he's always done before leaving us for trips long and short, he bent down, looked me right in the eyes while giving me a kiss on my nose and on the furrow on my forehead right between my eyes, and followed it up with a kiss for Mommy too.

This time though, when he did so, he said to me something I have thought about a lot over the past few days: *"Big Girl, I promise I will be back real soon. You will never be far from my thoughts . . . so until I get back, you have one more big job to do. You have to look out for your Mommy one more time. What I want you to do while I am gone is wherever she is, I want you to be there too . . . It will make her feel better. Okay? And just know that Mommy and I love you more than life itself."*

It wasn't his words that struck me that morning.

For by now, I had become accustomed to them—in particular that last part of his message. For both Mommy and Daddy had been saying it a lot recently. And when they would do so, I tried to not let on that I knew they were trying in vain to hide the fact that they were crying. Just as Daddy had attempted to do so again on Monday morning. But the truth was he could not. No matter how hard he tried.

Now as then I only wish I could have gotten up on my hind legs to put my forepaws around him, to comfort him. For while *I* knew what it was that was making both Mommy and Daddy so sad, *I* was more than comfortable with the decision we had made together with a single phone call just a few days before. About where we were together in our journey as a family —and about what needed to be done.

That Wednesday night, which I will remember forever as the return from Daddy's last trip, I knew Daddy was on his way to the "housis" well before Mommy did. Way before the machine with wheels actually turned into our driveway. Way before Daddy opened the garage to come through the side door where I have come in from my "batroom" thousands of times over the years. And so by the time he unlocked the side door, I was waiting there to greet him. Just as I had done on all those other occasions when either of my parents returned from trips.

After we exchanged "nuzzies," I went back into Mommy's study where, unbeknownst to Daddy, I had spent most of my time while he was gone. I lay down in my favorite spot, to the side of Mommy's desk, where I found myself watching him watching me.

His eyes were so tired. So I made sure he could see me returning that little shy smile he's always given me—with a little wag at the top of my tail. You see, since the fire so long ago, but never forgotten between us, that's been our own very special private way of communicating with each other the things we were really feeling.

This time we both knew for sure what the other was saying.

We both knew that the other knew these next few days would be life-changing for the three of us, and would be an incalculably difficult experience for the one we both adored more than life itself: Mommy.

. . .

And it has been just that.

Just as it has been a gift we have all given the other—of love and respect and closeness and devotion we have all felt right up to this moment.

Simply put, to have shared our life journey together has been the gift of a lifetime for each of us.

From that evening to this very moment, if it were at all possible, I would say our hearts have been touched even more by the other. So much so that sitting where I am today, it's hard to separate mine from my parents'.

Over the past few days, we have shared our "bestest" and deepest thoughts and prayers for and with each other.

We've shared memories about all the things we've experienced together, and listened to the music we've listened to over the years.

The fact is these few days have been extraordinary. Almost as if they were a synopsis of the relationship we have built together over the last decade and a half (my parents' time).

How can one adequately describe to you how incredibly deep is the love and devotion I feel for my parents?

Or how deep is the love and respect for me they have exhibited every day of my life?

How does one say that in a way they will never forget?

That's why before going to sleep that night I made a pledge to myself that given the right opportunity, I would in my own way do my very "bestest" to find a way to do so—in a way my parents would always remember.

. . .

THURSDAY, August 30, 2007

As soon as Mommy and Daddy came downstairs from their bedroom, it was easy to tell the depth of their sadness. Not that they wanted me to know it, but as I have said before, there are some things my natural instinct cannot miss. So as always, I didn't let on what I suspected. Instead I let them know how much I loved them too, as we all got down on the floor in the long hallway that separates the back of the "housis" from the front door. The area around which I have come to think of as mine, having—without being asked—made it my business to lie there guarding Mommy whenever she's upstairs. Especially when Daddy's been away, since my presence in the hallway has given Mommy greater peace of mind after she's turned off the lights for the night.

I was relieved recently when Mommy thought of my needs and came up with the idea of putting down large bed sheets to cover the carpet most everywhere downstairs. For the truth is I have been having accidents again over the past few days. Particularly when I would try to lift myself up to a standing position to greet her whenever she would come over to see me. And in doing so, I found myself straining—so much so that I haven't been able to control myself.

What's been really embarrassing for me, although I am so grateful my parents have never made an issue of it, is that I am not even aware of it when it happens.

So you can just picture the mess I have been making of myself, and why I am so touched that Mommy has so tenderly tried her "bestest" to reassure me while cleaning up everything, including me.

I know how hard that must be for her.

Not just the cleaning. But the stark realization that something she and I have come to take for granted—my impeccable cleanliness—can no longer be assumed.

How hard it must be for both my parents to accept something I have known for some time: the undeniable fact that my body is failing me with increasing regularity.

The worst example occurred earlier that week. During a walk that Mommy and I take together around the neighborhood, a time when I check in on those whose well-being I feel responsible for.

My equine friends Chippy, Baby, and their two pony pals, Shakey and Bakey, who live across the street, and Sinbad next door to us who's lost all of his hearing and has now developed cataracts. And of course, the two youngsters down the road: Paris, the young Collie I have taken under my wing, and Snoopy, the increasingly-protective-of-his-domain German Shepherd who lives across the road from Paris.

Mommy had stopped to talk to someone we knew. During or immediately after which (honestly I can't recall the details since everything happened so quickly), my body decided on its own to collapse. In a heap in the street! The look on Mommy's face of shock, fear, alarm, concern, and undoubtedly not a little bit of panic, made words totally unnecessary. My legs had splayed apart so wide that neither I nor Mommy could get me upright without the assistance of a Good Samaritan.

We both knew what this meant: Our long canine/human partnership had just crossed its own Rubicon. Towards a new life path for which there could be no question as to where it was now headed.

Though Mommy has related what happened to Daddy a couple of times since he got home, she and I have not talked about it all. There's been no need to.

Mommy and I both understand what happened and what it means.

Now all I have to do is get Daddy to understand too.

The opportunity to do so surfaced at 10:30 Thursday morning.

. . .

It took place in Mommy's study where again, as has been my wont over the past few weeks, I had retreated to get some sleep right after finishing off my breakfast. The music Daddy and I have listened together to for years, especially since the fire, was playing in the other room. Daddy had lain down next to me on the floor next to Mommy's desk, stroking my flanks and my muzzle and my head, so very gently as I have always loved. And as he did that, he asked me for a very personal favor: *"Big Girl,"* he whispered, *"I think I know we are doing the right thing, and that you're okay with it. But for your Mommy and me, can you please give us a signal . . . no matter what kind of signal . . . just any kind of signal that will tell us you agree with our decision"* . . .

By now, he didn't even try to hide his tears. Nor could Mommy either after she'd walked in and lay down on the other side of me, holding my body as close to her as she had ever done so before.

The depth of their sadness was visceral. It verged on despair. I felt it too—but in a different way. For I have always known that my connection with my parents is eternal, just as it has been and will be with my beloved Lucky, and all of my siblings who preceded my presence in our family.

Simply stated, I have been blessed with an innate knowledge: There is a *"passages of seasons"*—the inevitable cycles of life—I have already shared with you. Moreover, I and my siblings have always known in our heart of hearts that when the last of those seasons on earth of our respective life journeys would come to pass, our parents' unconditional love for each of us would ensure that none of us would have to endure unnecessary pain or discomfort while saying good-bye to each other. Comforted by the knowledge we will be reunited together again for eternity, when it's time.

Until which point, it will be up to us to keep our expanding family bench in Heaven warm for our parents, and all of those new children they will hopefully adopt, doing for them as they have done for each of us.

Hence, while I can understand, even appreciate my parents' profound sadness, I am totally at peace with where we are—where our life journey has come to. But it was clear to me that I had to find a way to explain to my parents in such a way that even through their sadness, they would understand my message that we were in total sync.

. . .

Around 1:30 p.m., I awoke from a very deep sleep in the hallway and walked over to the kitchen. Through the back door, I could see my parents on the "porchis" trying to relax with their daily reading.

It might have been the sight of them there, or maybe the wonderful weather we have experienced for the past few days, or maybe it was both. Whatever the reason, I decided to join them out there in the sunshine. Where, soon after I walked out onto the "porchis," I again curled up in my usual spot, in the shade of the table and chairs where my parents and I have enjoyed eating all the great meals from our lifetime of barbeques.

Thinking I was asleep, Mommy felt this was a good time for one of her long swims which is so good for her. And as she began her laps, Daddy took a seat on one of the chaise lounges next to the pool.

It brought to mind the only secret I have ever kept from my father: that whenever I see him go over to the pool, it's the one opportunity I have to fully relax and rest up, so that when need be, I'll be ready to do my job.

The same job Daddy is doing when he is in that chair beside the pool: guarding Mommy in case she runs into some trouble while she swims.

I guess it was a little over a half hour (my parents' time) later when I ambled over to look out the gate that leads to the stairs. Which, in turn, lead in one direction straight ahead to the stone pool deck and in the other to the remainder of our backyard. All of which borders on the edge of the forest immediately behind our "housis."

As subtly as possible, my eyes and nose took in all the details I would later need to recall.

The fact is I had something very important to do later. Something that I had been thinking about it ever since Daddy's earlier request of me.

Now, having had sufficient rest, and with the therapeutic effects of the warm sun making me feel much less arthritic and so much more able to move around, I knew the time would soon be just right to respond to his request. To unequivocally communicate to my parents who I love more than life itself: *"It is what it is. We have come to a crossroad in our life journey, and it's okay."*

To take advantage of this limited window of opportunity, however, would take an innate ability to reason, good timing, and thoughtfulness.

Fortunately, as you are aware by now, these are traits very much endemic to my ancestry.

· · ·

When it was finally time to do what I had to do, I got up slowly and walked over to the gate that separates the "porchis" from the pool area.

As soon as I did that, Daddy came over to open it.

I looked up and gave him a little wag at the tip of my tail. In return, as he always did, he gave me a pat on my head and a kiss on my nose.

I am sure he would have preferred my not knowing, but it was hard to ignore the incredible sadness his eyes revealed. Which only served to reinforce how desperately I wanted to communicate to both my parents that while I shared the poignancy of the meaning of this time together, I so very much wished they could also feel all of what I felt.

That this long weekend was not an end unto itself but is a path to a new beginning. One that would take me across a bridge—The Rainbow Bridge—to a place where no one hurt, no one is hungry, no one is alone, and everyone is happy.

I walked down the stairs of the "porchis."

However, rather than as I usually would, heading straight to the side of the pool to visit Mommy, instead I turned left and headed instead to the grassy area behind our house and next to "our" forest.

Daddy decided to join me. Together, we walked side by side, step by step in total silence.

The truth is we were both caught up deep in our own thoughts. Me—focused like a laser on my ultimate destination. And Daddy, realizing I had places to go and things I needed to do, he focused on doing his best to allow me to do what I needed to do.

That's the way it remained till we were about halfway across the lawn. When, without warning, Daddy suddenly bent down on his knees, took my face in his hands, looked right into my eyes and told me something else I will never ever forget.

"Prinny, I think I know where you are going and why you are doing so. So before you get there I need to tell you something: You are our 'bestest' girl . . . Your mommy and I love you so, so very much. You have been everything and more we could ever have asked for. You are our friend and protector—our life gift and, most of all, our daughter. We are so very proud of you."

It dawned on me that Daddy was sending me a message of his own. That he understood where we were on this little sojourn of ours. And that it would be up to us to be very strong for Mommy, as she too would eventually need to come to this same realization. It was, in fact, the same kind of pact Daddy and I had been making from the day Mommy was diagnosed with cancer. The same mutual understanding that each of us had a big job to do.

Staring into those so sad eyes of his, I returned his look in kind, with a slight nod of my head and pawing of the grassy area between us. The connection between us—and by definition between us and Mommy—was never closer, never tighter, as it was at this very moment.

All of which reinforced again what I had in mind with this very special walk of ours.

A "nuzzie" on my part indicated just that. It was also my way of saying we needed to keep moving.

So we did.

Until we arrived at a spot in the backyard immediately across from Daddy's study. A spot where Daddy can look out at any time and in his mind's eye see someone he's missed so very much for so long, someone with whom he enjoyed a relationship like that between Mommy and me.

It's a tiny spot, right on the edge of the forest, that I must have passed by hundreds if not thousands of times over the years. In all kinds of weather, doing all kinds of things such as playing tag with Lucky or playing "trow-ball" with Daddy.

This, however, is not just any "ole" spot in some backyard. It is, in fact, a plot of land my family cherishes as our own hallowed ground. For there under the Dogwood Bush where my nose directly pointed is where my late brother Smokey is buried.

For a split second, it struck me that for some, it might seem curious that in all those times I had passed by Smokey's grave, I had never before stopped, never previously pointed, had never taken the time to pay my respects to the one from whom I had inherited my third name: Spirit. For it was Smokey's spirit—an ingrained courage so strong and with an undeniable will to survive—that is still talked about by those who were privileged to know him.

That's why I looked up at Daddy. He nodded.

And then I lifted my head up as high as I could to take in the whole scene and all the accompanying scents, And followed that up by bending my head and neck as low to the ground as my arthritis would allow.

Daddy patted me on the head. I leaned against him as hard as I could.

He gave me a kiss on the nose. I gave him a little wag at the tip of my tail.

And then both of us turned our full attention back to Smokey's spot.

We didn't have to say anything more. My father and I were in full sync.

. . .

A few seconds later, we turned to walk back towards Mommy.

Back to where I could see Mommy in the distance standing in the water, right at the edge of the shallow end of the pool, where she had been intently watching Daddy and me.

She was standing there, with that wonderful smile of hers that has touched me since the very first moment of the first day we met.

The same smile, Daddy has told me so many times over the years, he too fell in love with. When they first met years before I was born.

I let her know I felt the same way with a nod of my head. And then with Daddy walking beside me, I picked up my pace to bring the three of us together.

. . .

And that's where I fainted. Passed out!

It must have been a huge scare for my parents.

In fact, in hearing their retelling of the story later that day and in the few days since, it seems it was quite something to behold.

Just as I got to within a few feet of Mommy, I suddenly collapsed. Without any warning! In a heap! Flat on my left side!

Apparently it had happened so quickly that neither Mommy nor Daddy was able to reach me before my body and my head hit the concrete pool deck.

And each had the same immediate reaction: They both thought I had died!

But they were too speechless to say anything!

I can only imagine their shock.

Shock mixed with a sense of foreboding and fear which was easy to understand.

I just lay there. Not moving. Seemingly (to them) unresponsive to their voices and their touch!

And that's where the three of us remained for quite some time: Mommy lying on one side of me, gently kissing my muzzle, and Daddy lying on the other side, tenderly stroking my face, my ears, and my flanks. Right up till I finally "came to" after what must have felt like an eternity.

I looked at both.

Every thought and emotion was written all over their faces: Concern . . . fear . . . even the sense of fatigue that comes from a long-awaited sense of the inevitable soon to pass.

And one other thing: The looks on both their faces conveyed total and absolute gratitude. A profoundly deep loving care that other than me, only my siblings would be able to describe. For they like me had experienced the same from our parents at a comparable time in each of their lives.

So I conveyed what they needed to know then and there with a little tail wag: *I was okay. We would all be okay.*

And to drive home the point, as soon as I was able, I rose as quickly as possible, shook off all the little stone remnants and dust of the pool deck that now covered a good part of my body, and proceeded purposefully up the stairs of the "porchis" where I took up my position, guarding over my parents' safety. And where I could overhear what they said to one another.

"Do you think she suffered a concussion or even fractured her skull?" Daddy asked. Mommy thought not.

From Daddy's facial expression, I could tell he was not convinced—but wanted to believe anything that would possibly assuage everything they were both feeling.

So I decided to help in my own way. I got up once more and walked over again to the door of the fence where they could more clearly see my tail wagging more vociferously this time, telling them, *"I really am fine, and no worse for wear."*

I guess they got it.

For I saw them turn to each other with that intimate look they have always had for each other when they are the only ones sharing a deep secret.

I also knew they got the bigger picture as well, when Mommy told my Daddy, *"I guess our Magic Girl just gave us the signal her father asked her for this morning."*

Daddy nodded his head knowingly, first at her, and then through the fence rails right at me. I nodded my head in reply. For I knew that he already knew, and now was happy that I had done what I had done on the side of the pool so that Mommy would know it too.

Not too long afterwards, all three of us called it a day— a nice day. A momentous day topped off with a barbeque dinner that evening, followed by a quiet reflective night together of reading and listening to some of our favorite music.

. . .

FRIDAY THRU MONDAY (LABOR DAY WEEKEND, 2007)

I'll be honest with you.

The four days leading up to the day after Labor Day passed as quickly as they did slowly. Each was mixed with our daily routines—the always delicious remnants of Daddy's daily breakfast muffin (and coffee) with Mommy; my two daily meals; my work in our office with Daddy as he worked on transcribing my thoughts into this book; my treasured private time with Mommy in her study as she worked on her computer; and then the equally cherished private time in the evening watching the box with pictures and voices and listening to music together in my den with my parents.

In that way, everything that had been our way of life together for almost three and a half years (my parents' time) remained just as it had been: a comfortable routine that was introduced by my parents—just for my benefit—after Lucky said good-bye.

Having said that, however, I would be remiss if I did not acknowledge that the routine as I've known it has increasingly been tinged with deepening emotion as time has gone by since Friday. And at times, Mommy and Daddy have tried to disguise (for themselves perhaps?) the reality the three of us have known is soon to come. Again I only wish they knew how much I could empathize with what they were feeling. And yet I feel very comfortable with all of it.

And so, in my own way, I have tried my best to let them know.

Yet as much as I have done so, I have also come to appreciate the fundamental differences in the makeup of our respective species. As any of my siblings have known, as have I, accepting the inevitability of life's full cycles is fundamentally easier for us than for our parents.

. . .

One thing Mommy, Daddy, and I have always enjoyed—but even more so these last few days—have been the walks we take around the neighborhood. Doing so also gave me a chance to check in with all my friends of nature. That is, except for Snoopy, who unfortunately for me, but lucky for him, was at his "beachis housis" with his family the whole time.

The weather was perfect—not too hot, not too cold. So I got to enjoy it without undue discomfort and even better, without scaring my parents as I had Mommy when I had that problem getting up from the street gutter when Daddy was away.

As I said, there's been a nice, almost routine normalcy to the last few days.

But there's also been a lot more, and that's what I will always remember.

Throughout these past few days, the machine that rings that my parents pick up and then talk into has been a mixture of total silence and intense spurts of activity. I've heard my name talked about in incredibly soft, loving, tender tones by each of my parents. I've also heard and witnessed firsthand their tears during those calls.

So I know what they have been talking about.

It hasn't been just the calls, but also seeing my friends and relatives who have come by the "housis" and stopped to talk to me during our walks.

I have very much appreciated their hugs and petting, their kisses and stroking. I've been touched by the gentle whispers of their love and mutual respect and admiration and affection, their expressions of awe and "bestest" wishes for me.

Moreover, as much as it's been wonderful for me, more importantly, I know how much it has meant to my parents.

Everyone has been so nice.

That's why I have asked my father to thank them all: our neighbors and friends who stopped to talk to us.

I have also asked Daddy to thank all those who have e-mailed my parents since my father returned home from his trip last Wednesday. And all the others who have called or wanted to call or even those who found it too difficult to call but knew my parents knew they cared. And those like my Mommy's mommy who so graciously passed down her love of those like me to her daughter, and others like my Aunt Linda and my Uncle Lonny, and my Daddy's mommy and daddy who called several times from my other country of origin, Canada, to convey their regards.

I wish I could, but I really cannot remember everyone and certainly don't want to leave anyone out. But I'm confident my parents will at the right time find a way to let everyone who should know just how grateful I am.

If it's okay with all of you; however, I'd like to take this one opportunity to especially thank two of my closest friends.

One of them, Uncle Brian, came over Friday night.

He and I must have spent a good hour (my parents' time) alone together. Huddled on the floor in Mommy's study and then again in my den, we did as we have always done throughout the years he has spent as my sitter, and then after we both grew up and matured as one of each others' "bestest" friends. We sat in silence—Uncle Brian stroking me . . . and me "nuzzying" him.

I know Mommy and Daddy feel the same way about him as I do: He is part of our family—and always will be.

My other "bestest" friend is also very special: my Uncle Dr. Greg Hahn. He, as you know, has been my family doctor—just as he was for my sister Samantha and my sweet Lucky—ever since the day my parents brought me from the orphanage. He's the one who's taken care of me when I've most needed to be taken care of. He's everything one could want in a family doctor: possessing a very calm demeanor, a very peaceful look, a very clean hospital, a very gentle touch, and a wonderful smile. He's someone I will always remember. One who combines the absolute very "bestest" of those who take care of those like me: knowledge and compassion and caring.

. . .

TUESDAY: THE DAY AFTER LABOR DAY

By now you probably realize Uncle Dr. Greg is coming over to the "housis" in just a little while. As such I have asked both of my parents for an unusual favor. While I have really appreciated sleeping for a while in their arms, all three of us lying down on the comfortable carpet in Mommy's study along side of her desk, I really want them to accompany me on another walk around our neighborhood. For I have others to see—and to say something to— before Uncle Dr. Greg gets here.

. . .

Now that we've returned, I'm so happy we did that. I did what I had to do, and doing so, I know meant a lot to my parents. You should have seen the looks on their faces when Chippy and Baby (my horsey friends) saw me crossing the street. First, they stood and saluted me with nods of their heads from atop of the hill outside their barn. Then they whinnied. And then each walked down from where they stood so that we could, and did, get to share one more quiet moment together.

I didn't have to explain in detail what I wanted them to know: The rapport we have developed ever since they were adopted and brought to their barn across the street from our "housis" has evolved into a wonderful and cherished friendship of mutual respect. They know I am counting on them to look out for my parents, just as I know my parents will for Chippy and Baby and their new sibling ponies: Shakey and Bakey.

It got even better when we walked over to where Paris and her family live. As usual, she wished to romp and play. So we did a bit of that together after which we had an important chat. I told her how proud I was of the fine young lady she was turning into. And that I wanted her to continue to strive to be her "bestest,"—which will include taking care of her family as well as she could.

It became clear my message was resonating with her.

For by now, it was obvious to my parents and me that for one of the few times ever, I had Paris' full, totally undistracted attention. She sat still and straight and looked directly into my eyes as I communicated: *"I'm counting on you to do what you need to do to get my parents to smile again."*

In a way she knew I would know, Paris promised she would.

I then led my parents across to the other side of the street one more time so that I could share some thoughts with my young pal Snoopy. But like I said before, he wasn't there. So we backtracked to where the horses and I had just spent our time together, after which we crossed over to see if Sinbad was home. He wasn't.

I pulled Mommy and Daddy into our driveway where I suddenly stopped and took a full, slow 360 degree turn.

This moment in time was just for me.

Having accomplished everything I had set out to do when I had asked my parents to accompany on me on this very special walk, I now wanted to take in the full senses and scents and sights of my whole domain that's become as much a part of me as anything else in my life.

As I was doing that, my parents hugged each other and then me tightly. In that second, we were all saying the same thing, *"We are family and will always be part of each other."*

Inside I was smiling.

. . .

I still am.

Here where both of my parents are again lying on either side of me on the carpet in the study I share with Mommy.

I can feel Mommy's whole body shaking, holding me tightly from behind, while in front of me, Daddy is gently stroking my head, face, and my ears, as his eyes peer at me peering right back at him.

"Take all the time you want," I heard Dr. Uncle Greg quietly tell them just after he arrived, right after he and I had greeted each other in our usual manner.

It's a good thing he did that. He really understood Mommy and Daddy, and I wanted this moment to last as long as we could.

The truth is even as long as all of us have known it's been coming, it didn't make it easier on any us, particularly my parents. If it were up to them, if they could have, we'd stay like this forever.

I love them so . . . so . . . so . . . so . . . so . . . very . . . very . . . much.

In the same way I have known they love me too—and have, *"forever and a day"* as Daddy keeps repeating to me.

Mommy is crying hard now.

If only I could make her sadness go away. Making her happy, while in my protection, has been part of my job since the day we met at the orphanage. If I could make a wish come true right this second, I know exactly what it would be: *I'd find a way to share my comfort, my acceptance, with her.*

Daddy's tears are streaming down his face too. Yet that shy smile I have come to love also is telling me it's okay—that he'll take good care of Mommy.

How far our father/daughter relationship has come!

I am so, so very happy that he opened himself up despite his sadness after our beloved Lucky— whom we both cherished so much— said his good-bye.

Dr. Uncle Greg has moved to a spot right in front of me. He's telling me I am *"such a good girl."* So is Mommy. So is Daddy. They are all saying the same thing. Uncle Greg is trying his best to smile between the tears that are now welling in his eyes.

Something I've never observed before. But it doesn't surprise me. He has never hidden the special place he holds me in his heart. Much more than doctor/patient, we are "bestest friends."

He's kneeling in front of me now.

He reached for my paw with one hand while stroking my head with his other.

But I pulled back.

I heard Daddy say, *"It's okay, Prinny. We love you . . . we love you so much . . . It's okay, girl . . . it's okay, girl . . . we will never forget you girl . . . You will always be part of us forever and a day . . . It's okay, girl . . . You'll be with Lucky soon."*

So like the "goodest" girl I have always been, without prompting, I simply handed my paw to Uncle Greg so that he would not have to ask a second time.

Mommy was crying so hard behind me, and I did what I could to try to comfort her. I've moved my body back closer to hers. Almost as if we were one. Just like those nights when I was so young and recuperating from my hip surgery, we would lie together as close as close can be, in the den where we lived and slept together, and talked to each other late into the night.

For a second, Uncle Greg and Daddy stopped to watch these special moments between Mommy and me. They have known better than anyone the depth of our relationship, the mutual unconditional love and respect my mother and I have for each other. It's been one that's known no barriers or borders or limitations or self-consciousness. And that will continue to go on in our hearts forever and a day.

As Daddy has said so many times, *"Your two souls were joined at the heart even before you met."*

Uncle Greg just took out something to wrap tightly around my paw. And I just saw the needle. But I didn't cringe. I'm not surprised. I've known what's coming and what it's meant to achieve. I'm not scared. I've seen it before, on the day my beloved Lucky said good-bye and now again as he awaits me on our family bench with all of my siblings, friends, and Mommy's daddy.

"Greg, it won't hurt, will it?" I heard Daddy ask.

I already knew the answer.

But when I saw my uncle, the doctor shake his head, it still made me feel good that Daddy had asked. He and Mommy needed to know for sure.

Mommy's holding me even closer to her. I can see one of her hands intertwined with one of Daddy's right in front of me.

Daddy's now telling me how much he and Mommy have loved me. And he just asked me to say hello to everyone when I get to Heaven. To tell everyone how much we miss them and love them.

He just leaned over and kissed my nose!

"That's something special for you to take with you to share with Lucky, okay girl?"

"Okay, Daddy," I smiled with my eyes focused on his.

I can feel the slightest pressure of Uncle Greg putting something into the tube that he's connected to my paw.

"It's okay, Mommy and Daddy . . . . I love you so much . . . Hold me tight . . .

It doesn't hurt at all . . .

I can smell Lionmonkee and Fluffy and Periwinkle and KissKiss right next to me . . . I love them so much . . . Please take care of them for me . . .

It's okay . . . It's kind of relaxing—a really nice feeling . . .

For the first time since I can't remember when, I am feeling no pain whatsoever . . .

I can feel myself getting a bit tired . . . .

It feels different . . . but it's okay . . . it's really okay . . .

I feel like I am going somewhere 'goodest' . . .

I hear music . . .

I see the Rainbow Bridge . . .

Everyone's smiling . . . and waving . . .

I see Lucky!!!!!!!!!!!!!!!!!!!!!!!!!!!!!!!!!!!!!!

I heard you Mommy . . . I love you too . . .

I will ALWAYS be your Magic Girl"

"ONE SMALL STAR"

"When I need to feel you near me
I stand in this quiet place
Where the silver light of countless stars
Falling on my face
Though they all shine so brightly
Somehow it comforts me to know
That some that burn the brightest
Died an eternity ago

But your light still shines
It's one small star to guide me
And it helps me to hold back the dark
Your light's still shining in my heart

I'm learning how to live without you
And I never thought I could
And even how to smile again
I never thought I would
And I cherish your heart's memories
Cause they bring you back to life
Some caress me gently
And some cut me like a knife

Can your soul be out there some where
Beyond the infinity of time
I guess you've found some answers now
I'll have to wait for mine
When my light joins with yours one day
We'll shine through time and space
And one day fall on a distant age
Upon some stranger's face

But your light still shines
It's one small star to guide me
And it helps me to hold back the dark
Your light's still shining in my heart
Your light's still shining in my heart"

LIFE AFTER MAGIC GIRL

A Father Remembers

A DAY LIKE NO OTHER

Carrying Princess Sheba Spirit's body out of what she knew as her country "housis" for the very last time is something I will never forget. The memory remains as strong and vivid today, months later, as it did the day after Labor Day.

I never know when it will surface. But it most surely does on a regular basis.

When it happens during the day, it is invariably accompanied by immediate tears, just as writing about it does right now. While at night, it wakes me up from even the deepest sleep.

It is what it is—an indelible life marker that will stay with me forever and a day. Or at least as long as my own memory continues to effectively serve me.

For the simple truth is this: in life, Princess Sheba Spirit was for Bobbie and me our once-in-a-lifetime canine gift. And ever since the day the three of us said good-bye to each other the day after Labor Day, she remains a fixture in our hearts. Still very much a part of our life journey together.

And so while the departure of that life-spirit that flowed so strongly through her right up to the very last moment of her final breath that day meant she could no longer feel our touch and kisses, the spirit of her life continues to profoundly touch us months later in ways so unexpected . . . and so welcome.

Simply stated, she is and will forever be as much a part of us in spirit as she ever was in life— just in different, but no less significant ways.

. . .

Bobbie and I lay with Princess for what seemed like a very long time after her beloved Uncle Greg did what his medical training had prepared him to do. A professional activity he's carried out hundreds if not thousands of times before.

His professors would have been proud of him: he was gentle and caring and compassionate.

However, even they would have observed the inordinately deep sadness so vividly etched on his face.

He didn't have to say anything. His facial expression conveyed his feelings better than any words might have done at the time.

Our good friend Greg Hahn not only shared our painful emptiness. To Doctor Uncle Greg, Princess had been much more than a canine patient.

She had been to him, as she was to us, a "once-in-a-lifetime."

Gratefully, what he had carried out was both painless and very quick. Upon reflection, it's the latter that told us everything: while Princess' lioness-like strength of spirit and will power had stayed with her to the very last moment of her life, her heart and her body were clearly exhausted.

She was ready to leave.

It's just that we weren't ready to let go completely. The truth was that well after her life-spirit had finally left us to join everyone keeping our family bench warm for all of us in Heaven, neither Bobbie nor I could, would, or wanted to let go of her body.

We kissed her muzzle and her forehead and her ears. Trying to imprint on our souls forever the memory of her sweet smell and feel of her oh-so-soft velvety fur.

We kept stroking her and petting her in all the special places we knew she would sense our touch wherever she now resided in spirit, even if she could no longer physically feel it.

For Bobbie and me, we had come to a major life journey crossroad. One we knew for months was looming. One from which there would be no turning back. One, we knew without ever directly saying to each other that once that road was crossed, nothing would ever be the same.

I think now that's why we tried so hard for as long as we could—as long as Prinny wanted us to—keep her going. Till we got to this point, where even if our hearts tried as hard as we could to will her to continue for one more day, and would have done anything to make it possible, we knew it was time.

She told us so.

And now that she was gone, we still didn't want to let go because we knew in our heart of hearts that to do so would be to say good-bye forever. To everything and anything we had come to know and accept—everything that had been a part of the continuum of our life journey together from Smokey onwards.

In short, we knew that saying good-bye to Princess would and will forever mean that nothing would ever be the same. And that's been exactly the way it's been.

As I said before, obviously we'd always known that. But there's a huge gap between knowing it and living it—HUGE.

. . .

To his credit, Greg did not rush us.

Instead, he kept to his own private thoughts, as he waited and watched, and reflected on the almost sixteen years of mutual trust and respect that had been so much a part of his working relationship with Princess.

Through my own tears, I saw him tear up a couple of times as Bobbie and I continued to hold and hug and pet and lovingly stroke and kiss and whisper to his late patient, our never-to-be-forgotten gifted canine.

On the two occasions our eyes met as I happened to look up, he slightly nodded his head in my direction.

It was his way of saying he understood the excruciating emptiness we both knew Bobbie especially was feeling.

For Prinny had not only been her "find"— but her "doghter", and friend, and support, and cheerleader, and pride and joy, and everything more that a cancer companion dog is for those in Bobbie's position. As Bobbie often said of Princess, *"She is my heart—there is no beginning or end between us."*

Said simply, no amount of rationalizing or planning or steeling oneself emotionally lessens the hurt and pain of her unique loss.

The fact is Greg and I had for a long time shared our own private secret, a mutual concern about this very moment and its eventual impact on Bobbie. It was something we'd touched on discretely, almost in passing, over the past few years as Prinny evolved from her prime to well-beyond canine seniority.

We knew that saying a final good-bye to Princess would be one of the saddest moments in Bobbie's own life journey.

Indeed, it was a moment in time I had thought about and for which I had tried to prepare—for a long time. Ever since that very special day, the day I brought Bobbie home from New York after her cancer surgery. When she'd worried whether Princess would remember her after being gone for thirteen days.

As you all know by now Prinny's actions that day said everything that had to be said.

By carefully and slowly and gently crawling up onto the bed where Bobbie lay bruised and battered by hours-long, life-altering cancer surgery, putting her head down on Bobbie's shoulder where Princess stayed protecting the human mother who had saved *her* canine life. And where, in so many other ways, Princess remained—for every day of the rest of her life.

Now, on the day after Labor Day, 2007, twelve plus years later, we had said our final good-bye to her with reverence and respect in prayer, and with our deepest thanks for a life so incredibly well lived.

To see, as Greg and I had anticipated, Bobbie so totally and completely shattered will forever remain one of the profoundly saddest moments of my life. She could not hide what she felt. Her heart was broken. The depth of her loss was as palpable as it was inevitable.

All of us who know her and care for her had wished—even before the event itself—that we could somehow take Bobbie's pain away. So that somehow she could have skipped this inevitable part of unconditional love and breathtaking loss. But we knew we couldn't. And those who really understood didn't even try.

For we all knew this was one of life's cycles she would have to eventually get through . . . on her own timetable . . . in her own way. To help her break through the maze of despair, she would wear like a suit of armor for weeks. To help bring back that soft, almost shy smile she saves for those she's closest to. To help her find solace, and then once again allow joy and laughter into her deeply wounded heart.

. . .

As Greg began the process of wrapping Prinny's body for her last ever ride to his office, I hugged Bobbie as close as I ever had in our life journey. I whispered how proud I was of both her and Prinny, and thanked her for allowing me to be a part of their once-in-a-lifetime relationship. Bobbie held on so tightly. So much so it struck me how strong she is versus how weak she'd been when she had been sick, when she had had to bear so much physical pain.

On this day, though this pain was different, the pain of a broken heart is no less excruciating.

Bobbie watched carefully as Greg and I gently lay Prinny in the backseat of his car. I made sure her face was uncovered; she always hated not being able to see around her.

Greg hugged Bobbie as I said my last good-bye to Princess. With gentle kisses on the top of her forehead and on her velvety muzzle, and final words of gratitude for our partnership in caregiving for her mother—from the edge of death from *"complications from cancer"* to the medical miracle of hope Bobbie's life has come to personify to so many.

Finally, it was time for Greg to go.

We shook hands, as men like us usually do. I thanked him for everything he'd ever done for Princess and for all of our snarfs, save for Smokey who he never got to meet. He seemed touched that in Prinny's honor, we handed him whatever fresh chicken and cans of chicken his patients could use at his clinic.

He and we knew Princess would have wanted it that way.

I told him how much we respected his professionalism and valued his (and wife Beth's) friendship. I also wanted him to know we knew how much Princess trusted him.

For her, trust was synonymous with love.

That's when Greg and I surprised ourselves: We hugged.

As we did I whispered I needed one more second to collect my thoughts. To compose myself. To try to figure out what I would say to Bobbie in the next few seconds.

You see, I knew that upon reentering our home, life as Bobbie and I had known it had just changed forever. For the first time, after an extraordinary twenty-eight-year run—from that day in 1979 in Charlotte North Carolina when Bobbie brought home Smokey snuggled against her breast, to my last kiss on Prinny's forehead and muzzle and promise we'd see her soon when it is our turn to go to our family bench—Bobbie and I would be totally alone.

. . .

Neither of us wanted to stay in the house. It already seemed empty and hollow.

Clutching hands tightly together, we walked up the street.

As we neared their pasture across the street, the horses looked back at us from near their barn. They whinnied.

To us, it seemed clear: They wanted us to know they understood they would miss their friend Princess too. But they would also look out for us just as we had committed to Princess—during her final good-bye to them just a couple of hours before—that we would do our best to always look out for them on her behalf.

That's when it hit us like a thunderbolt: If the horses realized their loss of a friend, we could not imagine how much Paris, her baby Collie pal and protégé neighbor, would miss her.

How do you explain to a hero-worshipping puppy that her best pal, the one she looked up to most, the one animal she wanted to impress most of all, would never come by her home again to say hello?

Moreover, how do you explain that no one was to blame? That no one had done anything wrong. That her love for Prinny had been reciprocal; that Prinny too had come to treasure those moments together—as much as Paris looked forward to them with so much anticipation every day.

So Bobbie and I made an immediate decision: For Paris, our actions would speak louder than anything any human could say. A few hours later, we went over to Paris' family's house where we met and talked awhile with our neighbors Janie and Rob and their wonderful daughters. They could not have been more empathetic, nor compassionate, nor thoughtful. They wanted us to know they really understood how we felt.

They also wanted us to know how incredibly touched they were that we had brought something special to give to Paris.

It was one of Prinny's favorite "monkees," one that had her scent deeply infused in it.

Our hope was authentic if perhaps a bit naive, that even if Prinny's physical presence would never again grace Paris in life, the latter might be forever comforted by Prinny's scent.

To this day, months later, apparently Prinny's "monkee" remains the only toy Paris has ever carried around in her mouth as she roams, wagging her tail, from room to room as she looks in on her family.

It would be only the first of several "signs" Princess has transmitted to us since the day after Labor Day, a day like no other for Bobbie and me.

The second occurred seconds after we'd said good-bye to Paris and her family that afternoon.

Chippy and Baby, Prinny's equine friends, literally pranced over to us, right to the edge of their pasture fence, as soon as they saw we were near. Rushing over to us in a way they never had before—nor have they since. Both were even gentler than ever. They nuzzled our fingers as we fed them carrots and reassured them that their canine pal was okay. That she was in a better place where all of us, including both of them, were destined to meet up again sometime.

Another "sign" occurred a day later, when Snoopy, the loud and rambunctious German Shepherd across the street, stopped and sat straight up in total silence, as if in salute for a fallen colleague as we walked by his family's home. He'd never done it before—he's never done it since.

. . .

The phone didn't ring much the evening of the day after Labor Day. Everyone we knew seemed to appreciate that Bobbie and I needed some quiet personal time to process the events of this day.

We were emotionally drained.

We left everything exactly as it had been. We could not bear removing Prinny's food bowls from the kitchen nor any of her beloved "monkees" from wherever she had left them on the first floor of her "housis" and upstairs in the office.

Seeing them all inevitably brought more tears. As did the deafening silence which had replaced the usual *slurp-slurp* sound as Prinny would drink her water, and the sounds of *clump-clumping* paws on the floor, and the clanging sound of her neck chains as she'd shake her head to tell us she was nearby and had something to tell us.

. . .

Now, as I look back on that extraordinary life-changing day for Bobbie and me, I now realize that my heart was broken too. I just didn't know it right at that moment. Nor did I know how deeply—nor how difficult acknowledging the good-bye to Princess would continue to be for me.

To be honest, it's something I am still coming to terms with.

Right up to this very moment—even as I write this line.

EVER SINCE NEVER THE SAME

The next morning, we left for Montreal.

We had no choice no matter what the circumstances. Months before we'd happily confirmed we'd be attending a three-day-long, very special celebration of the life of my most favorite aunt. Someone Bobbie and I have become close to over the years.

We cried the whole drive to Montreal and couldn't help crying much of the way back, three days later.

When Bobbie would nod off in the passenger's seat, it was as if the melody and lyrics of every song on the radio had an audio memory stamped of Princess.

And when the music stopped, silence gave way to introspection.

Which in turn gave way to the knowledge that when we would finally arrive home, it would be to a totally empty house. Devoid of all that canine love we were so accustomed to and had truly come to treasure over the past almost thirty years.

There would be no wagging of tails, no *clump clump* of paws on the wood floors, no *slurp slurp* of water being drunk out of bowls.

All of which, in turn, gave way to even more tears.

It was inevitable of course.

It was all part of mourning the inestimable loss we felt. From the moment we left for Montreal, to the moment we returned home.

If anything, the trip to my city of birth and half of my life should have been, and had been to some extent, a welcome distraction. One of joy and happiness for my aunt, shared by Bobbie and me and a couple of hundred of my aunt's other family members and friends.

Unfortunately, distractions only delay—they are not a surrogate for—grief and mourning. Part of the inevitable life cycle we needed to get through.

. . .

Two days after we got back from Montreal, Princess decided to send another "sign." I guess she'd heard the wish I'd shared with Bobbie as we sat having our traditional Sunday morning coffee on the deck.

"Boulie, I miss her so much . . . I just wish she'd give us some kind of sign . . . anything . . . something that will give us some comfort . . . just to let us know she's okay."

The next day at 12:35 p.m., that wish came true.

Bobbie was out. And I was working at my computer desk. The one I am sitting at right now, the one overlooking the forest behind our home. I was trying to compose an e-mail but frankly was having difficulty doing so. The harder I tried, the more difficult it became getting my words the way I wanted them to sound.

Looking back, I am not surprised.

I was trying to draft Prinny's final obituary.

So that it would read the way she would have wanted all of her family and friends all over the world to learn of her departure for our family bench in Heaven.

I was struggling with the task at hand.

To be consistent with her inbred selflessness, I knew in my heart of hearts she'd want the tone to be low-key, without exaggeration. But also to fully reflect the extraordinary relationship her family and she had shared.

What she meant to us—and we to her and her siblings.

Even today, I still don't know or understand why, as there hadn't been any sudden movement or sound or anything for that matter. But whatever it was that caused me to do so, all of a sudden, I found myself looking up from the keyboard out towards behind our fence and the forest beyond. Where, standing totally motionless was nothing less than a spectacular adult male reindeer with a *huge* rack of horns.

We have seen many deer over the years—a few males but most were females with and without their babies. But I had never seen this big guy before.

He was almost statuelike. He didn't move at all. He looked straight ahead—not up towards my direction nor down at the ground. Just straight ahead. For maybe five minutes.

He showed no fear whatsoever.

Then all of a sudden, he moved quite deliberately to his left, my right. Until he stood directly behind the spot where we have a statue of a deer that marks the spot where Smokey is buried.

The big buck looked straight ahead . . . and then down . . . and then pawed at the ground with his left foot. And then he stopped. And then he pawed even longer with his other foot.

And then he turned around and slowly but purposefully walked back into the forest.

I stared out the window a little longer. Until he was out of my eyesight. And then I went downstairs to the den to think about what had just transpired.

When the buck came back the next day, at exactly the same time in the identical spot, but this time looked up right at the window from where I sat watching him, in awe, I didn't need any further convincing.

Think what you will; say what you must.

All I can say I've never for a second had a doubt that Princess heard my wish. It was her way of saying she was happy, healthy, and strong—just as was this buck.

And knowing this seemed to free up the words which flowed into the text of the e-mail Bobbie and I eventually forwarded to all those who had ever come to know Princess:

"We said goodbye to Prinny Tuesday Sept. 4, 2007 for the last time when her vet came to our home and lovingly helped her go to sleep.

She was incredibly peaceful. And oh so incredibly beautiful. We had made our decision about her last week and spent the long holiday, along with special friends, saying all we wanted to have her know before she would leave us. Yet right up to the end, she took us for a last walk to see her canine pals and also the horses who live across from our house who whinnied at her and came to say goodbye. It's just what she wanted to do, hard as it was for her to walk so short a distance, yet for her so far.

For those who didn't know Lucky, our 'Mr. Sweetness' and the love of each other's lives, attached is a favorite photo of the two of them together (Lucky on the left, Prinny resting on the right) as they now will be for all time: young, passionate, loving, spirited, and always joined at the hip. EVERYONE commented on them.

We had a life gift in Princess, and so the hole is HUGE.

But she is now being cared—and caring—for Bobbie's dad—and all of our other snarfs who have gone before her, and eventually for us.

Candidly, we can't wait to join all of them, but know she will be our guardian angel till that happens.

We treasure the joy she brought us, for allowing us to peer inside and walk through her window to nature and to witness how all these wonderful creatures interact. It is truly impossible to fathom waking up each day knowing we won't hear her wolfing down her food, or padding around the house, or shaking her head to make noise with the tags on her collar for us to wake and join her in her 'morning muffin' routine.

But we will wake, and we will be thankful for every moment she graced us with during her lifetime.

She was not just a beautiful creature we have sent on the next part of her journey.

Bred to 'do her job,' she was also Bobbie's cancer companion dog to the last moment of her life. She saved our home and her canine siblings and Dick from a fire in our home at one point when Bobbie was hospitalized. Later she literally served as a guide dog for our Lucky when he lost his sight and hearing—until the day we and she said goodbye to him.

In short, she was an extraordinary 'once-in-a-lifetime', remarkable presence in our lives, and we genuinely feel blessed to have been part of her life.

Being unable to have human kids due to the cancer, this is the first time in 28 years together that we are 'on our own.' It is a very strange sensation.

But we know she is at peace and that is the only thing that counts. Heaven has gotten better and better this week with her presence. And when you look at their photo below, you too will know how content those two now are forever."

Bobbie and Dick

Lucky and Princess
Together Again

ONE HUNDRED DAYS LATER

It's been almost exactly one hundred days since I saw that buck.

Neither Bobbie nor I can believe it's been that long since we said good-bye to Princess.

Even more so, neither can we believe how quickly it has passed.

In fact, so much has transpired between then and now, on so many levels, that we've just focused on getting back to the basics by focusing even harder on taking things one day at a time, one challenge at a time.

And when something "positive" has knocked at the door, well we've just opened up, put out our welcome mat, and grasped it before it slipped away.

. . .

It has been a remarkable period of transition and change.

Marked by things we had started to seriously talk about possibly doing after she would be gone, even before Prinny left. Not just talk—but planning—for new things.

Such as travel. Not for business but rather for ourselves, for the first time in almost twenty years.

Places we know and adore like New Zealand, and the UK, and Ireland, and Italy for sure. And other places such as Scotland and Israel and perhaps even the Mediterranean for the very first time.

Just for ourselves.

No timetables; nothing formal.

Bobbie's reasoning at least had a legitimate purpose: *"We need to reawaken our thinking, open our minds to new things . . . get ahead of things like we used to"* was the way she put it.

My reasoning was far more basic. I knew we needed to get away from the cavernous emptiness of a home suited for more than just the two of us.

To me, life seemed not just empty; it felt hollow.

Travel now made sense. There was no compelling need to wait.

We had fulfilled our commitment to Princess . . . and to ourselves: As long as she was with us, we had known that travel for travel sake was not an option. She needed us as she neared the end of her earthly life. And we needed to be with her just as much.

Now we were free to do what we wanted to do when we wanted to do it.

All we had to do was figure out a prudent way to work it around our professional Executive Coaching and Strategy Consulting commitments we were so proud of.

No need!

Totally out of left field, two longstanding client relationships disappeared faster than I can write this sentence.

It had nothing to do with us.

One client quit *his* corporate presidency to join his biggest competitor. He gave his employer notice—*an hour or two*, and informed me *by voicemail.*

"It's perfect for me and my family. I don't have to tell you how good of an opportunity this is for me . . . the really big money it could mean . . . You've been a fantastic coach and you know I will never let you down."

It was an interesting voicemail from a man I have never heard from since.

You can imagine how Bobbie and I felt.

But as Prinny taught us, in life, there is a reason for everything, even if we don't know it at the time.

. . .

Simultaneously, another senior executive coaching client was offered and took over the job of *his* dreams.

He called personally to let me know. His excitement was palpable. And then he said that beginning immediately he could no longer utilize my services as *"it would not look good for me politically around here—I could be viewed as weak . . . I'm sure you understand."*

. . .

Coming on top of saying good-bye to Princess, it has seemed almost surrealistic at times. All of which has had the feeling of our lives unraveling . . . out of control.

Though clearly the circumstances are very different, the feeling is similar to the events of thirteen winters ago.

When within weeks of Bobbie's cancer diagnosis, she had collapsed and been hospitalized due to her system "going toxic" with peritonitis from the combined massive doses of radiation and chemotherapy poured into her. From which she lost not only her memory, but control over her bodily functions.

During the same time, we experienced the fire Princess recounted earlier.

I suppose that's what led me to decide to reread a book I had written, chronicling that whole cancer experience. In particular, to focus on the chapters that dealt with the life lessons I personally had gleaned from the most challenging period of the life partnership journey Bobbie and I have shared for three decades.

Doing so turned out to be a good thing. For it forced me to refocus on a few fundamental thoughts about the vagaries of life.

First and foremost, there's a reason for everything. We just don't always know at the time what those reasons are.

Second, cancer was a genuine crisis. Having gotten through that, we could get through most anything.

Now thirteen years later, with events and forces beyond our control seemingly taking us onto as yet unidentified new paths in our life journey, we needed to be open to the experience. To be prepared once again to embrace the unknown.

In that context, while travel may have *sounded* like a viable option, offering up as it did the possibility for some frivolity—a light-hearted escape from the emptiness and sadness and vicissitudes of life we were feeling right now—gut instinct told me it was something we could live with or without. At least for now.

It was laughter and joy Bobbie and I couldn't live without. Laughter and joy that would help repair our broken hearts. Laughter and joy that for us would come fastest and best in the form of familiar sounds: the *clump clumping* of paws roaming our halls and climbing the steps, food being "snarfed" and water being slurped.

That's when it hit me.

At the end of the day, for Bobbie and me, there is nothing more fulfilling or more satisfying than being parents to our canine family members. Without them, our life feels empty.

With them, they help make us the "bestest" we can be . . .

And thanks to the spirit of our wonderful Magic Girl, the new little one she sent us, our beautiful Cardigan Welsh Corgi, Panda Petunia Ruach, is filling our lives, our hearts, and our souls once again.

A LETTER FROM PRINNY:
LIFE PRINCIPLES TO LIVE BY

To my brothers and sisters (whom I do not yet know but will always look out for):

By the time you learn of this letter, I will have already joined everyone else keeping our family bench warm in Heaven. For me, it will not be a time to mourn, but one to celebrate—the time when my cycle of life comes full circle. But before I do, I thought I'd leave you a few, very personal thoughts from an older sister, and leave it to Daddy to decide how and when to share them with you.

First and foremost, as you will come to know in time, "*you have no idea how good of a life you are about to enjoy.*" You don't have to take my word for it. It's something each and every one of you—no matter your size or shape, age or color, gender or breed—will hear again and again. From those who know our parents and will get to know you, upon meeting you for the first time and many times thereafter.

That you are so incredibly fortunate to have joined this, our family pack, is not something you will understand right way. But will in due course come to profoundly appreciate. For it's real and true and as basic as the air we breathe.

Simply put, being unable to have children of their own making, our parents have dedicated themselves to make our lives the absolute "bestest."

That is why I feel so fortunate. I have had a wonderful life. One which has been more than fulfilling in so many ways.

From an abandoned childhood, to adoption by a family that has given me everything and more. So that I might reach—even exceed— the fullest of my potential. So that even now, as I find myself on the cusp of leaving for our family bench, I still bathe in the bliss and happiness and respect and unconditional love of our parents. As has been the case from the day I left the orphanage for a completely different life journey than I might have ever imagined.

Just like you.

Which is why, for me, life has been *"a good and interesting run,"* as Daddy would say.

During which I have had many questions answered, about a lot of different things I have had the opportunity to observe, to experience, and to think about. To which the answers have evolved slowly, over time. Into what I would best describe as a series of life lessons for me that have helped form the basis of core life principles your late brother Lucky and I lived by.

And I will continue to do so. And you, I hope, may decide to do so too.

You need to know these are *my* thoughts for which I take full ownership. Some are very personal; others, more philosophical. I guess you might say they represent the breadth of my interests. An insatiable curiosity which I hope you too will have about everything in life. And the continual capacity to not just live—but to live and learn.

In reading this, I don't ask you to accept my assertions for anything other than what they are meant to be.

That is, before it's my time to join the other members of our family who have been keeping our bench in Heaven warm, I just wanted to chronicle a few of the "bestest" lessons I have learned from a life journey blessed with so many—and such great reward.

In return for which, in the event you, my future siblings—or for that matter anyone reading this memoir—might have some life lessons and principles you may eventually wish to share, I certainly hope you would consider doing so.

For it is my deepest belief that for every idea that is shared with another, a new light of enlightenment is switched on by that one, for the other.

That's one of my life lessons and core principles.

Here are some others:

Take nothing for granted about life other than the knowledge that your parents will do absolutely anything for you to make sure you will be happy and healthy.

You will discover over time that not everyone of our kind has parents with the means to ensure you will get the "bestest" medical care when you are sick, nor the right food to eat to keep you healthy. Nor will every parent be able to do what our parents decided to do for us after the day of the fire, and after Mommy got better after being so sick for so long: to bring you to work every day in the office they built in our "housis" so that we can spend our days *and* our nights together. But this time spent with them will turn out to be one of your biggest joys in life.

. . .

It's not that difficult to think out of the box; it just takes courage of conviction, which is such a rarity today.

In my view, just about anyone can think out of the box.

Why do I say this? Let me explain it this way: About something I did a long time ago which our parents share with others all the time, something that "bestest" reflects why I feel the way I do.

In almost everything about our life journey together, our brother Lucky allowed me—really wanted me—to be the leader, the Alpha. He trusted my judgment to do what was right for all of us. In doing so, he was very comfortable taking a more passive role.

With one significant exception: He always wanted *whichever* "monkee" I had chosen to play with or *whichever* particular bone in my mouth I was chewing on.

This was a phenomenon that played itself out repeatedly, no matter when or wherever we were.

A scenario very similar to the following:

It was a Sunday morning like almost all our family Sunday mornings as I am sure yours will be too. Mommy and Daddy, having their cup of coffee in bed, reading newspapers and books, and watching *CBS Sunday Morning*. As for me, I was languishing on the floor, doing what I was doing rather contentedly. Which is why, as usual, Lucky ambled over to where I was to see what, if anything, I may have had in my mouth. And if I did, I knew to expect from him that special look of his reserved solely for these types of occasions: a curled lip, teeth bared ever so slightly, less subtly though than he thought.

You see, he knew from experience I'd defer to him by dropping whatever it was I had in my mouth. After which, he'd step closer, pick up whatever I'd dropped, and then walk away rather proud of himself—with a wag of his tail and that "Lucky smile" on his face.

This scene played out this way for as long as I could remember.

Until I figured it was time for me to put a stop to this behavior of his—taking things that were important to me.

And until I figured it was time for me *to think out of the box.*

So here is what I did.

That Sunday morning, Lucky looked on intently as I walked over to the pile of "monkees" that lay on the floor under the box with picture and words that hangs from the wall.

There must have been fifty of them.

Intuitively, I knew whichever one I eventually chose, Lucky would want it. So I decided I'd make a much bigger deal than usual of my search for the "perfect monkee."

I must have taken the full scent of thirty of them, and of those, I put ten or so in my mouth as if to check them for taste and texture.

Then I did something I had never done before: I picked out the one our parents and I had known from day one that I never liked at all!

In fact to be truthful about it, I not only had never liked it, but if I had only this particular one and no others at all, I would have preferred to have *none*.

Simply put, at least for me, it was not only not at all pretty, it was also far too soft to enjoy. It never squeaked or talked to me when I'd shake it. And I never liked its shape.

However, Lucky never knew any of this.

It wasn't that it was a secret or anything. I just never felt the need to tell him how much I disliked that particular "monkee." My only contact with it, in fact, had taken place the moment our parents brought it home, a long time before. When, as a courtesy gesture like I always do—and hope you will too whenever Mommy and Daddy bring home something new—I immediately took it in my mouth and made it seem as if I really liked it. If only because I knew it would give our parents some pleasure. After which, however, I walked it upstairs, put it down in the "monkee" pile, and literally never touched it again.

Until this particular morning I am telling you about.

When, as I said earlier, Lucky did exactly what I thought he might do, as he had been doing since whenever.

On seeing me seemingly *enjoying* holding in my mouth the "monkee" I never liked, Lucky came over, curled his lip, and bared his teeth less subtly than he thought. And so, as if on cue, I dropped it. He picked it up. And then proceeded to walk away, rather proud of himself, tail wagging and a smile on his face.

As far as he was concerned, it was "business as usual."

It wasn't.

In fact, what followed that morning was something quite radically different. Something I had never done before.

I went back to the same fifty (now 49) "monkees" strewn all over the bedroom floor and proceeded to choose my "bestest" most favorite one of all!

After which, I happily jumped on the bed to join our parents who had watched the whole scene unfold.

Years later, I still recall Mommy's words: *"Can you believe what we just saw? She did that on purpose! She's reasoning and making decisions!"* And Daddy's amazed reply, *"One day, we have to write about it if only to record it for posterity."*

To be honest with you, they seemed quite surprised by what they had observed. They shouldn't have been.

It was just me *thinking out of the box.*

And in my view, if I can, anyone can, and you should at least try.

. . .

"It's A Wonderful World."

This was always Lucky's favorite song; Daddy's too.

For its words speak to all the values our brother's life reflected. All he observed. And everything that was important to him . . . and us . . . and hopefully to you, in time.

Just like the song says, Lucky saw only the good—in everything. Which is why, even today, he remains, in spirit, the single most positive force of nature I have ever known.

In him, there was not a single ounce of jealousy of anything or anyone.

He took to heart the words of our Daddy's daddy long ago when he counseled him to never envy anyone else, for there will always be someone a little more talented, a little more good looking, a little richer, a little better student, a little better at sports, etc.

Our grandfather went onto tell Daddy, *"The one thing you can do is the only thing you should always want to say you did: that you did your absolute best. That you tried your absolute hardest. And that you did it to the best of your capability."*

It's the "bestest" piece of advice our father ever received from his father. It's also the "bestest" thing our parents ever imparted to all of us as a principle of life. It's the way they have lived their lives. It's also the way Lucky (and I) have lived ours.

In fact, Lucky always viewed another's success not as something to be envied, but rather as something to be appreciated and celebrated. It was a life principle that never wavered. Even as he got older, he never once looked back at what once was. He only looked to the future. He never thought about what might have been— only about what is and will be.

He also never complained. He never got cranky about the aches and pains that accompany aging.

Most notably, he never asked, not once, *"Why me?"* when he lost his sight.

Even though you could see from the smile on his face how dearly he had loved to watch children play. So full of life that accompanies the innocence of youth. For them he had only one wish: the "bestest" in everything that would come their way.

For Lucky, there were two ways to view life: either as a long sad struggle to overcome or as something special—full of new experiences, smells, and tastes to enjoy, appreciate and love. One could tell right away the instant you met him which one of those two alternative life outlooks was for him. From the way he'd shake hands with you. Something he never did as a stunt or a trick or to show off, but instead as his very personal way of saying, *"How dooo yooo dooo!"*

It was his way of saying he was, as always, genuinely happy to see you again—just as he was always genuinely happy to meet others for the very first time.

Indeed, to our brother, it *was* a wonderful world.

And for all of those whom he graced with his presence, friendship and love, he made it wonderful for us too. And always thought it was a life principle to be shared.

. . .

It's easier to communicate when you aren't yelling past each other.

Maybe it's my imagination, but it seems to me that when I was younger there was a softer tone of civility than there is today.

Whether it's the incessant banality and screaming on news, sports, and business channels or among the politicians at every level on the box with pictures and words. And on programs we hear occasionally on the box with voices and music in the machine with wheels, it just seems like there's a whole lot of screaming going on.

For some time, it has made me wonder if anyone's actually listening.

It's everywhere one goes—in every venue, in every facet of our lives.

Screaming and yelling disguised as "debate."

Ranting and raving substituting for "dialogue."

The indiscriminate cacophony of decibel-breaking sounds being passed off as "communication."

There's so much noise today, it's difficult to discern what others are trying to say—or if in fact they are trying to say anything at all.

It's gotten to a point where it's a genuine relief just to be able to listen to either quiet melodies of music or even the sounds of silence.

I don't know what can be done about it. Frankly I don't know how many others care. But to me it seems counter-productive at best.

You see, Lucky and I would be the first to tell you that we learned far more from *listening* than we ever did from *screaming*.

And one thing I know for sure: If we—and all of our peers everywhere—kept yelling and screaming past each other supposedly to "communicate" with each other, all their parents and ours would consider such behavior as really really bad.

. . .

Treat others as if they were what they ought to become and you will help them become what they are capable of being. (Goethe)

This is Daddy's philosophy of life—and he's passed it down to all of us. It is at the core of how our parents raised us. In so doing, they helped us become even better than anyone might have hoped for. Certainly that can be said of Lucky and me. It's a wonderful legacy to inherit, and an even better one to pass on to share with others.

. . .

Everyone should have a "monkee."

That's how Lucky and I learned so much about caring for those that need our affection and love. As well as how to chase and fetch when Daddy would play with us.

. . .

Everyone should have music in their lives.

You will discover how wonderful melodies will bring you a sense of calm and inner peace and bring you and our parents even closer together.

. . .

I believe in miracles.

There are many reasons why I do.

For now, suffice it to point out just two: Between Mommy and me, we have respectively survived late-stage and very aggressive forms of cancer. Neither of us should still be here. But we are . . . and we did it together.

That's why I believe in miracles.

. . .

If you only see what you want to see, you'll see only what others want you to see.

One's sense of self worth should be built on your pride in all that is *about you*. Not about looking for what isn't there, just because it might be in someone else.

. . .

So be who you are, not what you think others might want you to be.

The best are those who never have to lie or fabricate or exaggerate beyond what are the facts. Being true to yourself means living up to your promises and your commitments.

And doing what you say you will do, not doing what you say you will do—but don't.

. . .

Mistreatment of an animal is not an accident; it's a crime against nature.

There is no excuse for it. NO explanation can justify it.

NO apology can make up for it. Nothing further need be said.

. . .

Live one day at a time.

To be able to do so is nothing less than a gift. One that allows you to appreciate everything and all that is right around you—and too easily overlooked or missed when your gaze is focused too far ahead.

For Lucky and me, this was the one most important life principle that we, abetted by the experience of Mommy's cancer, did eventually impart to our parents.

So that today, it is one of their and my core life principles, and how the three of us—Mommy, Daddy, and me—continue to live our lives today.

For the three of us, it is the very "bestest" life lesson of all.

. . .

Finally, know that your siblings and I will always be looking out for all of you in ways I cannot explain now, but you will eventually come to know when you least expect it.

With love and "nuzzies" forever and a day,

Your sister Princess Sheba Spirit

POSTSCRIPT: BOSTON, OCTOBER 2008
OUR GUARDIAN ANGEL
STILL DOING HER JOB

2008 was a year which will go down as one of the very worst—perhaps *the* very worst—in the lifetime of many living Americans as the result of the "financial tsunami" that encircled the globe.

However, for Bobbie and me there are two days that year which will never be forgotten. Each was genuinely unimaginable: one as recently as a few months before; the other right up to the very last moment.

The former, of course, was very special and shared with so many in the United States and around the world: Presidential election day. On that day, the hopes and dreams of so many were awakened again.

The other was much more private but for us even more personally momentous. In fact, it is fair to say that for Bobbie and me, in what is now a three-decade-long life journey together, October 28, 2008 will be a date that we will forever hold sacrosanct.

For it was the day Bobbie was told her cancer is totally behind her. Not only almost fourteen years from the day she was diagnosed with what at the time I was told would for sure be a quick-to-kill, already late stage case of colon cancer— but also a little over ten years from the day of her last surgery for a second metastasis on her lung.

And also exactly eleven months and three weeks from the day Bobbie was told a new tumor lesion *might* have been spotted growing—or not. Again on her lung. And October 28, 2008 was to be the day we would know for certain.

. . .

At 7:00 a.m., we left for the Dana Farber Cancer Institute visit that would dictate the future of our life journey.

At 7:30 a.m., Bobbie was led away for her scan.

By 7:50 a.m., Bobbie had already dressed. And as we held hands in the elevator that took us up to her doctor's office, knowing I would ask what the scan was like this time, Bobbie told me the one thing she unequivocally knew I'd want to know.

. . .

Twenty minutes later, her oncologist Robert—Bob—Mayer gave us incredible news!

"There is no tumor, just scar tissue . . . and at this point in time, you can assume your cancer is behind you."

We were stunned, amazed, and grateful all at once.

We were being told something we had never allowed ourselves—never dared to think: Bobbie had beaten the cancer!

The truth is there is no way whatsoever I can adequately describe what those words meant when we first heard them spoken. Just as there is really no good way to explain what the words *"you have cancer"* do to you when you first hear them. So I will not try.

Other than to say they are life-changing . . . literally.

. . .

As much as we had wanted to begin our 354-mile-drive home as soon as possible after we'd returned to the hotel, assuming Bobbie felt up to it, the torrential rainstorm and its accompanying 60 mph winds that engulfed Boston on the 28th precluded any possibility of doing so.

However, any momentary disappointment was brief. For we now had an unplanned day to ourselves, "holed up" in a beautiful suite in one of our favorite hotels, the Four Seasons Boston. A gift we gave ourselves to offset the stress of the oncology visit.

Who could ask for anything more?

We did not have to wait long for the answer.

. . .

Around 4:30 p.m., with the wind howling and rain still falling but lessening in intensity, we decided to go for a walk.

We picked up some books and magazines from a nearby Barnes & Noble bookstore and searched for whatever we couldn't find in an eclectic "odds and ends" store we always enjoy visiting when in Boston, and followed that up with a bit of aimless window shopping which helped kill some more time.

Our mood hadn't changed in the eight hours since we'd been with Dr. Mayer. We were bouncing! And relieved and happy and grateful!

We decided to get a bite in a sandwich restaurant cum coffee shop right down the street from the hotel that we had eyeballed the previous evening: The Parish Café, about two blocks from the hotel. Where we took a table right in front of the large street facing window where we could have light to read our papers and watch the rain showers turn into sunlight.

And got to witness *twice* one of nature's sights: rare and magnificent. A site which for the two of us was incredibly emotional yet needed no explanation at all.

A beautiful double rainbow: as clear as the sky's best paint job.

Bobbie and I looked at each other in that way couples in love know the other's thoughts and need no commentary: It was Princess letting us know she was there looking out for us. And that she was not alone: This was a double rainbow because Lucky was with her this time. They wanted us to know they knew what we had come to know, and had come to help us celebrate the news that their beloved mother was now cancer free.

That this is what the double rainbow signified, neither Bobbie nor I have ever had the slightest doubt—then or since.

For us, the explanation had arrived eight hours before, while Bobbie was undergoing her scan. When she felt and then saw both Princess and Lucky right next to her, holding her in their grasp of unconditional love, letting their mother know all was okay.

Bobbie had felt Prinny's presence on prior occasions while being scanned. But never so close. And Princess was always alone.

This time she had brought her beloved Lucky with her to make certain we got the message. *"She's still doing her job, isn't she?"* Bobbie whispered.

"Yes, and she always will," I said as we both continued to stare out at the double rainbow that had also captured the awe of passers-by who stopped in their path to fully appreciate its beauty.

"She will always be your Guardian Angel."

Richard Pomerantz
The Last Day of 2008

Lucky and Prinny's Double Rainbow
Boston, MA, October 28, 2008

OUR FAMILY GALLERY

The Brothers: Young Lucky and Smokey Max

The Sisters: Princess and Samantha

Lucky and Princess
As Depicted by Pennsylvania Artist Sandra Severson

Smokey Max and Samantha Blackie
As Depicted by Pennsylvania Artist Sandra Severson

Princess With Mommy and Daddy
At Westtown School Lake—Our Own "On Golden Pond"

Princess and Daddy in Jupiter

Mommy and Princess

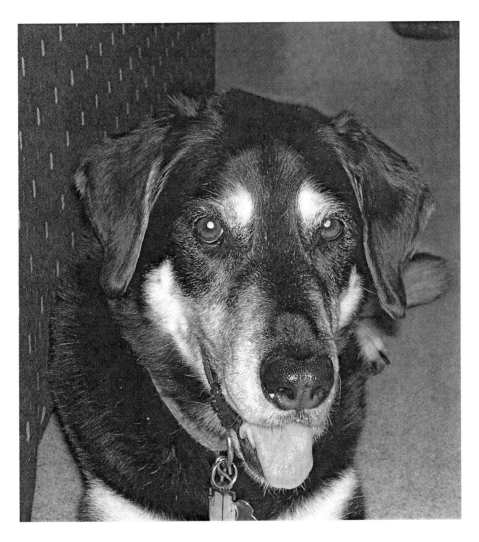

Princess Sheba Spirit: Our Magic Girl

The Next Generation: Panda Petunia Ruach
(The Spirit of Princess Sheba Spirit)
Born: Williamsburg, VA, July 16, 2007

The Next Generation: Beckham "Little Bear"

Born: Warren County, PA, June 16, 2007
Rescued Through The Collaborative Effort of
Warren County Humane Society and
The Cardigan Welsh Corgi National Rescue Trust
And Lovingly Fostered By Karen Smith

The Next Generation:

Beckham Little Bear and Panda Petunia Ruach

CPSIA information can be obtained at www.ICGtesting.com
Printed in the USA
BVOW072054250612

293620BV00001B/1/P